T5-DGT-859

© THE BAKER & TAYLOR CO.

Television's
Classic
Commercials

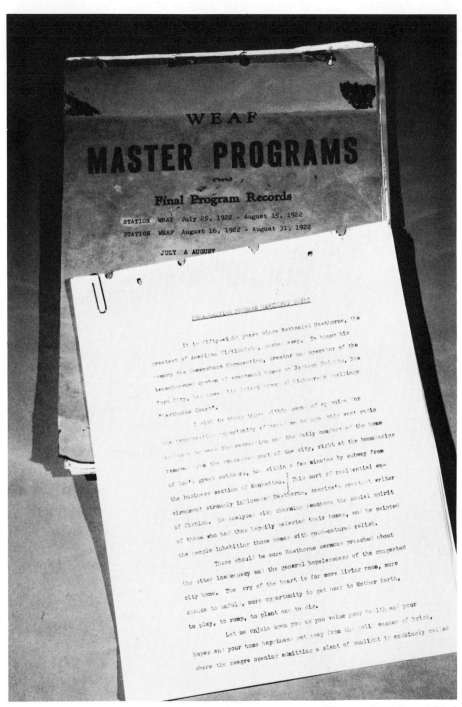

WORLD'S FIRST COMMERCIAL

This initial radio "ad"—broadcast to New Yorkers on a summer evening in 1922—gave rise to what eventually became our multi-billion dollar television commercials industry.

Television's Classic Commercials

The Golden Years

1948-1958

by

LINCOLN DIAMANT

Past Vice-president Broadcast Advertising
Producers Society of America and Chairman
I.R.T.S. TV Commercial Production Workshop

COMMUNICATION ARTS BOOKS

HASTINGS HOUSE, PUBLISHERS
New York 10016

This book is for Joan.

First Edition
Copyright ©, 1971, by Lincoln Diamant

Published simultaneously in Canada by Saunders of Toronto, Ltd.,
Don Mills, Ontario

ISBN: 8038-7103-1

Library of Congress Catalog Card Number: 79-150018
Designed by Al Lichtenberg
Printed in the United States of America

Contents

PART ONE

Development of the American Television Commercial

PART TWO

The 69 "Classic" Television Commercials, 1948-1958

(Chronologically Arranged in Categories)

FOOD

COFFEE & TEA

BEER, WINE & SOFT DRINKS

TOBACCO

HOUSEHOLD PRODUCTS

MEDICAL PRODUCTS

TOILETRIES

Acknowledgments

Preparation of this book has been a long labor of love—and perhaps some kind of a funny Valentine to the outpourings of a gigantic industry that did not even exist 25 years ago. The material was put together mainly in stolen off-hours, so I voice appreciation to those near and dear—and some now even gone—for their patience and fortitude with a "struggling writer."

Inevitably, writing any kind of a book induces a change of perspective toward one's material. This book—relating to a profession in which I have been immersed for almost three decades—offered no exception. If evidence is apparent of any sea change in my professional attitude while bringing the manuscript to completion, the reader should make the most of it.

The "newest" commercial described herein is at least a dozen years old; have things changed much since 1958? The reader as a TV viewer can answer that for himself; the moral, if any, may be found in Appendix D.

Two particular salutes are in order: to my friend Wallace Ross for initiating the American Television Commercials Festival, which in turn accepted the original responsibility for the "Classic" cachet on the 69 commercials gathered in this book; and to Irving Sachs and Neil Matz of Syncrofilm, Inc. for generous technical assistance that made certain portions of this work practical.

Also, for quiet encouragement that carried me hopefully onward beyond too many missed deadlines, very special thanks to my Hastings House editor, Russell Neale.

Extracts

"The trade of advertising is now so near to perfection that it is not easy to propose any improvement."
                                                                    —Dr. Samuel Johnson

"In America three-quarters of the enormous newspapers are filled with advertisements. The remainder is occupied by gossip and anecdotes."
                                                                    —Alexis de Tocqueville

"It is inconceivable that we should allow so great a possibility for public service as broadcasting to be drowned in advertising chatter."
                                                                    —Herbert Hoover

"If I were starting life all over again, I would go into the advertising business; it has risen with evergrowing rapidity to the dignity of an art."
                                                                    —Franklin D. Roosevelt

"Commercial television has truly opened up our American way of life."
                                                                    —Brig. Gen. David Sarnoff

"Television makes everything simpler or more dramatic or more immediate than it really is. If you watch television, you really can't find out what's going on in the world."
                                                                    —Walter Lippmann

"Television is a triumph of equipment over people."
                                                                    —Fred Allen

"The basic premise of the commercial is that it is a game everyone is willing to play. How pleasant it is to have a problem presented and solved before our eyes; it is inconceivable that the breath not be sweetened, the hands not softened. The American television commercial is the last stronghold of formula playwriting."
                                                                    —*Television Quarterly*

"Even before Marshall McLuhan, I was drawn to the gray shadows of the cathode tube. In fact, I was sufficiently *avant-garde* in 1959 to recognize that fact that it was no longer the movies, but the television commercial, that engaged the passionate attention of the world's best artists and technicians. The result of their extraordinary artistry is this new world, like it or not, we are living in. The relationship between consumer and advertiser is the last demonstration of necessary love in the West, and its principal form of expression is the television commercial."

—Gore Vidal, *Myra Breckenridge*

"Watching television is like making love—not a reasoning activity."

—*Television Quarterly*

"To the poorer blacks, the lily-white commercials act not only as an affront, but also as an ironic encouragement to violence. On the shows, gunfire is commonplace; it is necessary, it sells products. Virtue triumphs, but the outlaw is mighty attractive. Every day, every hour, he is sanctioned—by the pretty white girl in the commercial lighting up and taking a deep puff as a preliminary to romance; or caring about her soft hands even when washing the dishes; or naked in the shower behind the ripple glass, arms raised to the white, white lather in her blond, blond hair."

—John Hersey, *The Algiers Motel Incident*

"Television is the supermarket of the soul."

—Eric Bentley

"Television leaves half the American people dead in the water each night. It force-feeds external additives like hair color, deodorant, mouthwash, headache and sleeping pills, coffee, cigarettes and beer to a bewildered people in search of 'more'—instead of stimulating them to live the kind of life that alone can bring the satisfactions they seek."

—FCC Commissioner Nicholas Johnson

"Ask people about a commercial they saw last night and they tend to have amnesia."

—*Life Magazine* Promotion Dept.

"I can't talk about ecology out of one side of my mouth—and sell a pollutant out of the other."

—Arthur Godfrey

"It may sound corny, but the time has come for broadcasters to re-orient their thinking. Competition is limited. Broadcasting is not 'free enterprise' as such. Frequencies are held as a public trust."

—*Southwest Advertising & Marketing*

Introduction

THERE seems no question now that something is very wrong with our society. Materialist infection was always with America; but it is no accident that it started festering in the years immediately after World War II, when television took hold of home after home and—almost without exception, like a narcotic—mind after mind, sliding us nightly into a flickering era of national schizophrenia.

Beginning in the late '40's, American television, through its advertisers and their agencies, pursued the perfection of the little one-minute art form known as the TV "commercial." Ensuing years saw the principles and practice of this bit of instantaneous mass marketing raised to undreamed-of heights—and profits. By 1970, as three-fourths of America watched television every night (were they finally "peaking-out"?), the cost of a single "prime-time" minute on a network had risen to almost $70,000!

In the late '40's and early '50's, as commercials came to golden flower, American life began to balance on a fulcrum of *things*. Things that could be bought, used, swallowed or puffed—all sold at a frantic pace day and night by the most accomplished practitioners of the huckster's art. In 1959, a personable young man named Wallace Ross decided to reward annually the most artful of these TV commercials (and their craftsmen) with special "Festival" awards (now called "Clios").

By so doing, he and a professionally selected board of judges recognized only the shiniest tip of the iceberg; the vast mass of television advertising was then—and has been since—too dull, uninspired (and often dreadful) to merit anything better than death by drowning.

COMMERCIAL "CLASSICS"

To get the first Festival off to a running start. Mr. Ross asked his judges to honor "the best" of the past commercials that had been seen on American television since 1948—and continued this practice into subsequent years. It is the earliest of these "Classics"—69 of them, produced from 1948 to 1958—that make up the substance of this book, *reflecting the seedtime of a permanent TV style.*

Only in the mass (and in the manner that these "classics" represent a still greater mass) can these commercials be considered as social documents. That fact, indeed, may be more obvious to the reader than it was at first to the author, whose original intention was to provide an historical and detailed audio-visual study of 69 major TV commercials that would be of general interest to advertising craftsmen; and at the same time evoke uncanny—and perhaps uncomfortable?—memories among general readers. In the mass, however, something quite different seems to emerge.

Perhaps the social historian of tomorrow may be able to use this collection to pinpoint ways in which these advertising messages—and a million others like them—set our society off on its "fast . . . fast . . . fast" search for some mythical grail?[1]

For some right now, it may be enough to look at these 69 "spots" and simply say, "This is the way we came." Others may want to move to higher ground, and study the perceptive suggestions of a television observer like "Sedulus," writing in *The New Republic:*

> TV has *again* been discovered as the great brain washer . . . but we can't beat the wash one hankie at a time. We need to get down to elementals like the infinitely repeatable one-minute commercial. We need to understand how that commercial works, and then *we need legislation to keep it from working so well.* We need less talk and more information about what the tube and the other media are doing to us. Particularly we need to understand how the tube's salesmanship (starting with the one-minute commercial and working up to Nixon's appearances) works. My impression is that our reformers think the process is a rational one. Every mature brain-washer knows better.
>
> The reformers, for example, have recently been hightailing it after the deceptive advertising of drugs, breakfast foods, cars and the like. This is worthy of them, but deception by fact and reason is a relatively trivial factor on the brainwash scene. Our eight-year-olds know the ads are frauds, but they (like us) keep buying the snake oil. Rational?
>
> Furthermore, most of the fraudulence is not factual at all; that is, not assessable in terms of claims made for products. It is *atmospheric* fraudulence, hoked-up circumstances, verbiage rather than facts. My favorite ad at the moment, for a dry-skin remedy, brings us a scholarly, bespectacled geezer who takes a medical book from his five-foot shelf, sits down at a dignified desk, recites a gentle and melodious patter about the ailment and the remedy (with no claims at all), and then launches into his key testimonial: "*X* provides ephemeral relief in mild cases." *X provides ephemeral relief in mild cases!* It could be said of dirty crankcase oil.
>
> I am reminded of P. T. Barnum's come-on under the big tent: "This way to the Egress." Ain't no court gonna find fraud here—we are, suh, playing a fine old American game. Some of this selling is even truthful (heavens to Betsy), innocent as pie, except that it comes at us ten times an hour. With none of it are we persuaded by argument; *we*

---

[1] Like pollution, the madness is now international. *The New York Times* reported in 1970 that: "After a TV commercial on a Finnish cheese was run in Moscow, the demand for the brand shot up by 70%."

simply drown in product awareness. These are the conditions of brainwash that we need to fear; wash that goes beyond true-false, right-wrong, and puts things in our heads as arbitrarily and mechanically as a robot spoon stuffing a goose.

With commercials, the only kind of legislation I can imagine that would effectively reduce brainwash would limit the frequency of commercial appearance; by law Pepsi-Cola could hit me no more than once a day on any one channel; by law Winston could give me only one chorus of its bloody song, etc.[2] The law would be, in effect, an anti-assault law; once we get around to acknowledging that the tube has unlimited assault potential, the law would not seem so exotic or frivolous. It would be a negative law, saving us from concentrated, long-term assaults—yet democratically keeping no single claim, position, argument or product from us, no matter how crummy.

Drastic suggestions for improvement such as this may appear to violate American traditions of "free enterprise"—but the U.S. Marketing Establishment itself (with commercial television as willing accomplice) has already raped that principle out of all recognition. Less than 2,000 firms, owned by about 100 conglomerate corporations, now employ one-quarter of the total U.S. labor force and create more than 80% of this country's gross product! Hardly "free enterprise," and in many ways, it makes this a mighty strange era to be living in.

But it's also an era with some promise of change in TV "software"—with the growth of local CATV programming; only four commercials to the half-hour and no advertising in station breaks, promises *Broadcasting Magazine* in the Fall of 1970.[3] And a change in "hardware," too—as a raft of brand-new TV home playback equipment begins to lift American viewers out of the rut of watching only what happens to be "on the air." There are even stronger views: Video cassettes, says Tony Brown, producer of NET's *Black Journal,* may eventually "put the white racist play toy of commercial broadcasting out of business."

Everyone is straining to peer ahead to what will happen. It could be important to see where it all began.

---

[2] This article appeared in 1970, before the FCC ban on all cigarette advertising took the Winston song *completely* off the air.

---

[3] Although the same issue reports straightfacedly that one CATV facility, in Melbourne, Fla., now "carries a commercial every 30 seconds."

PART ONE

Development of the American Television Commercial

S ALES-CREATING "sponsored" messages have been part of the economic pattern of American broadcasting since August, 1922. At that time, New York's WEAF, owned by the AT&T subsidiary Western Electric, had been broadcasting for less than three weeks, all the while coyly soliciting advertising use of its new medium. The Griffin Radio Service commissioned four 15-minute (!) commercials at $50 apiece for its client, the Queensboro Corporation.

This was a New York real estate firm extolling a back-to-the-soil concept of living they attributed to Nathaniel Hawthorne, in an effort to fill vacant apartments in "Hawthorne Court," their cooperative housing project in Jackson Heights, Long Island. Queensboro's first "commercial" was broadcast at 5:00 p.m., Monday, August 28, 1922. Sandwiched between a soprano's recording of "Carry Me Back to Ol' Virginny" and a studio pianist's Paderewski minuet, this advertising interruption set what has since become an accepted broadcasting pattern.[1]

Half a century later, the *television* commercial descended therefrom offers advertisers the easiest, fastest (and perhaps least expensive) way to splatter mass markets, even at costs that now approach $70,000 per minute or more than $40,000 per half-minute. The *Saturday Review* has estimated that every member of the current crop of U.S. high school graduates has already seen about 100,000 television commercials—"a relentless input of visual data."

---

[1] For historic interest and study, the commercial—one of the longest and least expensive on record—is shown in the Frontispiece and in Appendix D, and indicates how little broadcast advertising hyperbole has changed in half a century.

1

Sponsor payments to create and broadcast such messages and the programs surrounding them have totalled, since the end of World War II, about $50 billion! This activity has now become the largest source of revenue for every major American advertising agency; in 1969, commissionable U.S. advertising agency billings on television activity alone totalled $3½ billion.

All these dollars have encouraged the creation of some rather extraordinary facilities for instantaneous public communication between more than 200 million Americans seated in front of 80 million TV sets—almost half in "living color." America is the only country in the world where the apparent slum luxury of television reception is instead considered an absolute necessity, and where one of every six families existing on less than $5,000 a year enjoys its TV in color!

All these viewers have been legal witnesses to the television commercial's *enfantement;* in a sense, midwives. As American consumers, they have always responded generously to this concentrated little audio-visual sally, eager to be interested, entertained and persuaded to buy—in the briefest of selling moments. By definition, of course, commercial "broadcasting" has been wasteful; only a small portion of the audience for any commercial is in a position to take useful buying action, and a Gallup Poll in the Spring of 1970 reported that viewers paying the most attention to TV commercials "are often persons for whom they are not intended—older, less affluent, less educated." But no other advertising medium has ever offered manufacturers such a vast audience of *potential* action-takers.

COMMERCIAL FORMAT

The convenient length of radio's 60-second "word from our sponsor" appears in the National Association of Broadcasters' "Code of Ethics" as follows:

A 5-minute program is permitted 1 minute of commercial time.
A 10-minute program is permitted 2 minutes of commercial time.
A 30-minute program is permitted 3 minutes of commercial time.
A one-hour program is permitted 6 minutes of commercial time.

These original "Time Standards for Radio Advertising Copy" were carried bodily over into television in the late 1940's.[2] In TV's early years, the most-used

---

[2] Adherence to this NAB Code was voluntary for member stations until 1970, when the FCC finally stepped in with regulations of its own. The new rule indicated the extent to which TV stations had been violating the NAB "standards"; from now on, no more than *16 minutes* of commercial time in any hour! What is still not controlled is the *number* of commercials, which is more of a problem than the length of time they take up. It creates what *Life Magazine* has called: "The hurly-burly of the station break: the dozens of products flung pell-mell, the tumultuous piling on of images, the frenetic salesmanship. The *din.*" For example, during a typical sports event, there are now 34 commercials; during a movie, 32. This quantity of noise is generally transmitted, for complicated technical reasons, above the sound level of the surrounding program. No matter how "creative" all this may be, it is mind-boggling; it is questionable that the audience can remember more than one or two of the products being advertised. In fact, the Gallup Poll mentioned above noted that more than 100 of its 1,500 interviewees could not even remember if they had watched television at all the previous night. All this finally led General Foods, the nation's second-largest TV advertiser, to propose—in the Spring of 1971—a $1.5 million "commercial clutter" study.

commercial length was the one-minute spot—but rising time costs and the growing need for versatility have changed all that. Today, less than 35% of all commercials are one minute (or longer). Lengths now in use are:

10-second messages (only in the station identification period—known as "I.D.'s"[3]). These represent about 5% of the number of commercials on the air.

20-second messages—about 10% of the commercials on the air.

30-second messages—the most popular length—about 50% of the commercials on the air.[4]

40-second messages—an odd length—less than 1% of the commercials on the air.

1-minute messages—about 34% of the commercials on the air.

2- or 3-minute messages used within programs—a favorite length with a few "institutional" advertisers like Xerox and Hallmark who like to offer "uninterrupted" holiday or special-event programming.

Almost all of these commercial lengths are used in two equal ways; either as "network" commercials within the body of a television program, or as "spot" commercials, during the station break period.

The reader (along with broadcast researchers) may speculate on the possible difference in loyal audience impact between the identical commercial presented in either context. In days of old when the "sponsor" was the man who paid the bill to bring you the program—it was Secretary of Commerce Herbert Hoover who first suggested the advertiser's name be mentioned at the beginning and end of each broadcast, an idea he apparently later regretted—there most assuredly was a difference in listener loyalty.

It is not splitting hairs to point out that only the advertiser who presents the *program* is today continuing the social theory and practice of American broadcasting—public programming privately underwritten.[5] The advertiser who places his commercials in *station breaks* is merely supporting the financial operation of a local broadcast facility.

If any impact edge still remains between "program" and "wild spot" use of the same or different commercials, it is becoming increasingly dulled by media practices of alternate sponsorship, participating sponsorship, off-week billboarding, and such cut-in "spot carrier" network programming as NBC's *Tonight* and *Today* programs. Advertisers are carefully watching the way this difference dwindles; the

---

[3] The "I.D." usually allows only 8 seconds of video and even less of audio, to accomodate the other mechanical needs of a station break.

[4] It took only a few years for large corporate advertisers to demolish TV station resistance against counting two dissimilar "piggy-backed" :30's as a single :60 spot.

[5] TVB (Television Bureau of Advertising) statistics indicate this type of sponsorship now represents a shrinking minority of all TV commercial advertising.

talent unions still continue to insist on premium re-payment for *program*—as opposed to *wild spot*—use.[6]

BIG SAM IS WATCHING

The growth of American television broadcasting has been subject to fits and starts of government control. The present 525-line U.S. TV transmission is equal to a picture scanned along 525 horizontal sweeps of the frame every 1/30th of a second. This system, frozen by the FCC in the '40's, is so archaic in potential quality that even the tiny cameras we sent 60 million miles to Mars in 1970 worked on a 704-line system, and gave pictures with 78% better line resolution. The current European standard of 625 lines represents a 20% improvement, but the FCC apparently has felt that what was good enough for the U.S. in 1941 is still good enough in the '70's—and with 80 million sets now in use, it is really too late to do anything about it.

TV station expansion was suspended during World War II, and slowed in the years immediately thereafter by a raging argument over what form *color* television broadcasting should eventually take. The Columbia Broadcasting System opted for a spinning *color wheel* in front of every picture tube; RCA pushed for the more electronically-sophisticated *color signal* transmission (which has since been adopted).

This knot was cut by the FCC in 1948, with a decision that the American viewer was not yet ready for color TV at all. In addition, the Commission added, the 36 black-and-white television stations already on the air were creating serious problems of signal interference. On this basis, the FCC promulgated its famous "temporary" freeze order of September 1948, which refused to accept applications for new TV station construction for almost three-and-a-half years.

This did not, however, cancel applications previously approved, so the number of stations able to get on the air rose to around 100. Meanwhile the networks took advantage of this three-and-a-half-year moratorium to consolidate their historic programming position as the heart, nerve and sinew of what was eventually to be pronounced a broadcasting "wasteland."

By April 1952, after innumerable hearings, the FCC sorted out enough major technical problems to "unfreeze" further station construction on twelve channels (2 through 13) in the VHF—Very High Frequency—waveband. The government also established a UHF—Ultra High Frequency—waveband of seventy channels. In theory, these new UHF channels (14 through 83) were meant to encourage practical construction of 2,000 additional commercial and non-commercial TV stations, thriving competitively and independently throughout the United States.

---

[6] A study of "commercial audiences" in 1969 by the research firm of C. E. Hooper, Inc. suggested that the "ideal" commercial is still the 60-second message (or perhaps even longer) appearing alone as the middle commercial of a fully sponsored, highly-rated musical variety program some time after 8:30 p.m., preferably in the 9:00–10:00 p.m. block. By the same standards, Hooper suggested that the least desirable prime-time commercial might be 20-seconds or less in length, scheduled in second position or later in a group of two or more commercials back-to-back in the last five minutes of a low-rated science-fiction or adventure program early in the evening.

Unfortunately, it did not work out as planned. Today, there are too few commercial UHF outlets in operation, and all but a penny or two of every broadcast advertising dollar is channeled into the 677 VHF stations now on the air. Program control—despite valiant FCC attempts to unlock it—still remains firmly in the hands of the networks; opportunities for viewer selectivity are held to a minimum. Even government legislation that forced inclusion of UHF tuning equipment in all TV sets sold in the U.S. after 1962—a step Japanese portable manufacturers took first—did little to move public service forward in this area.

To the advertiser, of course, this has been half a boon. Within a narrowed marketplace, media decisions are simplified, and far less physical advertising material—scripts, film prints, video tapes, etc—must be prepared for broadcast use. Tacit government acknowledgement that its UHF legislation had failed to break the TV broadcasting mold came in 1965, with a new FCC request—for reaction to a proposal that would cut "prime time" from 3½ to 3 hours per night and legally limit network participation in program preparation to 50% (still under litigation in 1970).[7]

The reaction from the networks was, to put it mildly, negative.

But also in the '60's, when the inventive Bundy-Friendly-Ford Foundation communications satellite plan for national exchange of good non-commercial programming came out, the networks' initial stand towards this proposal was surprisingly positive, although later modified by reservations suggesting fear that non-commercial satellites might eventually divert a significant number of commercial viewers.[8] Such pessimism was to some extent refuted by a 1966 Louis Harris poll, showing—within the sophisticated precincts of New York City—that 57% of the viewers of the metropolitan area's sole non-commercial VHF channel would be perfectly willing to accept commercialization as one means of alleviating the station's sporadic financial distress.[9]

This was also the period in which TV commercials appear to have come of age. At least, people started saying with a perfectly straight face at church socials and cocktail parties: "You know, the commercials are better than the programs." Either U.S. TV programming had gotten much worse, or this was indeed a case of the tail wagging the dog.[10]

How did this happen?

---

[7] Another proposal brought to the FCC in 1970 by Action for Children's Television (ACT), would ban all TV advertising for children, while compelling stations to devote at least 14 hours a week to commercial-free children's programs. The passing of children's show advertising might be welcomed by parents who find the current price of $24.95 toys a bit steep. The FCC Chairman admitted to ACT that American television "has nothing to boast about" in the children's area. The best the NAB Toy Code has to offer broadcasters is: "Avoid employing irritating techniques to demand the child's attention." (Guideline III-B-1).

[8] *New York Times,* August 2nd and 23rd, 1966.

[9] WNDT, Channel 13; now merged as WNET with the National Education Television Network and presumably solvent on the basis of (well-advertised) "corporate grants."

[10] The reader may wonder whether TV commercial advertising from other parts of the world has a better or worse history than U.S. efforts. The author has judged hundreds of European and Japanese commercials for several international festivals; in his opinion, national restrictions on commercialization of European television seem to have restricted their "advertising creativity." For example, British TV spots—limited to half-minute lengths—

BUY ME, BUY ME

An advertiser—usually by commissioning his advertising agency—creates television commercials to serve one of four major sales purposes:

1. To introduce his new product; his improved product; or his old product in a new form. (21 of the commercials in this book.)
2. To switch viewers' market preference from another brand to his brand. (44 of the commercials in this book.)
3. To help create or maintain his brand or corporate reputation. (4 of the commercials in this book.)
4. To do the same as *3*, by implication, with some form of "public service" message. (None of the commercials in this book.)

Often TV commercials try to accomplish several of these tasks at once.

The earliest television commercials (c. 1948) in any of these four categories were known then (and are still called) "stand-up spots." The announcer seized the advertised product in his right hand, carefully guarding the label from obscuration by his fingers, and then stood up and said his piece directly into the TV camera lens—like the medicine man, carnival barker or street salesman of old.

Unless the announcer or presenter was gifted with a phenomenal memory (what is known in show business as a "fast study"), all the advertising agency copywriter's carefully-selected words were pencilled for him in large letters on white boards held up at one side of the camera. Despite their almost universal use, these boards—ten or twelve to a commercial—were soon disparagingly dubbed "idiot cards" (perhaps by a disgruntled Thespian).

Eventually, technology caught up; prompting continued, but with more sophisticated, motor-driven devices, projecting player-piano rolls of printed words onto a 45° mirrored surface directly in front of the camera lens. This made the presenter appear to be reading the TV viewer's mind, perfectly re-establishing the "eye-contact" Mr. McLuhan infers to be essential for any intense personal selling effort.[11]

From time to time during such *live* commercials, an electronic "feed" could be added from other cameras to provide titles ("supers"=superimpositions), close-up demonstrations of the product, packages, etc. Slides with dealers' names, small photographs (called "balops" and "telops" after the manufacturer of the equipment used in their projection), and other graphic material could also be inserted using separate electronic sources.

Where it proved impractical to supply an important piece of action "live," it could be pre-recorded beforehand on (usually silent) film, and "rolled in" on cue by motion picture projectors shining into modified TV cameras.

show only rare flashes of wit; German minutes, lumped at one time of evening, are stodgy carbon copies of U.S. work; French advertising film is inventive, but is produced mainly for motion picture theater consumption—French TV only permits commercials on agricultural products, textiles and electrical items.

[11] Starting with LBJ, a pair of these devices became standard equipment at televised Presidential press confrences.

The advantages of this by-now ancient form of television advertising—the "live commercial"—are obvious. It was simple, relatively inexpensive to produce, and subject to day-to-day marketing alteration as desired. Most important, perhaps, the live portions possessed an electronic "look of immediacy"—a feature soon lost from those early days of television, and only recaptured by the advent of video tape recording.[12]

Often, the program's star was required to deliver the advertising message. Some of those efforts were memorable, and even find a place in this book. Costs, as mentioned, were minimal—until craft and talent unions began fleshing-out crew and actor payments. For live network shows, the "live" commercial made excellent sense.

On current advertising participation programs such as *Today* and *Tonight*, where the host's selling personality plays a big part in attracting sponsors, the television advertising "pitch" of 1948 may still be seen in operation. The appeal of this type of commercial has never been adequately acknowledged; why does it seem so refreshing?

A TV audience is made up of amateurs. A perfectly filmed or taped commercial is the ultimate in professionalism; the audience can never actively empathize with it. The live "stand-up" spot, often with bumbled lines and sticky refrigerator doors (see page 206) equals the audience in its amateurism; emotional participation (identification with the goof) is quite easy.

FILM TAKES OVER

But limitations of the "stand-up" spot bothered advertisers. All action had to be confined to the TV studio. Any live demonstration in the commercial had to work perfectly each time (and as commercials became more competitive, demonstrations became more complicated). There could be no allowance for lapsed time. There could be no "re-takes"; even after complete and perfect rehearsals, the advertiser often had to settle for fluffs in his on-the-air commercial performance. Perhaps more important, when performers were able to respond with a brilliant reading, it was ephemeral. They had to come back and do it all over again—perhaps badly—the next day or the next week.

Until the advent of video tape recording in 1956, it was impossible to pre-record a good "live" commercial. All you could do was use a motion picture camera to photograph the face of the TV tube as the commercial went out on the air. The results of this *kinescope* (or "kine") *recording* were indifferent, but many commercials that were preserved for the analysis of posterity, including five in this volume, owe their existence to this admittedly imperfect technique.

---

[12] It is interesting (and to some degree important) to note the genuine difference in appearance, on the face of the TV tube, between sharper *video taped* and "softer" *filmed* commercials. Even the least sophisticated viewer will agree that a video tape commercial, repeated a thousand times, still suggests the spontaneity of the original "live" TV camera performance. Film, however, interposes translation and storage of picture information from an *electronic* into an *optical* medium, then back again; somewhat akin to translating Shakespeare into Russian and then back into English from the Russian.

Once TV commercials became more creatively complicated, the *filmed* commercial took center stage. *With a film camera, your studio was the world.* Commercial scenarios were limited only by the copywriter's or art director's imagination. Casts of thousands—if the advertiser could afford them—were attainable. Also, the historic film technique of animation drawing could be exhaustively explored as a television selling tool. A hundred different optical effects could be used to move the commercial along, and hoary Hollywood tricks used to make things seem to happen that really didn't happen.[13]

Most important, of course, one could literally create the best possible performance of commercial material with a little film splicer, piecing together the best of a lot of bits of film that had been shot (or re-shot) at everyone's convenience.

Hand-in-hand with this film breakthrough went the opening up of "spot market" television advertising in one section of the country after another. Every TV station possessed 16mm projection equipment for filmed *programs*. In twenty-four hours, therefore, an advertiser could duplicate hundreds of relatively inexpensive commercial 16mm film prints and ship them out for broadcast all over the United States.

The '50's firmly established the era of the *film* commercial. Its keynote was not low cost, but *simplicity, versatility* and *control*. These are still the same reasons why nine out of ten commercials broadcast today are produced on film.

THE WHOLLY ELECTRONIC MESSAGE

In 1956, an important new TV programming development threatened film's dominance of the TV commercial production field. Out of the laboratories finally emerged a practical method of electronically recording the complicated picture and sound information that passed through a TV camera. Transmitted *later* to a picture tube, such recordings were absolutely indistinguishable from the original "live" performance.

Where such "live" quality was creatively important to a television commercial, the new video tape recording technique—then and now—proved invaluable. But certain serious technical drawbacks to this method had to be overcome:

1. Unlike film, the commercial could not be taped in "takes," or out of sequence, but only in one continuous, top-to-bottom 60-second performance.
2. Unlike film, no video tape material from a different source could be compatibly edited into the original recording.
3. Editing required physical splices, which caused electronic roll-over (picture tearing) on the viewer's home screen.
4. Heavier cameras and cumbersome video tape recording equipment made location work difficult.

---

[13] Until the Federal Trade Commission moved in the 60's to recover viewers' lost innocence with some celebrated "cease and desist" orders to advertisers and their agencies.

5. Labor and equipment costs were usually equal to film, often higher.
6. Unlike film, animation, or stop or slow-motion, was impossible.
7. Duplicates (and re-duplicates) of the "master" tapes—providing the air materials for broadcasting stations—were usually of indifferent quality. Transfers to film—for stations without video tape playback facilities—were worse.

Against this seemingly hopeless array of disqualifications stood one unique factor that literally kept TV video tape commercial production alive—while tape recording scientists busily eliminated, one by one, every one of the problems enumerated above. *Video tape commercials, when prepared properly, could be produced in a matter of hours, compared to the days required for film.* Where rush advertising and marketing schedules made it necessary, video tapes could even be—and were—duplicated and placed on the air on the evening of their day of production.

Video tape unfortunately oversold this obvious advantage. Advertisers who had no business being in video tape in the first place—it required stomachs strong enough to make instaneous production decisions—soon shied away permanently. Their adverse comments left others afraid of the medium and unwilling to experiment.

Whereupon the video tape industry, after a rosy initial expansion, shrunk. But time works wonders. As indicated, television is basically an *electronic*, not a *cinematographic* medium. Video tape's disqualifying challenges have been slowly, painfully and often expensively met. For example, video tape recording and editing techniques have now incorporated computer programming to generate non-sequential taped material from a dozen different sources, cameras and location—for striking "see it now" commercials.[14] Today, tape has no place to go but *up*; it is the "natural" medium for television.

Compact, mobile equipment has also eased the difficulties of video tape location work. Advertisers have pinpointed the economy areas of video tape use, as well as the wasteful ones, and costs have dropped accordingly. "Instant replay," stop motion, and even slow motion and animation are now possible.

Although the need for commercial film transfers has declined—because most of American television stations now possess video tape "playback" equipment [15]—film transfer technique, too, has vastly improved. And with the introduction of "high-band" video tape recorders, duplication quality has enjoyed an upward leap—although *costs* for a tape "dupe" are still about twice that of a film print.

The primary value of video tape, its *visual immediacy,* remains unchallenged by any other medium. Video tape commercials are produced with the opportunity to make required changes *on the spot*—instead of having to wait for a film laboratory to process a picture.

---

[14] Television scans a new picture every 1/30th second; motion picture film can only be edited to 1/24th second. Theoretically, therefore, video tape editing can be more precise.

[15] 98% of the U.S. VHF TV stations possess facilities for playback of video tape commercials.

With the almost universal use of color, video tape has come booming back in the TV commercial production race. There is no interposition of triple emulsions; the colors of a video tape commercial on the face of the viewer's picture tube are colors the TV camera actually sees—and not some later chemical interpretation thereof. Results are less open to a film laboratory technician's subjectivity, and are usually softer, truer and less garish. The often interminable wait while the film laboratory or advertiser rejects color answer print after color answer print—attempting to hit an elusive match of different takes, shot under different light conditions, on different days—is a problem that need never occur with properly-controlled video tape.

Intense competition between these two inherently dissimilar methods of television commercial production will go on. What of the software—the advertising agency storyboards that production house salesmen have been struggling (since 1948) to obtain?

WHAT'S UP THE FLAGPOLE?

Most American television commercials originate within and are controlled by the Creative Departments of U.S. advertising agencies. Depending on size, an agency's TV production operation in such a department will include from one to more than 100 employees. Most are organized with a Production vice-president, supervisors, producers, assistants and secretaries. On the client side, advertisers usually keep TV supervisory responsibilities inside their Advertising Department, limiting the number of personnel (or the time they are required to devote) in accord with TV marketing activity.

The long, involved, detailed and expensive process of getting a television commercial, film or video tape, onto the home viewer's tube, starts with the advertiser's marketing plans for a particular product or set of products.[16] These are transmitted to his advertising agency's Creative Department by the agency go-between, the account executive. In most agencies, TV production personnel are now included under the organization's "creative" heading, so preparation of the commercial idea—to express a consumer's interpretation of the client's marketing strategy—is usually a joint effort of producer, copywriter and art director (or their properly hyphenated equivalents).

Typical Checklist for TV Commercial Producers

The man responsible for coordination of this often mad group of creative people is the producer. After a while, he may end up mad himself. The author's check list for his producers while at Grey Advertising Inc. (a major agency with $200,000,000 annual client billings) may help explain why:

1. □ Have you discussed Storyboard with all Creative People involved?
2. □ Timed the Script or Board and verified its producibility?

---

[16] See the author's more specialized *The Anatomy of a Television Commercial* (Hastings House, 1970).

3. ☐ Prepared Bid Sheets for Production Companies?

4. ☐ Prepared Music Bid Sheet when necessary?

5. ☐ Given copies of Board to Casting, Continuity Clearance, Business and Fashion?

6. ☐ Prepared a Job Jacket for the Commercial?

7. ☐ Met with Business Department to prepare Estimates?

8. ☐ Discussed Casting Requirements with Casting Dept? Arranged Casting Session?

9. ☐ Do you have Approved Estimate?

10. ☐ Did you get Approval of Revisions which will change Estimate?

11. ☐ Do you have approved Continuity Clearance?

12. ☐ Have you arranged Pre-Production Meeting (with Script and Board for this)?

13. ☐ Prepared Production Schedule and issued it promptly?

14. ☐ Issued Minutes of Pre-Production Meeting to all concerned?

15. ☐ Are you sure Fashion Department knows Commercial Requirements and has estimated Wardrobe Costs?

16. ☐ Does everyone concerned know Time and Place of Shooting or Recording Session?

17. ☐ Do you have all Home Phone Numbers of Everyone attending Shooting?

18. ☐ Do you have approved Script and Board for Shooting?

19. ☐ Do you have Talent Contracts and Forms available on Shooting Date?

20. ☐ Do you have a Producer's Report filled out for Each Day of Shooting?

21. ☐ Do you have Music Lead Sheet and AFM Contracts for Business Department?

22. ☐ Have you scheduled Screenings? Creative; then Account?

23. ☐ Do you have a Complete Report for each Screening?

24. ☐ Did you clear with the Business Dept. any Revisions requiring Budget Changes so Revised Estimate can be approved and prepared?

25. ☐ Did you complete the Answer Print Form?

26. ☐ Did you prepare As-Filmed Scripts?

27. ☐ Did you check all Changes and Invoices prior to Billing of job?

28. ☐ Did you check First Sample Air Print supplied by Traffic Dept.?

29. ☐ Take every opportunity to contribute to the Creative Development of the commercial, while you were doing all the other things herein mentioned?

Creative First Principles

While it is difficult, perhaps impossible, to set down exactly what mental processes are followed under these circumstances of "creating" a commercial, there are some points that are usually kept in mind (front or back) by creative people as they go. Some years ago, the author contributed a *precis* of these points to

Effective Advertising (Grosset & Dunlap, 1964). Visual styles may change, but these principles are probably basic:

1. Capture the viewer's attention. Don't keep what you're trying to sell him a complete mystery. Show why he needs it, show why your product surpasses competition, show how easy it is to get some.
2. Don't think of *writing* a TV commercial; draw it. The *video* sets the mood, tone or style.
3. Maintain sufficient movement. As a rule of thumb, move something within each scene (or change scenes) every three seconds.
4. *After* you've plotted the various scenes in the commercial, write audio that EXPLAINS the picture; do not describe it: People can see for themselves. Tell the viewer *why* what he sees is important to him.
5. Keep things simple. Shorten. Condense. Tell half the story. Use optical shortcuts to get from one idea to another. Move from a broad view to close-up, from close-up to broad. Stay away from optical tricks that distract.
6. Make a storyboard. Use a new frame every time something new happens on the screen. Match your audio to your frames.
7. Record any audio on a tape recorder. Hear how it sounds . . . see if you like it. You'll probably want to change words, shorten sentences. Study the storyboard as you listen to the recording.
8. Use titles (words or trademarks superimposed on the screen) generously. If the advertiser has a logotype or design prominent on his product or point-of-sale material, splash it around generously on your commercial; if you have a slogan, superimpose it. Not just at the bottom, but wherever it will do the most good. Keep titles short. Never, never have your titles do anything but reinforce the audio. Never write one thing on screen while the announcer is saying something else; this only creates confusion and distraction.

What About Music?

Music is usually a key commercial ingredient, and plays a role in more than half the commercials in this book:

Emotional impact: Music sets the mood for pictures and copy and influences the way people "feel" about a brand.

Memorability: Music triggers recall—a slogan, selling idea, brand name, etc.

Distinctiveness: Music gives a unique sound—helps the commercial stand apart from competitive advertising.

Audience Selectivity: Music helps reach a special audience or market—especially age or ethnic groups to which it appeals.

Signature or Theme Music: Identifies the product being advertised; gives long-term continuity to a brand's advertising, promotes high advertising awareness.

Mood Music:

      a. *Underscoring:* Supports emotional content of the pictures or copy it accompanies; induces unconscious emotional reactions in viewers, aids understanding of time and place.

      b. *Effects Music:* Punctuates or highlights important words, pictures or ideas.

Musical Jingle: Copy set to music and sung.[17]

Storyboards and Scripts

Doodles and scribbled words are quickly transferred to a pad with a group of blank rectangles a few inches wide, known as a storyboard. There are 1,440 different frames of picture information in a 60-second film commercial. The storyboard attempts to distill them into only about two dozen frames, showing pertinent changes of scene, movements, titlings, etc., necessary to properly present an understandably condensed version of the commercial idea.

Some form of storyboard in the production of a television commercial is as essential as getting a good road map for a long motor trip. This combination of pictures and words should be clear, understandable, and easily and inexpensively reproduceable in a size small enough to fit file folder or pocket.

The storyboard serves as a point of instant reference at every moment in production, and is kept completely up-to-date, particularly during the planning and review stages of a commercial, before a foot of film is shot. Practical master storyboards have easily replaceable video and audio panels, temporarily affixed with rubber cement.

No storyboard can exactly predict commercial filming conditions or camera angles in advance. The argument against rendering storyboard video panels too "tight" is in fear that this may effectively limit some spontaneous creative inspiration by the director and cameraman. Where this becomes a matter of advertising agency policy, storyboard panels are drawn quite loosely—or even cartoon-style.

Physical size and shape of the storyboard is open to variation. It can be merely a huge piece of cardboard with a dozen panels mounted thereon. Two or three of these boards are usually sufficient to effectively depict any one-minute commercial—and make an unpopular armful in a crowded agency elevator. Photostatic reduction to half-size makes them more convenient to handle, but brings original typewriter type down to the border of legibility. In a meeting, the big board is big enough to be seen from across the table (if the words are read aloud); the photostat can be studied later.

---

[17] David Ogilvy once pronounced that if a Macy's Basement salesman ever thought of singing the virtues of pots and pans at him, he'd flee. But Ogilvy & Mather still writes jingle commercials.

The storyboard concept is reviewed and re-reviewed with the advertiser in various unfinished and finished states.

Presenting a storyboard to a naive client is difficult. He may not realize that attention should be focussed only on one panel at a time—the way the viewer will see the commercial unfold on TV. All sorts of acrobatic ways have been devised to fold up or mask the other panels, in order to concentrate the client's eye on the panel under discussion; perhaps it is easier to educate the client in presentation technique.

When soliciting new business, most agencies prefer to carry suggested commercial storyboards further down the road to actual production. Short of test filming, these "lights-out" presentation approaches are most often based on color or black-and-white still photography, placed on an animation stand and shot as a 16mm motion picture, or placed on a filmstrip stand and shot as a multi-frame strip. In each case, soundtracks are transferred to film, tape or disc, after being recorded as close as possible to a finished commercial track—which is not difficult.

Sooner or later, a *script*, too, becomes essential to proper commercial production, usually just prior to recording or filming. Script audio is easily *readable* by talent, and gives the script clerk a place to make formal notes.

The film editor, too, can use a script as a convenient guide to exactly what goes where, once all of the commercial's useable picture and sound takes have been sorted out. After the commercial is completed, the script is easily revised into an "as-filmed" form (such as those in this book) that correctly describe all the camera moves and matching audio. It then becomes a permanent legal and file record, even handier than the film itself for network continuity clearance, future creative revisions, discussions of the medium, etc.

Color

The question of color is an interesting one; because color transmission is now universal, advertisers go with color automatically.

We live in a world of color, but humans have long been accustomed to accepting visual reports of it in monochrome. Since the first charred stick drawings on a cave wall, man has been able to abstract the essential qualities of an object—shape, texture, etc.—and reproduce them *without* reference to color. People recognize objects almost as readily by their shape as by their color, often *more* readily. Color, by and of itself, is not vital to a basic perception of the world; it only refines and heightens *certain* recognitions.

At other times, color can be a hindrance to recognition. For example, try and find, by color, a particular gaudily-colored detergent box on a shelf full of gaudily-colored detergent boxes. In that case, color is just clutter.

While the first few color commercials a family sees on their new color set may rivet their attention, the curiosity value dissipates sometime around the second night's eleven o'clock in-color news. Color is just *there*—nothing more miraculous than TV itself.

So the use of color becomes just another factor in the media mix. As such, it has to communicate—or it's a distraction.

Consider a headache remedy. The package viewed in monochrome may leave the advertiser disappointed. Viewers are unable to recognize its carefully (and expensively) designed high visibility for the point of purchase; those tastefully muted graphics of red, white and blue. But considering the synthetic central drama of the headache itself—and its depressing nature—perhaps the selling communication might be more compelling in monochrome. Or color might be saved for the moment of relief—a very effective mixing of monochrome and color that Eisenstein first used in *Ivan the Terrible,* and Antonioni, Bergman, etc. have used since. Oddly enough, few practitioners of the "one minute art form" have yet had the courage to really experiment with creative color use of this sort.

INTO PRODUCTION

When agreement to produce the commercial is secured, a decision is made on the use of film or video tape, etc. A production house is selected (usually under a competitive three-bid system) to create the final commercial, and final cost estimates are submitted for client approval.

Casting is done by the advertising agency, with the participation of production house director—who will, after all, be responsible for the performance to be obtained from the actors.[18] If the commercial is on film, it is carefully discussed in a pre-production meeting, and then shot in and out of sequence, in a studio or on location, or both. Filming is usually completed within two or three days. Each scene is shot several times; only the successful performances—or camera moves—are printed. These are carefully examined in a screening room soon after the shooting by everyone involved, and then re-analyzed on a complicated-looking but simple editing machine known as a "Moviola," which also can synchronize the recorded soundtrack.

From the best pieces of film and track, an initial edited version of the commercial, known as a "rough cut," is prepared by the production house editor, working with the agency producer, for screening in an "interlocked" (film with rough-mixed sound) condition. At this stage, the agency is ready to unveil the commercial film to an anxious client for comments, suggestions, changes—and hopefully, no additional reshooting. Delays and consequent costs engendered during this "hurry-up-and-wait" period are what make television production on film such a maligned and often costly business.

When final approvals on the rough-cut picture (it is by now called a "workprint") are secured, the film elements are turned over to the laboratory, to prepare the optical negative used in the final release printing.[19] Using edge numbers

---

[18] Television talent fees offer an amazingly important and large-scale subsidy to professional actors. View old commercials, and you'll recognize more than a few of today's stars, carried over their lean earlier years by TV commercial money.

[19] Although only a handful of U.S. television stations (in major cities) are equipped to *project* TV commercials from 35mm film, 95% of all film commercials are *produced* in 35mm

that are part of the original film emulsion and have remained constant through all the reprinting and editing processes, laboratory cutters match up the selected frames, printing "finegrains"[20] of each different selected "take" into a single strip of cellulose acetate negative, and add such optical effects as fades, dissolves, wipes, titles, etc. as printing progresses. Finegrains of more complicated optical effects—floating cigarettes, Hertz customers, etc.—are prepared separately on a complicated film printing machine known as an "optical bench."

Typography and Titles

Titling is an indispensable part of an effective commercial. Good titling is good as much for what it doesn't try to do as for what it does do; the technical limitations of the medium must always be kept in mind. Most of the commercials in this book reflect the following basic considerations, prepared by the author in the early '60's for David Ogilvy's Art Department:

Style and Size: Where possible, use the same typographic style and size throughout a commercial, to offer some visual consistency. Consider full-screen treatment for titles with many words; the visual interruption may be exactly right. Keep all titling well within the safety perimeter of the SMPTE standard; most TV receivers are not properly adjusted.[21] The height of letters in any line should not be less than 1/20 of the total height of the frame, to insure legibility at normal viewing distance. Small-size titles should be held on-screen at least half a second for each word to insure average reading comprehension. Larger titles may be shown more quickly.

Type Forms: The simple, classic typefaces are best for TV transmission. Even with poor reception ("ghost" images, etc.) a simple letter form may still be legible. Upper and lower case letters are more legible than all upper case ("all caps") typesetting. This is simply because the lower case letter form is more distinctive—less "boxy" and therefore more quickly recognizable—than its capital. In almost every alphabet design, it also occupies less area. Thus an upper case/lower case title can either cram more letters into the same area, or the same number of letters can be set visibly bigger. But remember that "all caps" can convey a useful newsy, heraldic effect. Punctuate properly; punctuation is a precise communications tool. Use italics with caution; legibility is the watchword.

Arrangement: Reading arrangement for the viewer should be logical; he has only a moment, with no time for visual hurdles. Bizarre layouts supress his normal

---

width, and then reduced—in either negative or positive form—to the smaller 16mm size. Use of a 35mm original improves final quality, is easier to handle, and permits greater optical flexibility.

[20] A "finegrain" is the reversed (positive) image of a selected section of original black-and-white negative footage (its equivalent in color film is called "interpositive"). It is used to *reprint* (again reversed) the basic commercial optical negative—which preserves the *original* negative footage intact for future use.

[21] Standards are based on *average* TV set reception. On new TV tubes, the ends and edges of titling squeezed up against "safety" margins will be lost. This is because the size of all TV pictures shrinks with age; set manufacturers postpone a service call by purposely installing tubes that "overscan" slightly.

cooperation. To concentrate attention, lines of type may be "rolled up" one line at a time through the frame—or "scratched on" one letter at a time. Horizontally-moving titles may "strobe"—an optical phenomenon that works against the very phenomenon of persistence of vision that makes motion pictures possible. Run a test. Titles either supplement video information, or can be almost an animated part of the commercial picture action. If they are static, it should be by design and not default; remember that a TV commercial is a *moving* picture.

Technique: Lettering should be "reverse" (white) against all but the lightest backgrounds. Television is a light source shining into the viewer's eye; white lettering offers the greatest degree of tonal drop-out against the gray scale of normal photographic values. A drop-shadow (a slightly-offset black rendering of the white type) will help separate title from complicated background. Be specific about the amount of shadow desired; optical houses can be disturbingly arbitrary about this detail.

Rendering: Render titles on storyboard frames in the exact size and style that will appear in the finished commercial, with careful attention to lettering safety. This will avoid a lot of later argument and extra cost.

Cost Estimates and Animation

From the point of view of cost estimating, sometimes complicated film effects are actually easier to work with than live shooting. It is much less complex to estimate the cost of animation, for example, than the cost of live filming. Such things as weather, per diems, travel, actors, teamsters, grips, and other unpredictable factors do not enter into animation calculations. The major cost is labor; material consists of paper, acetate, type, photostats, Xerox, paint, film processing, and that's about it.

Figuring the labor costs of animation is not the least bit mysterious—*provided* you know seven things:

1. Length of film.
2. Number of characters (and are they on screen together?).
3. Do the characters talk with lip synchronization?
4. Kind of animation action (complex, stylized? Disneyesque?).
5. Style of drawing and painting.
6. Background (Yes or no? Full or limbo?).
7. Rotoscoping? [22]

PUTTING IT ALL TOGETHER

Final soundtrack elements—synchronous and non-synchronous—are brought together much the same as the various pieces of the picture and incorporated into a single magnetic track by a re-recording process known as the "audio mix." Although television is primarily a visual medium, sound nuances must be carefully evaluated at this point; a good commercial can easily be spoiled by an inept mix.

---

[22] Rotoscoping is a method of combining animation and live action with traveling mattes.

Synchronous sound is fairly straightforward to work with. Non-synchronous sound presents the producer with additional decisions.

"Voice-Over" Recording

Two alternate methods are used to prepare a non-synchronous soundtrack for a television commercial. One is to *pre-record* the track, obtaining from talent as satisfying, comfortable and well-paced a reading as possible. Where a large number of words is involved, and picture cues are very precise, this method seems to work best.

With the pre-recorded voice track as a base, it is an easy matter for an editor to cut scenes against words. If the commercial has been properly produced, pictures will fit nicely. Where adjustment may be necessary, the voice track can be "opened up" (and pieces of "room tone"—a piece of quiet tape made at the same recording session—inserted). It is usually harder to "close up" a track, when there is not enough picture to cover words. The technician has to work so subtly that his finished track may have a splice every 3 or 4 inches.

Two arguments are held against pre-recording, neither of them final. The first; that television is primarily a visual art, and *pictures* should always control *words*—number of words, choice of words, and the speed with which they are delivered. That is to say, the editor should first cut the best-looking picture, and then words should be made to fit this cut.

The second argument; that voice-over talent cannot become sufficiently interested or excited unless watching the picture they are commenting on. This fails on purely professional grounds.

Where words are few and voice cues are not precise, the second method, post-editing *dubbing* (called *looping* on the West Coast), is often preferred. The edited workprint is projected on a screen outside a soundproof booth; inside, the voice-over talent records the words to match, often following light-bulb cues without even watching the picture.

One advantage inherent in this process is that it may usually be combined with the final audio mixing session. The editor's work to this point will then have been almost completely visual; minor adjustments can be easily made to the workprint picture later, to fit the final mixed track.

Most original music tracks are usually post-recorded; "counts" are taken from the final workprint, and a musical arrangement completed, to the precise frame. Stock music offers less flexibility.

Soundtrack "Pull-Up"

Because of the nature of film projection equipment, the audio section of a 16mm film commercial—of any length—must be at least 26 frames (1-1½ seconds) briefer then the video. This is because the picture must be intermittently *jerked* past the projection lamp, while the soundtrack must be *slid* smoothly past the sound reading head.

A distance equal to 26 16mm frames is required to effectively smooth out the initial intermittent jerking, utilizing a series of projector rollers and snubbers. To compensate for this by printing the soundtrack 26 frames *ahead* of the picture sets up a risk; careless splicing of several spots by a TV station may chop off the first words of the commercial.

To be safe, *the first second or two of every film commercial is always silent.*[23] This "pull-up" has been accepted as part of the art form by TV viewers; such silence may appear disconcerting only when extremely violent or noisy action is apparent from the very beginning of the commercial. Occasionally, this limitation is put to aesthetic use, re-printing the first, very active frame as a "frozen" still 26 times; then "unfreezing" it as sound begins.

The same problem exists in a less important form in video tape recording. There, too, the sound reading head is separate from the picture head, but placed only 9 inches "later." At the standard video tape speed of 15 inches per second, this represents a negligible delay of about ½ second which is normally not a factor in editing video tape commercials.

Sound Transfer

The mixed audio elements, now on one splice-free master tape, are transferred to an identical band of magnetic material striped onto clear 35mm ("mag stripe").

The final mixed "35 mag" track is eventually transferred to a piece of optical negative film, and the commercial is ready for composite (picture *and* soundtrack) printing. Sprocket holes maintain a synchronized sound/picture relationship.

An educated guess is made in the laboratory as to the different light (or color) densities required to make the commercial appear as if it was all shot in the same place at the same time. The result of this first guess is the "answer print"—and answer printing is continued until everything looks right and proper densities have been permanently recorded on a card that controls all future printing of the commercial.[24]

The commercial is then ready for final "release" (air) printing, and the advertising agency producer can relax.

VIDEO TAPE

If the commercial is to be produced on *video tape,* the pre-production meeting is usually much more detailed; it is more expensive to make "after the fact" changes in a video taped commercial. Studio or location taping usually goes quickly with video tape. Control room monitors show each shot as it is recorded in

---

[23] Thus a 60-second film commercial only has time for 58 seconds of audio; a 30-second commercial, only 28 seconds, etc.

[24] A relatively new device that breaks through color printing's "cut-and-try" straitjacket permits the operator to electronically add or subtract values of yellow, cyan or magenta with any scene, to obtain (and record) a subjectively satisfactory printing "formula."

or out of sequence; once it is performed perfectly, the crew moves on to the next shot. Optical effects—dissolves, wipes, titles—can be added *while shooting;* one of the great time-and-money-savers of the video tape process.

With the client in attendance in the video tape control room, it is practical to receive approval on the entire commercial even before proceeding to edit picture, sound, and music together—which is now done by some rather amazing computer hardware. The great value of this process lies in its speed and simplicity—but it requires impeccable taste and strong nerves, lest the entire project later be swept down the drain by some rambunctious client as "unsatisfactory."

Many People Are Involved

In addition to the advertising agency and client personnel involved in these two production processes—film and video tape—many other skilled (and usually unionized) craftsmen take part. In the case of complicated *film* commercials, these can include any or all of the following people:

Talent	Greensman
Director	Teamsters
Assistant Director	Wardrobe Mistress
Production Assistant	Make-up Artist
Director of Photography	Hairdresser
Camera Operator	Script Clerk
Assistant Cameraman	Stylist
Chief Electrician	Still Photographer
Second Electrician	Home Economist
Third Electrician	Nurse
Generator Operator	Animal Trainer
Chief Grip	Baby Teaser
Second Grip	Graphics Designer
Third Grip	Drivers
Special Effects Man	Watchman
Sound Mixer	Teamsters
Recording Engineer	Helicopter Pilot
Boom Man	Prompter Operator
Playback Operator	Music Arranger
Sound Effects Engineer	Music Conductor
Art Director	Musicians
Scenic Artist (Construction)	Editor
Scenic Artist (Shooting)	Editorial Assistant
Carpenters	Projectionist
Construction Grips	Optical Laboratory Technicians
Stage Manager	Developing & Printing Laboratory
Chief Property Man	Technicians
Second Property Man	Messengers
Third Property Man	Etc.

In the case of a *video tape* commercial, the crew and operational list is equally complex:

Staff Producer	Carpenter
Director	Assistant Carpenter
Assistant Director	Wardrobe Mistress
Lighting Director	Make-Up Artist
Audio Director	Hairdresser
Technical Director	Stylist
Video Director	Home Economist
Scenic Designer	Nurse
Scenic Artists	Animal Trainer
Cameramen	Baby Teaser
Floor Manager	Graphics Designer
Boom Operator	Drivers
Boom Pusher	Prompter Operator
Head Electrician	Music Arranger
Assistant Electrician	Music Conductor .
Property Man	Musicians
Assistant Property Man	VTR (video tape recorder) Operators

With such a high level of union labor involvement, it is not surprising that those 1,440 little ¾″ × 1″ cellulose acetate-and-emulsion rectangles in a one-minute film commercial—or the 75 feet of 2-inch wide ferrous oxide-coated Mylar in a video tape commercial—create such high production charges. "Producer's nets" of between $15,000 and $25,000 are common for even a slightly complicated TV spot. When the advertising agency has grossed up that production house bill with concomitant talent costs, internal creative expenses for storyboards, weather contingencies, travel, wardrobe, etc.—and then added the 17.65% commission standard with members of the American Association of Advertising Agencies, a client's "external" cost for a single commercial can fall between $25,000 and $35,000. Add to this salaries within his own advertising department, plus the cost of possible collateral promotion around the TV effort, and you can see why an accountant's heart grows sad.

It all begins to explain why small advertisers have had trouble budgeting even a single commercial; why even the largest advertisers have usually attempted to "pool" two or three spots in a similar creative campaign. And also, why the television viewer may see one particular spot repeated *ad infinitum,* or certainly more often than would be the case if the cost of producing alternates was not so high.

There is nothing new in this situation; it is a problem with which advertisers have lived since the earliest days of television. Any grumbling has been offset by the clearly apparent fact that successful television commercials have always proved to be worth every penny of even exorbitant production costs and more . . . *as viewers responded.* (See Footnote, page 39.)

Viewer Response

At first, viewer response was judged empirically. People either bought a TV-advertised product or they didn't. When they didn't, the manufacturer commissioned a new commercial that *would* catch their interest—a move that had to be made anyway when even a good commercial had "used up" viewer attention.

When swifter marketing judgments became necessary (and commercial production costs rose), this cut-and-try method became too chancy. A number of research test techniques were developed first for commercial *ideas;* then for *dummy commercials* inexpensively produced; and finally for the *actual commercial* itself—*before* it was placed on the air.

One such technique, "day-after recall," has been extensively employed by Procter & Gamble, Shell Oil, etc. Using thousands of personal telephone calls the day after a new commercial has been "sneak-previewed" in a particular market, people who actually viewed it are isolated, and their reactions graded against scores for previous commercials for the same product. A poor reaction may turn back for revision—or completely scrap—a finished commercial costing tens of thousands of dollars.

As viewer sophistication improved, it became apparent that commercial advertising sophistication would have to keep pace. Great clouds of dust were raised during this period by proponents of the "hammer-head" school of television spot production. Using trade speeches and learned books, many advertising executives pushed a doctrine that suggested the American TV viewer would buy anything if hit often enough, loud enough, and with the same sales message.[25]

By 1959, public distaste for this approach had mushroomed, fed by the TV quiz program scandals and irritated by the flood of "bait and switch" commercial advertising *ad nauseam* for storm windows, domestic appliances, etc. Commercials seemed to be running downhill. The time seemed ripe to start upgrading the image of an industry, and eventually, perhaps, the industry itself.

A FESTIVAL

At this moment in television history, Wallace A. Ross moved onto the scene with the American Television Commercials Festival and Forum. It was also at this moment that the question of which comes first, the commercial or the program, was finally resolved—with the straggling demise of the finest programs of TV's "Golden Age": *Studio One, The United States Steel Hour, The Armstrong Circle Theatre,* etc.

The point of television now became to sell things, and the medium was finally on its way to becoming one big over-commercialized selling message. And

---

[25] This argument failed to note that the product most involved, headache remedies, came from an industry whose use of inexpensive raw materials affords its manufacturers the luxury of earmarking 43 cents out of every consumer retail dollar for *further product advertising*. This is the highest such figure in all of American marketing experience; it is easy to see why such a dollar return provided a successful insulating buffer against advertiser sensitivity to any public distaste.

how infectious it could be; even a non-commercial, education program like today's *Sesame Street* sells children the letter "B"—or the number "9"—using the format and techniques of the TV commercial.

But any vision of *Sesame Street* was still far in the future for Mr. Ross, who is an intelligent, articulate young man with a professional background in public relations for the motion picture and broadcast industries. In the Fall of 1959, he simply had the idea that there might be some special value in a formal annual evaluation of good and bad American television commercial advertising. His announced, almost single-minded purpose, was to help reform the TV commercials industry.

The response from a number of leading advertisers and their agencies to Mr. Ross' idea was most encouraging; many prominent advertising executives volunteered time to this project (and continue their service up to the present moment).

The American TV Commercials Festival was an immediate success. Perhaps because of it, the general creative quality of commercials on American television—both absolutely and relatively—has shown considerable improvement since 1959.

Trade and public interest in the American Television Commercials Festival has grown steadily. After eleven years, the once comfortable luncheon program that screened Festival "winners" at New York City's Hotel Roosevelt has evolved, by way of the Waldorf-Astoria, to a jammed black-tie dinner and dance in the New York Hilton's Grand Ballroom—and thence to Philharmonic Hall in Lincoln Center.

But before each year's festivities must come each year's judging. This month-long period of evaluation and eyestrain becomes increasingly difficult each year as the number of submitted entries increases—almost 2,500 in 1969! For the first Festival, Mr. Ross personally approached, in the Fall of 1959, persons prominent in or associated with television advertising, enlisting their unpaid time, talent and professional judgment.

Two-thirds of the initial "Council of Judges"—31 men and 3 women—were employed in creative or management capacities by 24 of the country's largest advertising agencies. Most of these people were, at that time, directly involved in their agency's creative production of television commercials. The remaining members of the Council included representatives of 13 of America's leading national advertisers, the firms for whom the bulk of U.S. commercials are prepared.

Judges aimed for objectivity. A rotating attendance of 10 to 15 judges at each screening effectively reduced log-rolling, and no judge voted on a commercial with which he or his agency or company had any affiliation. In the case of the "Classics" this objectivity was further enforced by a substantial passage of time. No commercial was nominated as a "Classic" that had not been first broadcast some time prior to 5 years preceding the Festival.

In each annual Festival judging, sufficient honors are passed around—in the form of "Firsts," "Runners-Up" and "Special Commendations," etc.—to keep advertising agencies and production houses (who pay a substantial submission fee per commercial) quite happy. Scrolls suitable for framing, and since 1962, "Oscar-type" golden statuettes (somewhat inappropriately named *Clio*, after the

Greek Muse of History) have been passed out to bedeck walls and windowsills of glassed-in offices of hundreds of advertising agency TV producers, art directors, copywriters, production house employees—and their clients.

The "Classic" Commercials

Amidst all this public relations furor, the Festival's "Classics" category still stands a little apart. The spots so honored are only a tiny handful among the thousands of television commercials produced each year. They are examined and chosen by the Festival's judges with some circumspection. As the "best" of American television commercial advertising, they must appear to have met a test of time as spontaneous, interesting, imaginative, visually and aurally exciting examples of the commercial art. The Festival's suggested criteria are: "believability; tastefulness; copy line; demonstration; identification; longevity; memorability; influence on later techniques." Above all, they are pieces of sales communication to which American viewers have—beyond any doubt—overwhelmingly responded.

The 69 television commercials in the section that follows were selected by judges from the formative period 1948-1958 as "classic" examples of effective TV selling messages. They break down into 13 major marketing categories. In 1958, when the "youngest" commercial in this volume was produced and put on the air, these 13 categories accounted for all but 11% of the $1,078 billion invested that year by American advertisers in spot and network TV.

The Second TV Decade saw extensive quantitative but not qualitative change.

Ten years later, total annual expenditures had almost tripled, to $2,824 billion; this was spent by 2,194 advertisers to promote 3,984 brands. Both spot and network buys still shared the TV medium almost equally between them; but a number of small new product classes had arisen, reducing the market share of the original 13 categories to about 80% of all monies spent.

Also, some advertising category investments had increased at uneven rates during the decade. *Food Products* and particularly *Coffee & Tea, Tobacco* and *Appliances* were on the low side; *Household Products* were on the high. But American advertisers were still making the same general kind of TV investments. Manufacturers of nationally-distributed goods and services heavied up in *network* TV; local and regional goods and services were heaviest in *spot*.

The categories represented by this first decade of "Classics" are:

Food	Toiletries
Coffee & Tea	Apparel
Beer, Wine	Appliances
& Soft Drinks	Cars & Trucks
Tobacco	Automotive Products
Household Products	Gasoline
Medical Products	Consumer Services

As might be expected in the formative years of the TV medium, there is close correlation between the number of award-winning commercials recognized in each category over the period 1949-1958, and *total* TV advertising in that category.

Six rough commercial types are represented in this collection:

1. Slice of Life (12 commercials).
2. Problem + solution (22 commercials).
3. Testimonial (10 commercials).
4. Confessional (2 commercials).
5. Presumed authority (5 commercials).
6. Demonstration (18 commercials).

These types are self-explanatory. The curious thing to note is that almost half of these "best examples" from the earliest years of this *reality* medium include some form of *unreal* animation, photo animation or puppetry—perhaps a stage in the maturation of self-deception?

In studying (and remembering) these commercials, it will be wise to ask the question, where did they lead us?

PART TWO

The 69 "Classic" Television Commercials, 1948-1958

ABOVE all, television is a *visual* medium. Words no longer control meaning. After 500 years of printing, we witness a renaissance in human communication. The intellectualized, symbolic, linear, step-by-step transmission of human knowledge and ideas—I quote McLuhan—turns pallid beside the re-introduction of all the ancient complex richness of immediate face-to-face confrontation, sparked by the resonance of voice.[1] Television again makes this possible.

The words in the section that follows are no exception—they are a poor substitute for the actual viewing of the commercials they describe. But already this book (and its printing press) are being supplemented by the more advanced technologies of magnetic video recording. Soon the reader will be able to use either—or both. But until that Second Television Revolution, however, we still have to *read* about the effects of the first.

As one enters this section of the book, it is useful to note certain standard industry terms and abbreviations that have developed to indicate picture framing (composition), camera movement, and voice sources:

Video:

LS = Long Shot = Tiny actors against a vast background.
FS = Full Shot = The actors and the entire background scene are in frame.
MS = Medium Shot = The actors' whole bodies are in frame.

---

[1] Highly original research from UCLA offers a surprising breakdown of the three ways in which a TV personality communicates with his viewers: facial expression and physical posture—55%; vocal intonation and inflection—38%; verbal message—*only 7%!*

MCU = Medium close-up = The actors are waist-up.

CU = Close-up = The actors' faces.

ECU = Extra Close-up = The actor's features.

ZOOM (In or Out) = Rapid frame size change achieved by camera lens adjustment (without parallax alteration).

DOLLY (In or Out) = Slow frame change accomplished by moving the camera forward or backward (altering parallax).

TRUCK = Slow frame change accomplished by moving the camera sideways.

PAN (Left or Right) = Camera movement from a set position, along a horizontal arc.

TILT = (Up or Down) = Camera movement from a set position, along a vertical arc.

Audio:

O.C. = On Camera = Someone visible says something. (Also: LIP SYNC)

V.O. = Voice Over = Someone invisible says something.

* * *

The following editing terms describe techniques for montaging from one frame of picture information to another:

DISSOLVE = Fade-in of a new scene over the fade-out of the previous one.

CUT = Instantaneous replacement of a frame with one completely new.

WIPE = New frame material used as an edge or in some geometric shape, to "erase" or "push" old material off the screen. Wipe edges can be "hard" or "soft."

POP = (On or Off) = Instantaneous addition or subtraction of new information (usually artwork or titles).

LOGO = Logotype = The advertiser's individualized graphic design of his name, etc.

* * *

The following terms describe the audio effect of mixing various sound sources:

FADE (In or Out) = Raising or lowering a particular sound level.

SEGUÉ = Cross-fading or dissolving one sound source into its replacement.

CUT = Sudden cessation of a continuous sound.

EQUALIZATION = Alteration of the frequency range of a sound source, for practical or creative effect.

* * *

The commercial scripts in this book are transcribed with a simple system of cue notation, which numbers each new video cue consecutively, but only if it embraces a complete scene change. Otherwise the cue carries the number of the previous cue with an alphabetical subscript letter. This is video shorthand which enables anyone involved in TV production to see at a glance how many set-ups, camera positions, sound takes, etc. are required by a particular commercial.

Food

More television commercials have been produced to sell edibles to the people of America than in any other marketing category. The size of this section reflects both that fact—and a general level of recognized "creative" achievement.

As television commercials penetrated American homes after 1948 (in that year there were only 975,000 black-and-white receivers in the country) and food and much other shopping shifted from the corner grocery to the supermarket shopping plaza, a food marketer's fight for "shelf facings" in the new self-service chains reached undreamed-of heights. By 1970 Americans were spending almost $100 billion a year just in supermarkets!

To support his claim to the fleeting attention of cart-pushing housewives, each marketer plunged swiftly and deeply into television advertising—both to advance existing brands, and to quickly introduce and establish new ones. As should be expected, TV viewers in the '50's were always promised the tastiest, most easily-prepared, most wonderfully-appreciated family food dishes ever offered to an overweight public.

During this "golden age," commercial emphasis swung from canned goods and packaged products to the ever more gastronomically complicated (and ever more profitable) frozen varieties. "Now in your grocer's freezer" became the TV food watchword of the decade.

From the earliest days of this commercial category, the new (and skilled) craft designation of "home economist" became familiar on both live and film TV sets. This specialist was usually a woman, earning from $200 to $300 a day, responsible for preparing (in the most beautiful pans and on the most gorgeous china) the most delectable-looking food products ever to come full-blown out of a can, carton or oven—always in less than 60 seconds!

Also beginning at that time, a certain amount of simple deception—shall we call it "food magic"?—continued even into the late '60's, when as respected a television advertiser as The Campbell Soup Company finally agreed to cease and desist from their normal practice of putting "invisible" glass marbles at the bottom of steaming soup bowls, in order to "float" solid ingredients nearer the surface!

Perhaps the fact that we are—as mentioned—an overfed country, suggests that Americans simply cannot take commercials for food products as seriously as they might be taken by—let us say—a television viewer in India. So almost all food commercials in the U.S. (and *all* the food commercials in this "Classics" collection—80% of which involve some animation) are some form of *fun*.

With *one* exception—Feeding Baby. That's still a deadly serious area, where the hopes and fears of all new mothers were always—and will always be—effectively played upon.

Scene 8   *"Chicken Zoop"*

DETAILS

Live black-and-white kinescope film. 248 seconds. 512 words. Air date
1954.
Thomas J. Lipton, Inc., *Advertiser.*
Young & Rubicam, Inc., *Agency.*
CBS-TV Network (N.Y.), *Producer.*

CREDITS

Thomas I. Ford, Bill Whitman, Richard Zellner, *Creative.*

"CHICKEN ZOOP"

1. OPEN ON MS OF ARTHUR GODFREY SEATED BEHIND DESK MICROPHONE. PICTURES OF LIPTON PRODUCTS DRESS THE FRONT OF THE DESK. (:06 secs.)

GODFREY (O.C.): Now, it says that I'm supposed to have a tray with soup, and—

2. CUT TO FS OF TONY MARVIN COMING ON STAGE CARRYING TRAY WITH SOUP BOWL AND FLOWER VASE. HE HANDS IT TO GODFREY. (:03 secs.)

—ahhh! Bless your sweet heart—

3. CUT BACK TO MS OF GODFREY AS HE PUTS TRAY ON DESK. HE LOOKS SADLY AT VASE, STARES REPROVINGLY OFFSTAGE IN BOTH DIRECTIONS. (:30 secs.)

—oh, you handsome man, you! It is supposed to be a "slim, graceful vase of flowers." (LAUGHTER) It looks pretty short and fat and dumpy. (LAUGHTER)

3A. GODFREY REMOVES VASE FROM TRAY, TURNS BACK TO CAMERA. (:12 secs.)

Anyhow, you get the idea. Spring. April in Paris. May in the Bronx. (LAUGHTER)

3B. GODFREY STARES AT THE SOUP BOWL, TURNS TO CAMERA. (:16 secs.)

And a bowl of soup, and you. Fresh cut flowers and soup. Sure. That's a good springtime dish. A bowl of the freshest-tasting, most delicious chicken noodle "zoop" you ever had.

3C. GODFREY TURNS AWAY TO PICK UP CHICKEN SOUP PACKAGE, WHICH HE PLACES ON THE EDGE OF THE DESK. HE TURNS AGAIN TO PICK UP DISPLAY BOARD OF SOUP PACKAGE PICTURES. (:11 secs.)

And you make it out of an envelope that comes in a box like that; Lipton Chicken Noodle Soup. There are three envelopes in that . . . in that, uh—

4. CUT TO ECU OF CHICKEN SOUP PACKAGE. (:03 secs.)

—(V.O.) ah, we've got the whole business here, look.

5. CUT BACK TO MS GODFREY HOLDING UP DISPLAY BOARD. DOLLY BACK TO FS AS HE PLACES BOARD BEHIND PACK-AGE. (:18 secs.)

(O.C.) Everything is on a board. Those are all the brands that Lipton makes. So how about some of that Lipton Chicken Noodle Soup for Spring? You cook it in ten minutes. Makes four to six servings each, depending on whether you really love soup or not. You . . . just want a little bit.

5A. DOLLY IN TO MS. (:21 secs.)

All you want . . . all you want is just a little cup, a little bowl, as you start the meal. It's good for you, inside. There's plenty of noodles in there. And there's chicken there, too. You won't find it, but it's there! (LAUGHTER) There's chicken.

5B. GODFREY RAISES HIS HAND. (:20 secs.)

Guaranteed—There's chicken. Guaranteed. If you find any, uh, bring it to us, will ya? (LAUGHTER) But . . . it's there. It's delicious, really delicious, because you make it yourself, like you do all the other Lipton soups: Lipton Chicken Noodle Soup—

5C. WIDEN TO MS TO INCLUDE DISPLAY BOARD. (:07 secs.)

—Onion Soup; Green Pea Soup; Beef Vegetable Soup; or Tomato Vegetable Soup. And that Green Pea Soup, oh boy!

6. CUT TO CU OF PEA SOUP PACK- AGE ON DISPLAY BOARD. PAN LEFT PAST LIVE CHICKEN SOUP PACKAGE TO ONION SOUP PACKAGE ON DISPLAY BOARD. (:12 secs.)

They're all good. And the reason they're good is that what you buy here is ingre- dients. It's not a canned soup that you just add water to, and heat.

7. CUT BACK TO MCU GODFREY (:25 secs.)

No, no. You cook these ingredients. It takes eight to ten minutes, depending on the kind of soup. You cook it yourself. It's homemade, and therefore it has that flavor. And it has the flavor of the kind of soup that, ordinarily, if you were to make it the old-fashioned way, would take hours of simmering on a hot stove all day. You do it in ten minutes. Sure, I know—

7A. GODFREY GESTURES UP AND DOWN WITH HAND. (:27 secs.)

—when you go into the grocery store, there are all those cans that are so easy to pick up. And you have to go way on down until you find the Lipton envelopes. But do it one time. Remember to do it once, and try it, and I think you'll stick with it. You'll find that the difference is worth the little extra effort. They are delicious soups. Made by Lipton's. Try them.

7B. GODFREY PICKS UP BOWL AND SPOON. (:17 secs.)

Lipton always likes it if I take a taste. I will therefore take a taste. Oh, look, look! See all the noodles in there? Chicken? Chicken.

8. CUT TO ECU GODFREY STIRRING SOUP. (:04 secs.)

(LAUGHTER)

9. CUT BACK TO MCU OF GODFREY TASTING SOUP. (:17 secs.)	Chick, chick, chick, chick, chick. (NONSENSE LANGUAGE) (LAUGHTER) Oh, that is good, oh!
9A. GODFREY PUTS DOWN SPOON. (:03 secs.)	Let me put it down. I'd like to have some more later.
10. CUT TO CU OF CHICKEN SOUP PACKAGE. (:03 secs.)	(V.O.) I'll put this away so we can see our next Talent Scout, while I—
11. CUT BACK TO MS OF GODFREY PUTTING AWAY PACKAGE DISPLAY BOARD. (:03 secs.)	—(O.C.) guzzle this soup.

* * *

"It's homemade," says the Ol' Redhead, "and therefore it has that *flavor*." And so did every Arthur Godfrey commercial—a special homemade flavor that sent housewives all over America religiously flocking to purchase every single product he pitched. Advertisers fought to buy time on his radio and TV programs.

Godfrey started this amazingly successful broadcast selling career on a Washington radio station during World War II—and is still going strong. As of this writing, Colgate was using Godfrey as an exclusive spokesman (on TV, radio, and in print) to introduce a new detergent—and even point out its ecological hazards! Without doubt, he has been America's Great Pitchman, spieling a sponsor's products for minutes on end, titillating housewives with an occasional leer or minor innuendo.

His method of presentation deliberately defied the arbitrary, constrictive, pre-digested one-minute time slots of broadcast advertising; and this was his strength. Working from "fact sheets" supplied by advertisers, Godfrey could—and would—make mistakes, pause to pick up a cheap laugh, sip tea (?) from a cup . . . and otherwise successfully ignore all the standard commercial advertising conventions that imitators automatically (and unthinkingly) observed.

The microphone was always in plain view. Mistakes were always made *on*-camera. Everything was REAL! The result was an unrehearsed, rather remarkable one-to-one selling communication that many other spokesman-performers tried for—and rarely achieved. No surprise that Godfrey was soon a millionaire, with unparalleled political power in the network he served—and largely helped to build.

"Chicken Zoop" is a representative Godfrey commercial from the period when he was conducting, in addition to his morning TV and radio activities, a popular evening program of the '50's, *Arthur Godfrey's Talent Scouts*—in the Major Bowes and Ted Mack genre. The spot even includes a brief walk-on by his Sancho Panza foil, the ex-CBS staff announcer Tony Marvin.

This live commercial exists today as a kinescope, photographed on 16mm motion picture film off the face of television monitor while the program was actually going out over the air. Scheduled as a one-minute commercial performed from a fact sheet, it actually consumes four minutes and eighteen seconds and several spoonfuls of Lipton Chicken Soup—a handsome bonus for Lipton's advertising department.

It is a performance worthy of study. Godfrey is a born orator, and might have become one of America's great politicians had he achieved his fame a bit later—when dancers became Senators, actors turned Governors, and novelists even tried for Mayors. Godfrey had a relaxed (but far from unconscious) selling rhythm, almost reducible to this formula:

1. Make a joke at someone else's expense; ally your viewer. (The live audience's laughter serves as the "convincer.")
2. Set the mood with some light commentary.
3. Introduce the product visually.
4. Make a damaging joke about the product; so damaging that it cannot possibly be true.
5. Offer a warm, *deadly-serious* sales pitch for the product.
6. Make a personal plea to the viewer to buy, against all possible obstacles.
7. Say "goodbye," with still another joke.

Godfrey viewers—all 20 million of them—soon became terribly familiar with this antic formula, yet they continued to respond over the Godfrey Years with the delight of a bullring audience admiring the footwork of a favorite torero. Why? The Godfrey charisma included great self-identification—he *was* America: materialist, smart-ass, maudlin and vulgar. On occasion, he would even weep on the air.

No one his equal (with the possible exception of another weeper, Jack Paar) has yet passed by.

Scene 1B   "Hey, Hey, Hey!"

DETAILS

Limited animation black-and-white film. 20 seconds. 47 words. Air date
1954.
National Biscuit Co., *Advertiser.*
McCann-Erickson, Inc., *Agency.*
TV Graphics, *Producer.*

CREDITS

Robert Olds, David Lippincott, S. Rollins Guild, *Creative.*
Don Towsley, *Production.*

"HEY, HEY, HEY!"

1. OPEN ON FS SQUEEZE ACTION OF MAN IN KITCHEN PEERING INTO EMPTY RITZ CRACKER BOX. (:06 secs.)

CHORUS (V.O.):
Hey, hey, hey,
That guy with the Ritz
Seems on the fritz.

1A. WIFE ENTERS FROM LEFT FRAME. (:03 secs.)

WIFE (O.C.):
No, no, stop, darling,
Don't blow your top.

1B. POP ON RITZ BOX IN HER LEFT HAND. (:03 secs.)

I always keep another box handy.
HUSBAND (O.C.): Dandy!

1C. HUSBAND TAKES BOX AND STARTS TO EAT CRACKERS. HALO POPS ON OVER WIFE'S HEAD. (:05 secs.)

CHORUS (V.O.):
Those Ritz Crackers are richer, crisper,
And his mouth is full or he'd help us whisper,

1D. ZOOM IN ON KITCHEN CABINET AS WIFE OPENS DOORS TO REVEAL IT FILLED WITH RITZ CRACKER BOXES. (:01½ secs.)

"Only Nabisco—

2. CUT TO MCU OF TILTED RITZ CRACKER BOX IN LIMBO. (:0½ sec.)

—bakes—

3. CUT TO ECU OF SAME TILTED BOX. (:01 sec.)

—Ritz!"

* * *

This 20-second spot was an early example of the animation stand technique known as "squeeze motion." It was the first of a long line of new and different visual approaches which television commercials explored—and then eventually passed by.

This technique utilized live models photographed in a great number of extremely active poses by a still camera against a limbo setting. The resulting prints—after careful study and selection of poses that appeared to "flow" from one to another—were scissored up, and the silhouettes placed on an animation stand against hand-drawn backgrounds. Then they were re-photographed, sequence by sequence, on motion picture film—much in the manner of an animated cartoon.

The resultant commercials jumped about visually in a very interesting manner, highlighting key visual elements—such as the cracker box in this spot—and were most successful when the somewhat spastic visual technique was accompanied by an equally spastic soundtrack. Here a chanted chorus does that job.

Scene 6B   "#$%&()*"

DETAILS

Black-and-white animated film. 60 seconds. 103 words. Air date 1954.
H. J. Heinz Co., *Advertiser*.
Maxon Advertising, Inc. (Detroit), *Agency*.
Storyboard Films, Inc. (L.A.), *Producer*.

CREDITS

Leo Langlois, *Creative*.
Stan Freberg, *Production*.

"#$%&()*"

1. OPEN ON ANIMATED FS OF OFFICIOUS TELEVISION ANNOUNCER IN FRONT OF CABINET WITH "57" LOGO AND HEINZ FOODS. PUSH IN TO MS AS MIKE LOWERS AND CAMERA MOVES IN FROM SIDE. (:10 secs.)	(SOUND: CUE BEEP) ANNOUNCER (O.C.): Ladies, do you ever wish for a magic sauce to whip up that tired gravy or stew you're cooking?
2. CUT TO CAMERA'S PICTURE (HEAD SHOT, CU) AS ANNOUNCER REACHES OUT OF FRAME TO CABINET AND BRINGS IN HEINZ WORCESTERSHIRE SAUCE BOTTLE. (:06½ secs.)	Wish granted! Because that magic sauce is Heinz #$%&()*.
2A. ANNOUNCER'S FACE REDDENS AS HE POINTS TO LABEL AND SWEATS. (:07 secs.)	That's "Heinz #$%&()*...." Ha, ha, ha!
3. CUT BACK TO SIDE FS AS ANNOUNCER FRANTICALLY WAVES–OFF-CAMERA–TO CAMERMAN TO SWIVEL CAMERA AROUND TO FOOD SHOT. CAMERA SWIVELS. (:05 secs.)	You see, this dark, richly-spiced sauce is made to an authentic English recipe.
4. CUT TO LIVE BEAUTY FS OF TABLE SET WITH VARIOUS FOODS. (:05 secs.)	And what it does for fish dishes, chops, even your glass of tomato juice–
5. CUT TO ANIMATED FS OF ANNOUNCER TAPPING CAMERMAN ON SHOULDER. CAMERMAN SWINGS CAMERA BACK ONTO ANNOUNCER. (:05 secs.)	–is nothing short of miraculous. So ladies, be sure to get–
6. CUT TO CAMERA'S PICTURE: CU OF PROUD ANNOUNCER. (:04 secs.)	–Heinz Worcestershire Sauce! Ha!
6A. ANNOUNCER REACHES OUT OF FRAME AND BRINGS IN A CAN OF BEANS. HE LOOKS AT IT, DOES A DOUBLE TAKE AND DROPS IT OUT OF FRAME. (:04 secs.)	Heinz Worcestershire Sauce! Well . . . beans!

6B. HE REACHES OUT AGAIN AND THIS TIME RETURNS WITH THE SAUCE BOTTLE. HIS MOUTH TWISTS UP. (:05 secs.)

You'll love Heinz "#$%&()* . . ."

7. CUT TO SIDE FS AS ANNOUNCER WAVES BOTTLE. (:04½ secs.)

No matter how you pronounce it. say "Heinz" first!

8. CUT BACK TO CAMERA PICTURE OF ANNOUNCER AS HE BECOMES VIOLENT AND BRANDISHES BOTTLE CLOSE INTO LENS. FADE TO BLACK. (:04 secs.)

And-you-know-it's-good-because-it's-HEINZ!

* * *

By 1954, television commercials had passed the first milestone of becoming an art form—they started to make fun of themselves. This is one of the earliest and still one of the best (and freshest) of these self-spoofs. It coupled the irrepressible comic talent of Stan Freberg with the animation genius of John Hubley. All the classic ingredients of the early "stand-up" TV commercial are present: the pompous announcer, the off-camera product which must be handed-in and brandished toward the camera lens at the proper moment. Even the "cut-away" *de rigeur* product-in-use food shot is amusingly rendered *live* in this otherwise animated commercial.

That the Heinz client stood still for this memorable garbling of his product's name is a tribute to both his patience and understanding of good marketing. The commercial played throughout the late '50's and never wore out its welcome.*

---

* Against the background of American economic (and creative?) inflation, compare the production cost of this commercial—less than $5,000—with the $150,000 cost of another 1-minute Heinz commercial (introducing Great American Soups) only a decade and a half later.

Scene 6C   *"Dot's Peanut Butter"*

DETAILS

Black-and-white animated film. 90 seconds. 106 words. Air date 1954.
Best Foods Division, Corn Products Corp., *Advertiser.*
Guild, Bascom & Bonfigli, Inc, (San Francisco), *Agency.*
TV Spots, (L.A.), *Producer.*

CREDITS

Alex Anderson, Dave Bascom, Sam Hollis, *Creative.*
Alex Anderson, *Production.*

"DOT'S PEANUT BUTTER"

1. OPEN ON ANIMATED WHITE DOT ON GRAY BACKGROUND. NINE MORE DOTS POP ON, GROW LEGS, CIRCLE AROUND, AND START TO LEAVE RIGHT FRAME. (:12 secs.)

(MUSIC: LILTING, THROUGHOUT) ANNOUNCER (V.O.): Fifty or sixty years ago, people were introduced to peanut butter for the first time.

2. CUT TO MS OF ORNATE JAR ON ART BACKGROUND. DOT PEOPLE PASS BEHIND IT. THREE OF THEM LIFT IT UP AND START TO CARRY IT OUT LEFT FRAME. (:12 secs.)

They looked it over carefully. The daring and courageous bought it—

3. DISSOLVE TO MS OF OPENED JAR WITH FIVE DOT CHILDREN BOUNCING UP AND DOWN IN FRONT OF IT. (:05 secs.)

—while children loved it.

3A. PAN RIGHT TO TWO DOT PARENTS PACING. (:07 secs.)

But Ma and Pa were more critical.

3B. PAN BACK LEFT WITH PARENTS TO OPENED JAR. ZOOM TO CU OF JAR. (:04 secs.)

They discovered it had several drawbacks.

4. DISSOLVE TO MS OF RADIATING RIPPLE LINES. (:03 secs.)

It became oily.

4A. LINES CONVERGE INTO STRANDS WHICH STRETCH AND DROP OUT OF FRAME. (:01 sec.)

Sticky.

5. TWO DOT FLOWERS GROW, BLOSSOM AND DROP THEIR PETALS. (:06 secs.)

And didn't stay fresh very long.

5A. FLOWER STEMS TIE THEMSELVES IN KNOTS. (:03 secs.)

It was rather hard to digest.

5B. DOT FLOWERS COALESCE INTO A PEANUT SHAPE, WHICH ZOOMS FORWARD TO CU. (:03 secs.)

It didn't taste like peanuts.

5C. PEANUT METAMORPHOSES INTO THREE CHEERING DOTS WITH BLACK PENNANT. (:02 secs.)

Grown-ups never became peanut butter fans until—

5D. ZOOM TO CU PENNANT. POP ON "1933" IN PENNANT. (:02 secs.)	—1933—
6. CUT TO JARS POPPING ON IN A CIRCULAR LINE. SKIPPY JAR POPS ON AT END OF LINE, CU. (:05 secs.)	—when a new kind of peanut butter started to appear in grocery stores.
6A. OTHER JARS DISSOLVE OFF. PARENT DOTS REAPPEAR. THEY EYE JAR. (:06 secs.)	It looked different.
6B. JAR TOP LIFTS OFF. SYMBOLIC ODOR DESIGN APPEARS. DOTS SNIFF IT. THEIR EYES WHIRL. (:06 secs.)	It smelled different.
6C. KNIFE ENTERS FRAME, WITH PEANUT BUTTER AND SLICE OF BREAD. BREAD DISAPPEARS IN BITES. ZOOM TO CU SKIPPY JAR. (:07 secs.)	It tasted different.
7. DISSOLVE TO CU JAR. (:06 secs.)	It had practically nothing in common with the old-style product. (MUSIC: END)

* * *

This minute and a half of abstract animation is still so fresh and delightful that it is hard to believe it was not done yesterday, but almost two decades ago. In both art and copy, it is the epitome of the "soft sell." The playful shapes and backgrounds tell a simple, somewhat institutional story of the history of peanut butter—and slowly get to the Skippy brand (in the video only!). Precisely because it abjures any tricky style, it does not age—as so many TV commercials do, very rapidly.

It is certainly artistic enough to put on the air again tomorrow. But it's 90 seconds long; in black-and-white; and everybody now seems to agree that the only way to sell peanut butter is to show kids in color slathering it over bread and wolfing it down. A pity.

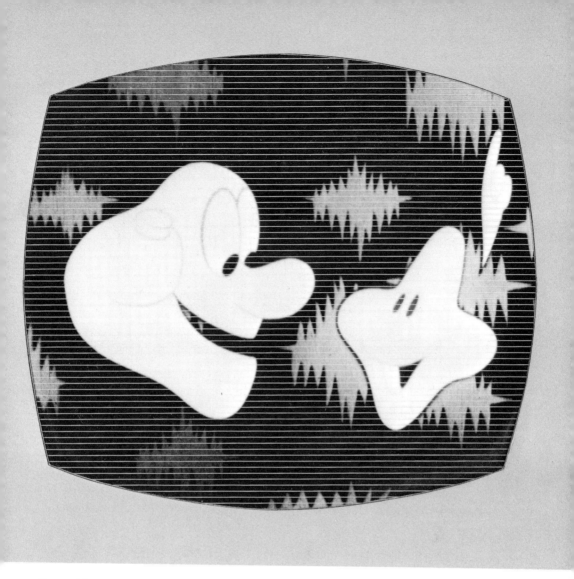

Scene 1A   *"Bop Corn"*

DETAILS

    Black-and-white animated film. 60 seconds. 164 words. Air date 1955.
    Top Pop Products, Inc. *Advertiser.*
    W. B. Doner, Inc. (Detroit), *Agency.*
    Storyboard Films, Inc., Producer.

CREDITS

    Phil Hower, Ben Goldstein, *Creative.*
    John Hubley, Stan Walsh, *Production.*

"BOP CORN"

1. OPEN ON LITTLE ANIMATED HEAD RICOCHETING OVER BACK-GROUND OF POPCORN MOTIF DESIGN. (:02½ secs.)

(SOUND: DRUM RIM SHOTS)

1A. POP ON SECOND (BIGGER) HEAD. (:09 secs.)

BIG HEAD (O.C.): Well, hello boy!
Now, whaddya' say?
LITTLE HEAD (O.C.):
Make with the popcorn, right away.
BIG: Too much trouble and bother,
Yes, indeed.
LITTLE: No, man, heat is all you need.

1B. LITTLE HEAD POPS OFF. ITEMS MENTIONED IN LYRIC POP ON AND OFF AROUND BIG HEAD. (:08 secs.)

BIG: You need more than heat, boy,
According to Hoyle,
You need popcorn, salt, butter and oil,
And a frying pan,
Or to be completely proper,
You oughta have a popper!

2. CUT TO MCU OF LITTLE HEAD. (:04 secs.)

LITTLE: I figure you ain't hip, old man,
Cause E-Z Pop pops in its own pan!

3. CUT TO CU BIG HEAD. (:02½ secs.)

BIG: E-Z Pop pops in its own pan?

4. CUT TO CU TITLE: "E-Z/POP" NEXT TO LITTLE HEAD IN LEFT FRAME. (:03 secs.)

LITTLE: Now you're swingin', daddy,
Crazy, man!

5. CUT TO PANNING FS OF LITTLE HEAD (WITH SYMBOLIC HANDS AND FEET) WALKING. (:02½ secs.)

Won't you make it with me to the grocery shop?

5A. POP ON BIG HEAD WALKING BEHIND HIM. THEY DISAPPEAR INTO STORE. (:04 secs.)

We'll both dig a pan of this E-Z Pop.

5B. THEY REAPPEAR CARRYING HUGE E-Z POP PACKAGE. ZOOM TO PACKAGE. (:03½ secs.)

(SCAT SINGING)

6. CUT TO PACKAGE. SQUEEZE-
MOTION SEQUENCE: PAN LEAVES
CARTON, TURNS, IS SHAKEN OVER
SYMBOLIC FLAME. PUFFS UP.
PUFFS OUT. OPENS TO REVEAL
FINISHED POPCORN. ZOOM IN. (:16
secs.)

LITTLE (V.O.): How, get up the heat good,
It's the wildest,
E-Z Pop's too much,
The neatest, the mildest.
We'll all have a gallon
In just about a minute,
Popcorn, salt and oil
And everything in it.
(MUSIC: DRUM BREAK)
BIG (V.O.): Whaddya know! No muss, no
fuss,
There's E-Z Pop Popcorn
For all of us!

7. CUT TO BACKGROUND. POP ON 11
POPCORN-LIKE HEADS, ONE AT A
TIME. (:02 secs.)

(MUSIC: DRUM BREAK)

8. CUT TO PACKAGE IN LEFT FRAME
WITH LITTLE HEAD. (:03 secs.)

LITTLE (O.C.): E-Z Pop! Man, that's
BOP corn!!!

* * *

This is another shining example of successful collaboration between a Detroit agency and John Hubley's 1950's Storyboard organization. These were still the early years of TV commercial production, before burgeoning agency creative departments usurped the imaginative perogatives of outside production houses. The animation is unusual and very lively, "scored" to a be-bop *recitative* soundtrack with the great Ray McKinley swinging on drums. Self-popping, self-seasoning self-contained popcorn was a dramatic marketing innovation, and this commercial was an equally dramatic presentation that carried the idea nationwide in a very brief time. It is a prime example of successful TV marketing.

Viewed from a purely technical point of view, the animation in this commercial was light years beyond anything else being done on television at that time. It had great influence on later animation styling, underlining the principle that *abstract* means anything but haphazard.

Scene 1   *"Busy Day"*

DETAILS

Black-and-white live action and animated film. 60 seconds. 123 words. Air date 1955.
General Foods Corp., *Advertiser.*
Young & Rubicam, Inc., *Agency.*
UPA, Inc., (L.A.), *Producer.*

CREDITS

Robert Margulies, Barbara Demaray, Gene Deitch, *Creative.*
Murray Hamilton, *Production.*

"BUSY DAY"

1. OPEN ON ANIMATED HOUSEWIFE ON KITCHEN TREADMILL. POP ON PHONE, KNOCKING HAND, BABY, POTS AND PANS IN SYNC WITH TRACK. ZOOM TO HOUSEWIFE'S DISTRAUGHT FACE. (:17½ secs.)

(MUSIC: HARMONICA)
FEMALE NARRATOR (V.O.): (IN CADENCE) Busy day,
Busy, busy, busy.
(PHONE: RINGS)
Too busy.
(SOUND: KNOCK ON DOOR)
Too busy.
(BABY: CRIES)
Oh, Herbert!
(SOUND: POTS AND PANS BANGING)
Dinner time,
Oh, dinner time!

1A. A VORTEX OF CIRCLING LINES CONCEALS HER FACE. (:07 secs.)

Too-late-to-make-desert.
ANNOUNCER (V.O.): Wait! It's not too late to make desert. Never too late, any more.

2. DISSOLVE TO ANIMATED OVAL ZOOMING FORWARD FROM INFINITY. BOX SHAPE FORMS AROUND OVAL. (:02 secs.)

Because now—

2A. POP ON "JELL-O" LABEL IN UPPER LEFT CORNER OF BOX. (:02½ secs.)

—the Jell-O family of famous deserts bring you—

2B. POP ON "New/INSTANT/PUDDING" INSIDE BOX OVAL. (:03 secs.)

—new Jell-O Instant Pudding, that needs—

2C. POP ON "No Cooking" INSIDE ARROW ON LOWER LEFT CORNER OF BOX. (:0½ sec.)

—no cooking!

3. DISSOLVE TO LIVE MCU OF WOMAN'S HANDS PREPARING PUDDING ON KITCHEN TABLE. (:06 secs.)

Just add to milk, and beat. In minutes, this terrific new "busy day" dessert—

4. DISSOLVE TO HER HANDS PLACING PUDDING DESSERT GLASS AT DINNER TABLE SETTING. (:06 secs.)

—is ready to eat . . . creamy, nourishing, so delicious.

5. LEFT-TO-RIGHT SOFT VERTICAL WIPE TO ANIMATED HOUSEWIFE, WALKING. PAN WITH HER AS ONE CHILD PASSES IN OPPOSITE DIRECTION WITH DISHES; STOP AS SHE COMES TO SECOND CHILD AT TABLE. (:07 secs.)

And so quick you can make it just before dessert time, while the children are clearing the table. Or let the children make it themselves. It's _that_ easy!

6. DISSOLVE TO LIVE CU BEAUTY SHOT OF INSTANT PUDDING PACKAGE. (:04 secs.)

New Jell-O Instant Puddings are at your grocer's now.

7. CUT TO MS BEAUTY SHOT OF ROW OF THREE PACKAGES. (:0½ sec.)

Stock up, with the terrific—

7A. POP ON TITLE: "NEW" IN UPPER LEFT FRAME, TITLE: " 'BUSY-DAY'/DESSERT" IN LOWER RIGHT FRAME. (:04 secs.)

—new "busy day" dessert. New Jell-O Instant Pudding!

* * *

To nobody's great surprise, once television commercial animation moved beyond the traditional hard-outline Disney cartoon style (where every hand had only four fingers—because five were too complicated), it tended to imitate a wide variety of sophisticated contemporary magazine cartoonists. This tendency continues to the present day.

In this combination of live and animated film introducing a new line of Jell-O puddings, cartoonist Saul Steinberg's thin spastic line falls a pleasant prey to the encroachment of television commercial creativity. It is a simple commercial, simply put together, and might have been even more effective had the announcer and his copy been slightly more sympathetic to the poor housewife, and less aggressive about the pudding.

Scene 1B   *"Cacklin' Fresh"*

DETAILS

Black-and-white live action and animated film. 60 seconds. 122 words. Air date 1955.
Kroger Stores, Inc., *Advertiser.*
Campbell-Mithun, Inc. (Minneapolis), *Agency.*
Animation, Inc. (L.A.), *Producer.*

CREDITS

Cleo Hovel, Don Grawert, *Creative.*
Earl Klein, Ed Barge, *Production.*

"CACKLIN' FRESH"

1. OPEN ON MS OF ANIMATED CHICKEN NESTING ON EGG. SHE CLIMBS OFF TO LOOK AT IT PROUDLY. (:06 secs.)	ANNOUNCER (V.O.): Isn't the chicken lucky . . . CHICKEN (O.C.): CACKLES HAPPILY. . . . that eggs are the shape they are?
1A. EGG IN NEST BECOMES CUBIC. (:01½ secs.)	Not square. CHICKEN: CACKLES FEARFULLY.
1B. CUBE GROWS TO TALL RECTANGLE. PAN RIGHT WITH CHICKEN AS SHE FAINTS. (:05 secs.)	Not rectangular. CHICKEN: FAINTING CACKLE. But perfectly egg-shaped.
1C. PAN LEFT TO OVAL EGG AGAIN. (:03 secs.)	And aren't you lucky, too, that the eggs you buy from—
1D. CHICKEN ENTERS RIGHT FRAME AND PLACES "Kroger" SIGN ON EGG. (:04 secs.)	—Kroger's are perfectly . . . CHICKEN: CACKLES HAPPILY. . . . egg-shaped?
1E. WITH HER BEAK, SHE ROTATES A "Fresh" LABEL ONTO FRONT OF EGG, WHERE IT FLASHES ON AND OFF. (:04½ secs.)	And as fresh as the hen can make them. CHICKEN: CACKLES HAPPILY. Cacklin'-fresh eggs—
1F. HAND ENTERS LEFT FRAME AND REMOVES EGG FROM NEST. (:02 secs.)	—from Kroeger.
2. DISSOLVE TO ANIMATED FS OF MAN AND CHICKEN LOADING "Kroeger/REFRIGERATED/EGG TRUCK." IT PULLS OUT OF RIGHT FRAME AS MAN AND CHICKEN WAVE GOODBYE. (:04 secs.)	Gathered fresh, and cooled on the spot. Then, (SOUND: TRUCK PULLS AWAY) whisked away in a real cool truck—
3. DISSOLVE TO ANIMATED MCU OF "U.S./INSPECTOR" CHECKING EGG AS CHICKEN WATCHES. (:04 secs.)	—for grading and dating by a government inspector.
4. DISSOLVE TO ANIMATED CU OF CHICKEN WITH KROGER EGG CARTON. HAND ENTERS FRAME TO PLACE DATING SEAL ON CARTON. (:04 secs.)	Every egg graded, every carton dated in a cool, cool grading room.

5. DISSOLVE TO FS OF ANIMATED CHICKEN ON GROCERY "DAIRY CASE." (:05 secs.)

From the hen to the Kroeger dairy case, they're kept cool all the way.

6. DISSOLVE TO LIVE CU OF EGG FRYING IN PAN. (:05 secs.)

So they're "Grade A" all the way. Guaranteed to ride high in the skillet.

7. DISSOLVE TO MCU OF ANIMATED CHICKEN ON CARTON. (:04½ secs.)

CHICKEN: CACKLES HAPPILY.
Guaranteed cacklin' fresh. Who but—

7A. CHICKEN PLACES "Kroger" SIGN ON CARTON. ZOOM IN TO CHICKEN'S FACE. (:07½ secs.)

—Kroeger sells cacklin'-fresh eggs?
CHICKEN: Nobody!!

* * *

The "anti-Disney" style of animated cartooning—more angular and simplified than any Mickey Mouse approach—was exemplified by this pleasant and innocuous commercial, aimed at increasing egg sales for a major midwest grocery chain. With the egg-layer herself as a mere bystander, the spot traces egg history from nest to supermarket dairy case. And then the chicken, too, has a line, at the end.

The copy is ordinary and full of the usual type of food promises. But the animation is cheerful, and certainly inspired ad agency TV commercial art directors to try more of the same.

Scene 1   "Life of A Baby"

DETAILS

    Live action black-and-white film. 60 seconds. 24 words. Air date 1955.
    Pet Milk Co., *Advertiser.*
    Gardner Advertising Co., Inc. (St. Louis), *Agency.*
    Sarra, Inc. (Chicago), *Producer.*

CREDITS

    Roland Martini, Beatrice Adams, *Creative.*
    Valentino Sarra, Ray Esposito, *Production.*

"LIFE OF A BABY"

1. OPEN ON MS OF BABY SLEEPING IN SHADOWY CRIB NEXT TO NURSING BOTTLE. (:12 secs.)

(MUSIC: BRAHMS "LULLABY")

2. DISSOLVE TO MS OF WAKENED BABY IN MOTHER'S ARMS, PLAYING WITH MOTHER'S FACE. (:16 secs.)

3. DISSOLVE TO ANOTHER ANGLE ON ABOVE SHOT. (:12 secs.)

4. DISSOLVE BACK TO SLEEPING BABY (SCENE 1) (:15 secs.)

ANNOUNCER (V.O.): Your baby. Yours to love, protect, care for. To be sure he gets the best of milk—

5. V-WIPE DOWN TO BEAUTY MCU OF PET MILK CAN AND NURSING BOTTLE AGAINST PATTERNED BACKGROUND. (:05 secs.)

—ask your doctor about Pet Evaporated Milk.

* * *

Half a century after Edwin S. Porter edited together his silent *Life of an American Fireman,* Pet Milk put together an equally silent little epic that surely may be entitled *Life of an American Baby.* Its form is even simpler and more naive than Porter's famous work; what made this commercial a classic was the welcome respite it provided from all the blaring, repetitious, spastic and poor advertising messages that blanketed the TV airwaves in 1955.

If you liked babies, if you liked peace—you loved this commercial. No plot, particularly. Only 24 words. Funny little optical for the final scene. Baby sleeps. Baby wakes. Baby plays. Baby sleeps. Can of Pet Milk.

Pet—and everyone else—could do a lot worse, even today.

Scene 5B   *"John & Marsha"*

DETAILS

Black-and-white animated film. 60 seconds. 26 words. Air date 1956.
Wesson Division, Hunt Foods, Inc., *Advertiser.*
Fitzgerald, Inc. (New Orleans), *Agency.*
Quartet Films, Inc. (L.A.), *Producer.*

CREDITS

Walter Collins, Art Babbitt, *Creative.*

"JOHN & MARSHA"

1. OPEN ON ANIMATED FS OF COUPLE AT DINING TABLE. WIFE PASSES HUSBAND A PIECE OF CAKE ON A PLATE. ZOOM TO HIS FACE AS HE EATS CAKE, AND FACE CONTORTS. (:10 secs.)

MARSHA (O.C.): (SOFTLY) John.
JOHN (O.C.): (SOFTLY) Marsha.
(MUSIC: ORGAN BACKGROUND)
(SOUND: TERRIBLE CRUNCH)

2. CUT BACK TO FS AS JOHN LEAPS TO HIS FEET AND ANGRILY GESTURES MARSHA OUT OF ROOM. (:07 secs.)

MARSHA: (ALARMED) John!
JOHN: Ulp.
(SOUND: CRUNCHING IN JOHN'S STOMACH)
JOHN: (SCREAMS) Marsha!
MARSHA: (CRYING) John.

3. CUT TO FS MARSHA'S MOTHER'S LIVING ROOM WITH WALL SAMPLER: "HONOR THY PARENTS." MOTHER IS SITTING IN ROCKER. MARSHA, WEARING HAT AND COAT, RUNS INTO FRAME. MOTHER PULLS SNOWDRIFT CAN OUT FROM UNDER HER SHAWL. MARSHA GRABS CAN AND RUNS OUT OF FRAME. (:11 secs.)

MARSHA: (SOBBING) John.
MOTHER: Snow-drift.
MARSHA: Snowdrift?
MOTHER: Snow-drift.

4. CUT TO FS MARSHA'S KITCHEN. SHE TAKES CAKE FROM OVEN AND PICKS UP SNOWDRIFT CAN. (:04½ secs.)

(SOUND: TIMER RINGS)

5. CUT TO MS OF DINING ROOM TABLE. JOHN, SEATED, IS STILL ANGRY. MARSHA ENTERS FRAME HOLDING OUT CAKE, WITH THE SNOWDRIFT CAN HIDDEN BEHIND HER BACK. (:05 secs.)

MARSHA: (COOING) John?
JOHN: (CURTLY) Marsha?
MARSHA: Johnnnnn . . .

5A. JOHN SEES CAKE AND LEAPS UP IN HORROR. (:02½ secs.)

JOHN: (APOPLECTIC) MARSHA!!!
MARSHA: (SWEETLY) John.

5B. MARSHA SLIPS CAKE OFF PLATE AND IT DRIFTS GENTLY DOWN TO THE TABLE. JOHN WATCHES IN ASTONISHMENT. ZOOM TO JOHN'S FACE AS MARSHA BREAKS OFF A BIT OF CAKE AND PUTS IT IN JOHN'S MOUTH. (:08 secs.)

(MUSIC: CELESTE GLISSANDOS)
JOHN: (SOFTLY) Love it.

6. CUT BACK TO MS AS MARSHA   MARSHA: (EXPLAINING) Snowdrift.
    SHOWS JOHN SNOWDRIFT CAN.   JOHN: (EXCITEDLY) Marsha!
    JOHN LEAPS TO HIS FEET AND
    SIEZES MARSHA PASSIONATELY.
    (:04 secs.)

7. CUT TO CU OF JOHN'S AND   MARSHA (V.O.): (SURPRISED) John!
    MARSHA'S FACES. HE LOOKS AT   JOHN: (V.O.): (PASSIONATELY) Marsha!
    CAMERA AND PULLS DOWN BLACK   MARSHA: (GIGGLES) (INDIGNANTLY)
    "WINDOWSHADE" CU OF SNOW-   John!
    DRIFT CAN TO OBSCURE FRAME.   JOHN (O.C.): Snowdrift, the Wesson Oil
    THEN HE RAISES THE SHADE AND   shortening.
    ADDRESSES CAMERA. (:08 secs.)

* * *

There was probably something terribly funny about repeating the names "John" and "Marsha" over and over again back in 1956, and Stan Freberg even cut a best-selling record that did nothing but repeat them with different inflections for three whole minutes. Somehow the record idea no longer seems so amusing, but this commercial—using Daws Butler, Freberg's original "John" voice—is still hilarious.

It has all the attributes of a morality play; ancient wisdom permits good to conquer evil, and everyone lives happily until the next station break. The animation, UPA-style, is a bit more cluttered than necessary, but that really doesn't get in the way of the (26-word) fun.

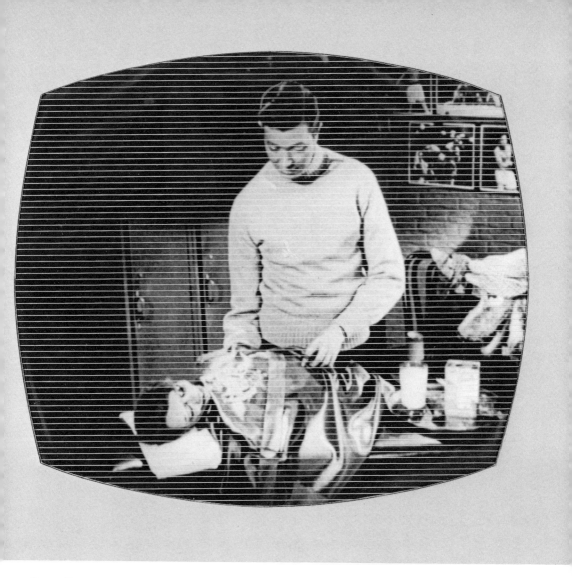

Scene 5   "Battlin' Danny"

DETAILS

    Live action black-and-white film. 60 seconds. 139 words. Air date 1956.
    The Nestle Co., Inc. *Advertiser.*
    McCann-Erickson, Inc., *Agency.*
    WCD, Inc., *Producer.*

CREDITS

    William LaCava, James Manilla, Patricia Grossman, Burns Patterson, *Creative.*
    Tom Dunphy, Marc Statler, *Production.*

"BATTLIN' DANNY"

1. OPEN ON LOW MS OF BOXING
   RING WITH JIMMY NELSON IN
   FOREGROUND, DANNY O'DAY
   (PUPPET) EXERCISING ON ROPES
   INSIDE CORNER OF RING. (:11
   secs.)

(SOUND: BOXING CROWD)
RING ANNOUNCER (V.O.): (ON ECHO)
In this corner . . . Jimmy Nelson and
Danny O'Day!
NELSON (O.C.): Now, remember what
I told you.
O'DAY (O.C.): "Chin out, eyes closed,
and Nestle's Quik for the referee."
NELSON: Yeah . . . uh, no, Danny!

2. CUT TO LOW CU OF NELSON'S
   FACE WITH PAINED EXPRESSION.
   (:01½ secs.)

(SOUND: BELL)
(SOUND: BLOWS)
NELSON: Too late, now.

3. CUT TO LOW CU OF FARFEL (DOG
   PUPPET), WHO PULLS EARS OVER
   HIS EYES. (:02½ secs.)

FARFEL (O.C.): I can't look.
(SOUND: THUD OF BODY)

4. CUT BACK TO LOW CU NELSON'S
   FACE. (:05½ secs.)

NELSON: Is it over yet?
REFEREE (V.O.): Eight. Nine. Ten,
he's out!

5. RIPPLE DISSOLVE TO HIGH CU OF
   O'DAY ON DRESSING ROOM
   TABLE. PULL OUT SLOWLY TO FS
   TO INCLUDE NELSON AND
   FARFEL. (:12 secs.)

O'DAY (O.C.): (MOANS) Quik, Quik,
shoulda' had my Quik, shoulda' had my
Quik.
FARFEL (O.C.): He's delirious.
NELSON (O.C.): Well, maybe he's right,
Farfel. After all, Quik and milk are great
for energy. Let's make him some.

6. CUT TO CU TRAY. HAND SPOONS
   QUIK FROM CAN INTO GLASS OF
   MILK, STIRS, AND INSERTS STRAW
   IN GLASS. (:07½ secs.)

(V.O.) Two spoonfuls in cold milk. A
little stir.
FARFEL (V.O.): I can see muscles
already!

7. CUT TO LOW MCU OF NELSON
   WITH GLASS IN HAND. (:03 secs.)

NELSON (O.C.): There you are, instant
chocolatey Quik.

7A. O'DAY SITS UP INTO FRAME AND
    SIPS FROM GLASS. (:11 secs.)

O'DAY (O.C.): Step aside, pal. Oh, Quik!
Nestle's Quik! It makes milk taste like
a million. Let me at 'im!
NELSON (O.C.): The fight's over.
O'DAY: Really, who won? Ohhhhhh!
(SINGS) N-e-s-t-l-e-s, Nestle's makes the
very best!

58

8.	CUT TO LOW CU OF FARFEL. (:04 secs.)	<u>FARFEL</u> (O.C.): Chaw-clit!
9.	CUT BACK TO CU OF QUIK CAN AND GLASS ON TRAY. (:02 secs.)	<u>O'DAY</u> (V.O.): He never laid a glove on me, Mom.

* * *

A particularly long-lived commercial puppet series was hosted by Jimmy Nelson. Broadcast puppetry began (in radio, of course) with Edgar Bergen. But Charlie McCarthy was never successful in the TV medium (carpers said Bergen's lips moved too much), and the children's popular favorite soon became Paul Winchell (with the puppet Jerry Mahoney).

Another friend of the milk-drinking generation was Jimmy Nelson's Danny O'Day and his dog Farfel, previously long-time commercial "pitchmen" on the *Texaco Star Theatre.* Nelson was soon signed to a contract with Nestle's and continued to produce these elaborately staged, highly expressionist commercials—each ending with the same spelled-out refrain: "N-e-s-t-l-e-s . . ."

Kids (of 21) will still sing it for you. Try them.

Scene 5A   "I Want My Maypo"

DETAILS

Black-and-white animated film. 60 seconds. 99 words. Air date 1956.
Maypo Division, Heublein, Inc., *Advertiser.*
Fletcher Richards, Calkins & Holden, Inc., *Agency.*
Storyboard Films, Inc., *Producer.*

CREDITS

Wyn Walshe, Jules Bundgus, Emery Hawkins, *Creative.*
John & Faith Hubley, *Production.*

"I WANT MY MAYPO"

1. OPEN ON ANIMATED MS OF CHILD IN COWBOY CLOTHES. PAN WITH HIM AS HE RUNS TO BREAKFAST TABLE AND CLIMBS ON STOOL. ZOOM TO MCU. (:07 secs.)

FATHER (V.O.): Come and get it. Big surprise.
CHILD (O.C.): Do you have a surprise for me?

1A. PAN RIGHT TO HARRIED FATHER WITH MAYPO BOX. HE SPOONS MAYPO INTO CHILD'S DISH. (:04 secs.)

FATHER (O.C.): Yessir! It's a new breakfast cereal, called "Maypo."

1B. PAN BACK TO CHILD. FATHER GRABS FOR HIS COWBOY HAT. (:04 secs.)

(V.O.) From now on, you're really going to like oatmeal. Take off your hat.

1C. CHILD STRUGGLES TO RETAIN HAT. FATHER GRABS IT OUT OF FRAME. (:03 secs.)

Your hat!!
CHILD: I want my cowboy hat!

2. CUT TO ANGRY FATHER HOLDING HAT. (:02 secs.)

FATHER (O.C.): After breakfast.

3. CUT TO INDIGNANT CHILD WITH ARMS FOLDED. (:07 secs.)

CHILD: I won't eat my Maypo.
FATHER (V.O.): You like maple sugar candy?

3A. CHILD PEERS INTO CEREAL BOWL AND SHAKES HIS HEAD. (:02 secs.)

CHILD: That's oatmeal.
FATHER (V.O.): Right.

4. CUT TO FATHER. PAN LEFT AS HE ATTEMPTS TO SPOON-FEED CHILD. (:05 secs.)

(O.C.) But it says here it's maple-flavored oatmeal.

5. CUT BACK TO HARRIED FATHER. WIDEN TO MS AS HE PLAYS ELABORATE CHARADE WITH CHILD. (:12 secs.)

FATHER: Tell you what. I'll be an airplane, you be the hangar. Open the doors, here it comes (WHRRRRRRRR) loaded with delicious (WHRRRRRR) maple- flavored (WHRRRR) Maypo!

5A. CHILD SNAPS HIS MOUTH SHUT NEXT TO SPOON. (:02 secs.)

Hmmmm!

6. CUT TO MCU OF FATHER. HE PUTS   Cowboys love Maypo. Giddyap, cowboy.
    ON COWBOY HAT, STARTS   (CLICKS TONGUE) Ummmmmm!
    WAVING SPOON, AND
    ACCIDENTALLY PUTS SPOONFUL
    OF MAYPO IN HIS MOUTH. HE
    SMILES WITH DELIGHT. (:06 secs.)

7. CUT TO CHILD. HE GRABS HIS   CHILD: I want—
    SPOON OF MAYPO AND EATS IT
    GREEDILY. (:03 secs.)

8. CUT TO MS OF CHILD CRYING AND   —my Maypo!!!
    FATHER GULPING SPOONFUL
    AFTER SPOONFUL OF MAYPO. (:03
    secs.)

* * *

The last line of this commercial became a temporary part of our language, whenever one felt like imitating funny television spots. It made a particular hit with members of the younger generation going through this same problem with *their* parents. The animation was by John Hubley, and represents perhaps the least imaginative visual work by his firm, soon after it was reestablished in New York. All the emphasis is on the humor of the situation and the quality of the soundtrack—which utilizes the talents of famous Broadway comedian David Burns, with Hubley's own son Mark, then four years old.

It was the start of Maypo's television campaign, and of Mark Hubley's successful career as a Maypo spokesman. It is interesting to know that this spot represented a "last roll of the dice" by Heublein on Maypo—they were about ready to give up this Division. But there was still enough budget for one last TV spot and Hubley was given his head. The result is cereal marketing history, and a nutritional bright spot in an industry whose most valueless products have steadily received the heaviest children's program advertising budgets.

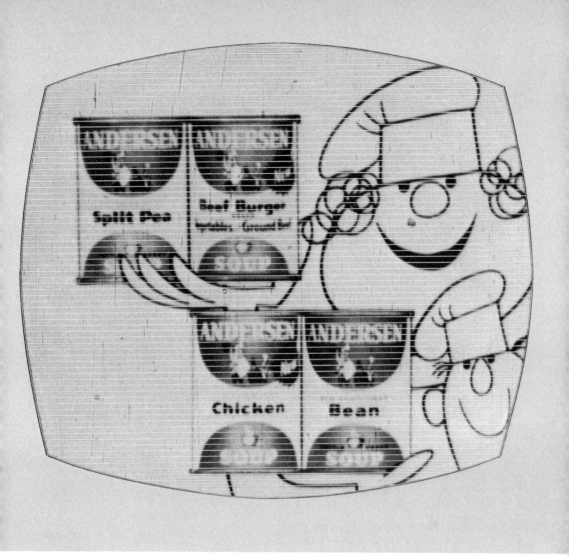

Scene 4   "Soup Twins"

DETAILS

    Black-and-white animated film. 60 seconds. 150 words. Air date 1957.
    Heublein, Inc., *Advertiser.*
    Fletcher Richards, Calkins and Holden, Inc., *Agency.*
    Goulding, Elliott and Graham, Inc., *Producer.*

CREATIVE

    William B. Templeton, Don Jordan, *Creative.*
    Ed Graham, Paul Kim, Mike Smollin, Albert Semels, *Production.*

"SOUP TWINS"

1. OPEN ON ANIMATED MS OF SOUP FACTORY OWNER WITH MICRO-PHONE. PAN WITH HIM TO FRAME TWIN COOKS AT BOTTOM OF FACTORY LADDER. (:09 secs.)	ANDERSEN (O.C.): Robert "Pea Soup" Andersen. . . . and here with me are the non-identical twins, Happy and Pee-Wee. TWINS (O.C.): Hi ya, soup fans everywhere.
1A. TWINS CLIMB LADDER OUT OF FRAME. (:05 secs.)	ANDERSEN: The gentlemen here are going to demonstrate how we split these peas, rather than crush them and lose their flavor.
2. CUT TO 2-STORY FS OF PEA-SPLITTING MACHINERY. ANDERSEN AND TWINS ARE ON DIFFERENT LEVELS. (:10 secs.)	(SOUND: MACHINERY) Notice the intricate machinery. The peas are being sorted.
2A. MACHINERY REACTS IN ALARM. (:05 secs.)	I thought that one was a dud. TWINS: That's an automatic reject feature of the machine.
3. CUT TO MS OF ANDERSEN. TWINS DESCEND LADDER INTO FRAME. (:11 secs.)	ANDERSEN: Unlike some soup manufac-turers, we're not much interested in how many cans we can crank out every minute, but more in how good our soup is.
3A. PAN WITH ANDERSEN AS HE WALKS BY LADDER. (:05 secs.)	When my friends say to me, "Robert 'Pea Soup' Anderson, how come no one else produces canned soups with real delicious homemade flavor?"–
3B. ZOOM TO ANDERSEN'S FACE. TILT DOWN AS HE OPENS HIS VEST AND HOLDS MICROPHONE NEXT TO WATCH ON FOB. (:06 secs.)	–I tell them it's because of an extra ingredient in every can. And that ingredient is time. (SOUND: WATCH TICKING)
4. CUT TO CU PEA SOUP CAN IN A TWIN'S HAND. WIDEN TO MS OF THREE OTHER CANS IN SYNC WITH AUDIO, HELD BY TWINS. TWINS' FACES IN FRAME. (:09 secs.)	(V.O.) It's in my delicious Split Pea, Beefburger, Cream of Chicken, or Old Fashioned Bean Soup. TWINS (O.C.): Try some (today) (tonight). 1ST TWIN: Today. 2ND TWIN: A week from Thursday.

By the Fall of 1957, Ed Graham had left Young & Rubicam to go into business with the two very funny men whose voices had made Graham's own Y & R "Bert and Harry Piel" memorable—Bob (Elliot) and Ray (Goulding). They began to mine what turned out to be a rapidly exhaustible lode of similar cartoon characters with voices supplied by Bob and Ray. Among the first efforts of the new firm was this commercial for Andersen's soups, with the non-identical soup-making twins, Happy & Pee-Wee—artfully drawn in somewhat Oriental style by Paul Kim.

The result was good fun that kept Andersen in more or less prominent supermarket shelf space for a while, but did not exactly put Campbell's out of business.

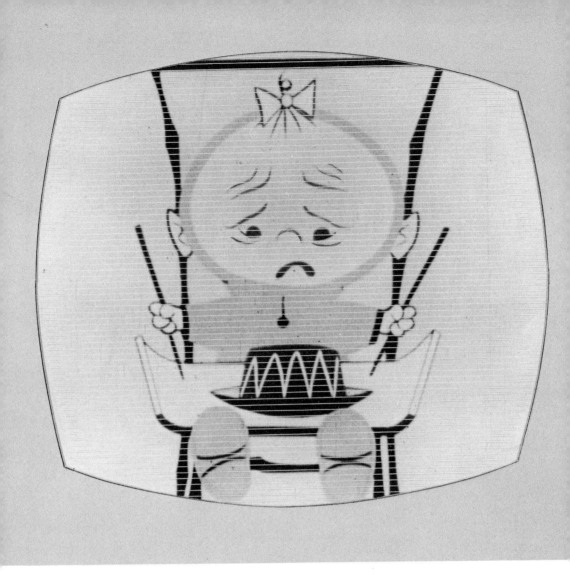

Scene 3   *"Chinese Baby"*

DETAILS

Black-and-white animated film. 60 seconds. 104 words. Air date 1957.
General Foods Corp., Jell-O Division, *Advertiser.*
Young & Rubicam, Inc., *Agency.*
Ray Patin, Inc. (California), *Producer.*

CREDITS

Barbara Demaray, William Lacy, Loren Collard, *Creative.*
Jack Sidebotham, Gus Jekel, Richard van Bentham, Ken Champin, *Production.*

"CHINESE BABY"

1. OPEN ON ANIMATED BAMBOO
   CURTAIN BACKGROUND. (:01 sec.)

1A. FOUR CHINESE IDEOGRAPHS DROP
    INTO FRAME, FORMING VERTICAL
    COLUMN. (:03 secs.)

ANNOUNCER (V.O. WITH COMIC
CHINESE ACCENT):
Beg to present, ancient Chinese pantomine—

1B. IDEOGRAPHS REARRANGE
    THEMSELVES HORIZONTALLY.
    (:01 sec.)

—just for fun of it—

1C. METAMORPHOSE IDEOGRAPHS
    INTO HAND-LETTERED "JELL-O."
    (:03 secs.)

—"Jell-O Tonight"! (MUSIC: CHINESE
GONG) Beg to present—

2. WIPE UP FRAME AS CURTAIN TO
   REVEAL FS OF ANIMATED
   UNHAPPY CHINESE BABY IN HIGH
   CHAIR, WITH CHOPSTICKS. (:02
   secs.)

—small Chinese-type baby, waiting for
dessert.

2A. CHINESE MOTHER ENTERS FRAME
    CARRYING PLATE OF JELL-O.
    BABY BANGS CHOPSTICKS AS SHE
    PLACES PLATE ON HIGH CHAIR.
    (:03 secs.)

Chinese mother bring baby . . . Jell-O—

3. CUT TO FS OF MOTHER AND BABY.
   SHE LEAVES FRAME. DOLLY IN TO
   CU OF FRUSTRATED BABY,
   TRYING TO EAT JELL-O WITH
   CHOPSTICKS. (:15 secs.)

—famous Western delicacy. Poor Chinese
baby! He unable to tell if this Jell-O is
Strawberry, Rasberry, Cherry, Orange,
Lemon, Lime, Apple, Black Raspberry,
Black Cherry or Grape. Jell-O come in all
ten flavors.

3A. BABY SCREAMS. (:04 secs.)

Poor Chinese baby! But—

3B. DOLLY OUT TO MS AS MOTHER
    RE-ENTERS FRAME WITH SPOON
    AND STARTS FEEDING BABY. (:06
    secs.)

—Chinese mother bring baby great Western
invention . . . spoon! Spoon was invented
for eating Jell-O.

3C. BABY SIEZES SPOON AND STARTS
    FEEDING HIMSELF. MOTHER
    LEAVES FRAME. (:05 secs.)

Baby find this is Grape Jell-O . . . deep,
dark, delicious new flavor.

4. CUT TO CU OF HAPPY BABY,   Chinese baby very happy. So end ancient
   EATING. DOLLY BACK TO FS. (:07   Chinese pantomime. Is pretty good
   secs.)   commercial—

5. WIPE DOWN FRAME AS CURTAIN,   —no?
   REVEALING WIND CHIMES. (:01
   sec.)

5A. METAMORPHOSE EACH CHIME   (MUSIC: ORIENTAL INSTRUMENTS)
    STRIP INTO SPARKLING LETTERS:
    "J," "E," "L," "L," "O." (:03 secs.)

5B. SUPERIMPOSE JELL-O PACKAGE
    OVER LETTERS. POP ON TITLE:
    "JELL-O IS A REGISTERED
    TRADE/MARK OF GENERAL
    FOODS CORP." UNDER BOX. ZOOM
    UP BOX AND TITLE. (:06 secs.)

* * *

"For fun of it" says voice at head of this black-and-white full-animation commercial, produced in Hollywood to introduce new product for one of America's oldest broadcast advertisers. "Chinese Baby" combined up-to-date and honorable tradition of American comic "sell" with ancient single-cel technique of animated cartoon photography (first attempted in America by J. Stuart Blackton in "Humorous Phases of Funny Faces" in 1906).

Popularity of poor baby struggling to get chopsticks (!) into new grape-flavored Jell-O soon established another American tradition, Chinese Baby Jell-O commercials. Three were produced, and viewed on television for years. With some clairvoyance, copywriter directs famous character actor Alan Swift (billed, with merit, as "Man of Thousand Voices") to inquire at end of spot: "Is pretty good commercial, no?"

Yes.

Coffee & Tea

It didn't need television to make us the world's largest nation of coffee-drinkers. Long before Dr. Vladimir K. Zworykin patented his TV transmitting tube, we were already gulping coffee at a rate that staggered every Brazilian plantation-owner's imagination. What television commercials *could* and *did* do—in the 1948-1958 period—was to take the innovation of *instant* coffee, and merchandise it to a fare-thee-well. Jennifer Cross suggests that instant coffee was among just 20 products heralded loudly as "New!" during two decades of TV advertising that in any way deserved the adjective.

Less than two decades later, "instant" brands now account for more than 25% of all U.S. coffee sales; Americans drink more than 117 million cups of instant coffee every day.

Coffee commercials in the '50's usually featured high-contrast, close-up photography of the steaming brew—sometimes with the help of a little dry-ice or cigarette smoke (the *tea* commercial here is no exception.) Simple, dramatic copy usually invited the viewer to "almost smell the coffee aroma" coming off his TV tube.

Different coffee nations pushed their own *unblended* product. Brazil was first. Colombia followed with its famous and dramatic "Juan Valdez' series. Even the Tea Council united its members long enough to produce an award-winning commercial. (But perhaps the most renowned coffee or tea commercial of all was yet to come—in 1959. This was the Maxwell House "Percolator Top," with its catchy *musique concrète* theme by the early electronic music expert, Eric Siday. This Maxwell House commercial was aired, in many updated variations, well into the '60's.)

Today's coffee marketing, both on and off TV, remains one of this country's most highly competitive areas—and from time to time each major manufacturer mounts a brand-switching campaign that sounds great but seems to produce something less than spectacular results. American viewers are truly creatures of habit with regular coffee (300 million cups a day), probably because 95% of them probably don't recognize a really good cup of coffee when they drink it.

Scene 1   "Flavor Buds"

DETAILS

    Live action black-and-white film. 87 seconds. 229 words. Air date 1956.
    General Foods Corp., *Advertiser.*
    Benton & Bowles, Inc., *Agency.*
    Filmwright, Inc., *Producer.*

"FLAVOR BUDS"

1. OPEN ON REX MARSHALL SEATED IN PLAYROOM EASY CHAIR. HE RISES AND WALKS TO TABLE WITH COFFEE-MAKING UTENSILS AND JAR OF INSTANT MAXWELL HOUSE COFFEE. HE PICKS IT UP, UNSCREWS THE CAP, AND PICKS UP A TEASPOON. (:24 secs.)

MARSHALL (O.C.): Say, who gets to make the coffee in your house? Well, you know more often than not, when it's coffee time in this household, I get to make it. Of course, the fact that my wife lets me make the coffee, tells you how amazing Instant Maxwell House must be. And believe me, this really is amazing. It's a completely different kind of coffee.

2. CUT TO ECU OF SPOON ENTERING JAR. IT IS REMOVED, FILLED WITH INSTANT COFFEE, AND MOVED UNDER MAGNIFYING GLASS. (:10 secs.)

Take a look for yourself, under this magnifying glass. Now you can see . . . it's not a powder, not a grind, either, but millions of tiny, hollow—

2A. ZOOM OUT SUPER TITLE: "FLAVOR BUDS" FROM INFINITY TO TOP FRAME. (:03 secs.)

—"flavor buds" of real coffee—

2B. DROP TITLE. POINTER ENTERS FRAME AND TOUCHES COFFEE IN SPOON. SPOON IS REMOVED. (:05 secs.)

—formed this way to capture and preserve that famous Maxwell House flavor.

3. CUT BACK TO PLAYROOM FS AS MARSHALL MIXES POTFUL OF INSTANT COFFEE, AND POURS A CUP. (:18 secs.)

Now, these unusual "flavor buds" burst instantly, the moment you pour in hot water, flooding the pot with that wonderful "Good to the Last Drop" flavor. I want to tell you, that is real coffee.

4. CUT TO HIGH CU OF COFFEE POURING INTO CUP. PULL BACK, PAN LEFT AND TILT UP TO FRAME JAR NEXT TO CUP. (:07 secs.)

As delicious as the best cup of coffee you ever brewed. What's more, with the large jar, you save money, you know.

4A. SUPER TITLE: "SAVE/75c" OVER CUP. (:06 secs.)

Up to seventy-five cents, compared to three pounds of ground coffee. Means that Instant Maxwell House costs you less per cup.

5. CUT TO MS OF MARSHALL. ZOOM TO MCU OF JAR HELD IN HIS RIGHT HAND. HE TILTS IT TO REVEAL STARS ON TOP, THEN HOLDS IT UPRIGHT AGAIN. (:14 secs.)

So this is Rex Marshall, reminding you that no matter who makes the coffee in your house, the secret of coffee that's "Good to the Very Last Drop," is right in this jar with the stars on top. Instant Maxwell House, the amazing coffee discovery.

A 14-second scene! An 18-second scene! *A 24-second scene*!! Those were luxury days for television commercials, when someone as famous as Rex Marshall could r-e-l-a-x in the simulated comfort of his simulated playroom—and make very real money telling you about all the benefits of the new "instant" coffee, s-l-o-w-l-y.

Today, a 24-second scene is almost an entire commercial. Even a 30-second spot has ten or twenty scenes (or set-ups)—not *five,* like this one. There is no time or money any more for a relaxed approach to TV selling, which may also be the reason why one doesn't see too much of Rex Marshall, either.

But in 1956, he was one of the most famous of the school of, "Hello there, I'm (USE YOUR NAME) . . ." TV announcing personalities who grew up in this broadcast medium only, and were never in any other area of show business. Marshall had a friendly, easygoing attitude toward the product he was selling, always sounding rather intelligent, and quite skilled in holding jars so that the label was always at right angles to the camera lens.

The only curious fact about this well-written "radio commercial" in the visual medium, is that Marshall never actually drinks his instant cup of coffee, after all his praise. In radio, the listener could have at least *thought* he was drinking it.

Scene 2   "Take Tea"

DETAILS

    Live action black-and-white film. 60 seconds. 60 words. Air date 1956.
    National Tea Council, Inc., *Advertiser.*
    Leo Burnett, Inc., *Agency.*
    Elliot, Unger & Elliot, Inc., *Producer.*

CREDITS

    Bob Richardson, Jack Hirschboeck, Jack Bramlette, *Creative.*
    Michael Elliott, Stephen Elliott, Don Tirrell, Bengt Sommerschield,
    Production.

"TAKE TEA"

1. OPEN ON ECU POURING TEAPOT SPOUT. TILT DOWN TO EMPTY CUP AND SAUCER, WHICH IT FILLS WITH STEAMING TEA. (:37½ secs.)

(MUSIC: ORIENTAL THEME)
ANNOUNCER (V.O.): This is tea,
(MUSIC: STING)
Filling a cup . . .
(MUSIC: STING)
Not with indigestion . . .
(MUSIC: TROMBONE SLIDE)
Not with nerves . . .
(MUSIC: JANGLING BELLS)
Not with sleeplessness.
(MUSIC: STRING FLOURISH)
This is tea. This is calm stomach, quiet nerves, deep sleep. This is tea. Steaming hot, hearty, delicious, invigorating.

2. DISSOLVE TO ECU MAN'S FACE. HE RAISES TEACUP TO LIPS AND SIPS. (:09 secs.)

The lift . . .
(MUSIC: STING)
. . . that leaves you with a nice warm glow. So good.

3. CUT TO HIGH BEAUTY MS OF TEAPOT NEXT TO EMPTY SAUCER. HAND REPLACES HALF-FILLED TEACUP ON SAUCER. (:05½ secs.)

So good for you. Make it hefty, hot and hearty.

4. DISSOLVE TO ARTWORK OF CU SILHOUETTED TEAPOT WITH LEGEND: "TAKE/TEA/AND SEE." (:08 secs.)

"Take tea, and see."

* * *

On the commercial-jangled airwaves of the late '50's, the respite offered by this Tea Council spot—only one word a second—was obviously welcome. But what makes it classic is the way its mood and form mirror the selling message of the product—a restful hot cup of tea. The dramatic close-up photography, starting tight with the very spout of the teapot, was daring work by an innovative cameraman/ director team, Stephen and Michael Elliot. It represented a breakthrough in TV commercial photography, akin to the moment in the 1890's when one of the Lumiere Brothers' employees first took a motion picture camera off its tripod and mounted it on the bow of a Venetian gondola.

As an institutional message—selling the *idea* of tea for a group of manufacturers—the commercial did well. But no individual tea manufacturer ever moved beyond this excellent concept.

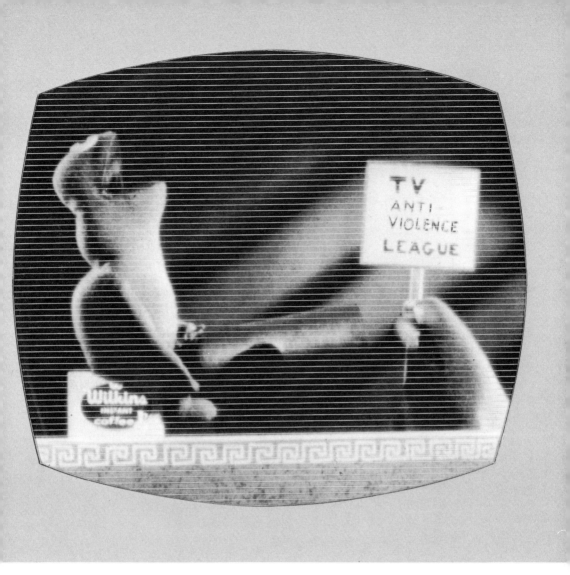

Scene 1A   "Cannon Shot"

DETAILS

   Live action black-and-white film. 8 seconds. 19 words. Air date 1957.
   Wilkins Coffee Company, *Advertiser.*
   M. Belmont ver Standig, Inc. (Washington), *Agency.*
   Rodel, Inc. (Washington), *Producer.*

CREDITS

   James Henson, James W. Young, *Creative.*
   James W. Young, James Henson, Jane Henson, Del Ankers, *Production.*

"CANNON SHOT"

1. OPEN ON FS OF MUPPET STAGE.
ONE MUPPET, NEXT TO CANNON,
SITS ON CAN LABELED "WILKINS
INSTANT COFFEE." SECOND
MUPPET ENTERS RIGHT FRAME
CARRYING PICKET SIGN
LETTERED: "TV/ANTI-VIOLENCE/
LEAGUE." HE SPEAKS. (:04 secs.)

SECOND MUPPET (O.C.): No, I'm not
gonna' drink any more Wilkins Instant
Coffee.

1A. FIRST MUPPET LAUGHS SOUND-
LESSLY. (:01 sec.)

2. CURTAIN LABELED: "ONE/
MOMENT/PLEASE . . ." DROPS IN
FRONT OF STAGE. (:01 secs.)

(SOUND: CURTAIN DROPPING)
(SOUND: CANNON SHOT)

3. CURTAIN RISES AGAIN, REVEAL-
ING FIRST MUPPET ALONE NEXT
TO SMOKING CANNON. HE TURNS
TO CAMERA. (:02 secs.)

(SOUND: CURTAIN RISING)
FIRST MUPPET (O.C.): Now he's not
gonna' drink any more coffee!

4. CUT TO CU OF JAR OF WILKINS
INSTANT COFFEE WITH SUPER-
IMPOSED TITLE IN RIGHT FRAME:
"Rich . . ./Rich . . ./Double/Rich." (:02
secs.)

* * *

The puppet show is as old as civilization. Javanese, Japanese, Chinese and the ancient Greeks loved puppets; Goethe wrote and Mozart and Haydn composed for the puppet stage. James Henson's unique TV "Muppets" have translated the eternal appeal of the puppet theatre for American television audiences in short bursts of syndicated advertising (in this case for a Southern coffee roaster). Sandwiched into TV station identifications across the country, these 8 seconds—with just 7 seconds of audio—are the shortest (and for tiny budgets, the least expensive) available units of TV advertising time.

The popularity of the Muppets and the advertising success of their humorous salvoes indicates that while TV commercial trends and styles come and go, the Muppets—in some local reincarnation or other—will probably continue forever. Right now, you can catch them on *Sesame Street* . . . where *The New York Times* calls them "essential to the success" of that children's program.

Beer, Wine & Soft Drinks

The brewers of America took the foaming promise of television commercial marketing to their hearts—and it has never let them down (their audience is currently swallowing 285 million glasses of beer a week). Hamm's produced the first commercial in this section almost twenty years ago, and Hamm's is still going strong on—and because of—TV.

Beer drinking has always been shown on television (in mostly regional advertising to match distribution) as the greatest sort of fun—the brewing industry has even produced two-minute national panegyrics attesting to beer's unchallenged place in our total national happiness.

Against such a slice of American reality it is curious to note that only one of these early beer award commercials—the most famous of which is New York's Piel Brothers' "Bert and Harry"—is anything more than an animated cartoon or a puppet show!

Were the TV producers psychologically hamstrung by the medium's unwritten law that foaming beer glasses may be lifted a million times in front of a live camera—but never once openly quaffed?* (In Canada, it should be noted, beer advertising is even more severely circumscribed, and has become mainly public-service advertising in which an advertiser may show only his *flat* beer label—not even wrapped around a can or bottle!)

* * *

In the soft-drink area, America's "cola" bottlers took the famous Schweppes Tonic TV success story to heart, and by the '60's had produced such a spate of happy, soda-swilling teen-age commercials, that they were crowding TV's beverage award-winner's circle.

And with the advent of the low-calorie drink fad, the soft-drink folks exploded their use of television (7 to 22 on-air brands in four years); and were horribly upset 10,000 commercials later when the Pure Food & Drug Administration blew the whistle with cancer warnings about Americans' over-ingestion of such artificial sugar substitutes as cyclamates.

Also meeting television's marketing challenge since the earliest days have been America's larger wineries. Wine commercials have always been a funny blend of hard-sell mixed with low-level gentility, as vintners excitedly pushed domestic wines with all the aura of their imported brethren. It still goes on.

---

* United States Brewers Association guidelines also stipulate that "TV beer advertising should not include scenes of riotous hilarity, or portray sexual passion as a result of drinking beer." Nor should they ever "show a beer drinker littering."

Scene 2D   "Bear Beer"

DETAILS

Black-and-white live action and animated film. 80 seconds. 110 words. Air date 1952.
Theo. Hamm Brewing Co., *Advertiser.*
Campbell-Mithun, Inc. (Minneapolis), *Agency.*
Swift-Chaplin, Inc. (Los Angeles), *Producer.*

CREDITS

E. P. Andrews, *Creative.*
Charles Chaplin, Howard Swift, John Abbott, *Production.*

"BEAR BEER"

1. OPEN ON ANIMATED/PROCESS FS OF RIPPLING MOONLIT LAKE. (:03 sec.)	ANNOUNCER (V.O.): This is the—
1A. SUPER TITLE: "LAND/OF/SKY BLUE/WATERS." (:05 secs.)	—Land of Sky Blue Waters . . . land of cool enchantment.
2. VERTICAL WIPE TO CARTOON FS OF BEAVER GNAWING DOWN TREE, BEAR WATCHING. TREE FALLS INTO LAKE. BEAR JUMPS ON IT AND BEGINS TO ROTATE IT WITH HIS FEET. PAN RIGHT. (:10 secs.)	Listen! (SOUND: TOM-TOM EFFECT OF BEAR'S DANCING FEET)
2A. BEAR'S FEET ROTATE LOG TO REVEAL TITLE: "FROM THE LAND OF." (:01 sec.)	CHORUS (V.O.): (SINGING) From the land of—
2B. LOG ROTATES AGAIN TO REVEAL NEW TITLE: "SKY BLUE WATERS." A DUCK FLIES INTO LEFT FRAME. (:07 secs.)	—sky blue waters. DUCK (O.C.): Wa-ters. CHORUS: Comes—
2C. LOG ROTATES AGAIN TO REVEAL NEW TITLE: "THE BEER RE-FRESHING." (:02 secs.)	—the beer refreshing.
2D. LOG ROTATES AGAIN TO REVEAL NEW TITLE: "HAMM'S." DUCK KNOCKS BEAR OFF LOG. (:02½ secs.)	Hamm's, the beer refreshing.
3. SPLASH WIPE TO HAMM'S LABEL ON GRAY BACKGROUND. (:03½ secs.)	ANNOUNCER (V.O.): Mmmmmmm! Hamm's!
4. DISSOLVE BACK TO RIPPLING MOONLIT LAKE. SUPER LIVE BEER GLASS AT INFINITY AND ZOOM FORWARD TO FILL FRAME. (:09½ secs.)	Yes, from the Land of Sky Blue Waters, to you . . . comes Hamm's; the beer refreshing as the crisp, cool land it's brewed in.
5. DISSOLVE TO MS OF LIVE BEER-DRINKING COUPLE ON MOONLIT BALCONY OVER LAKE. (:06 secs.)	—the beer that captures for you the wonderful refreshment of this enchanted Northland.

6. DISSOLVE TO BEER GLASS SUPERED OVER FS OF MOONLIT LAKE. SUPER WHITE "Hamm's" LOGO IN CENTER FRAME. (:01½ secs.)	Hamm's.
6A. EXTEND LOGO OUT OF FRAME ON BOTH SIDES TO REPEAT "m's." CONTRACT IT AGAIN. (:02 secs.)	Mmmmmmmmmm!
7. DISSOLVE OUT BEER GLASS. REPLACE WITH BEER BOTTLE WITH BLANK LABEL. ZOOM "Hamm's" LOGO BACK ONTO BOTTLE, CHANGING POLARITY, ZOOM BOTTLE FORWARD. (:06½ secs.)	Hamm's. Crisp, clean-cut to the taste. Refreshing!
8. CUT TO CARTOON FS OF BEAR DANCING ON LOG. DUCK SWIMS UP WITH SCROLL IN BEAK. (:06½ secs.)	(SOUND: TOM-TOM OF BEAR'S FEET) CHORUS (V.O.): If you're after something lovely. DUCK (O.C.): Hamm's Beer.
9. CUT BACK TO ANIMATED MOONLIT LAKE WITH SUPERED BEER GLASS. (:04 secs.)	CHORUS: And with sparkle in each glassful. DUCK: Hamm's Beer.
10. CUT BACK TO CARTOON OF BEAR ON LOG. HE TAKES SCROLL FROM DUCK AND UNROLLS IT CENTER FRAME TO READ: "Hamm's (logo)/THE BEER REFRESHING." (:06 secs.)	CHORUS: Hamm's, the beer refreshing, Hamm's, the beer refreshing, Hamm's!
11. CUT TO LIVE MCU OF HAMM'S BOTTLE BEING POURED INTO BEER GLASS AGAINST BACK- GROUND OF HAMM'S DISPLAY. (:04 secs.)	ANNOUNCER (V.O.): Refreshingly yours, from the Land of Sky Blue Waters.

* * *

"From the Land of Sky Blue Waters," sing the Hamm's choristers—but all Hamm's commercials might have been more aptly characterized "From the Land of the Silent Bear." Hamm's big, friendly, Disney-like cartoon bear appeared in all his spots absolutely mute. Even geese and ducks sang—but the bear never opened his mouth. There is nothing terribly distinguished about Mel Henke's music; the cartooning is middle-Disney; and the visual flow is interrupted by constant switches from cartoon to live action and back again—with some sort of optical effect breaking up every live scene. Add to this the incredible client claim that Hamm's and the agency actually edited 700 (!) later commercials to this identical sound track and you can see that we may be on the edge of an entry in the *Guinness Record Book*. Prosit!

Scene 12   "Hey, Mabel!"

DETAILS

    Black-and-white animated film. 60 seconds. 119 words. Air date 1954.
    Carling Brewing Co., *Advertiser.*
    Lang, Fisher & Stashower, Inc. (Cleveland), *Agency.*
    Storyboard Films, Inc., *Producer.*

CREDITS

    Alvin Fisher, Stan Walsh, *Creative.*
    John Hubley, Arnold Gillespie, *Production.*

"HEY, MABEL!"

1. OPEN ON ANIMATED FS OF TIRED BUSINESS MAN ENTERING TINY HOME. PAN RIGHT AS HE EMERGES OPPOSITE SIDE IN SPORTS CLOTHES, STROLLING OVER LAWN. (:14 secs.)

   MALE VOCALIST (V.O.):
   Ah home, sweet home, the little nest,
   Where after work a man can rest,
   Or take a peaceful stroll outdoors
   Doing little simple chores.

2. CUT TO MS OF HIS WIFE FURIOUSLY WEEDING GARDEN. (:01 sec.)

   FEMALE VOCALIST (V.O.):
   Weed the garden,

3. CUT TO MS OF WIFE FURIOUSLY MOWING LAWN. (:01 sec.)

   Cut the grass,

4. CUT TO MS OF WIFE FURIOUSLY PAINTING AND RE-GLAZING WINDOW. (:02 sec.)

   Paint the window, fix the glass,

5. CUT TO MCU OF WIFE FURIOUSLY SHEARING HEDGE. (:01 sec.)

   Trim the shrubbery,

6. CUT TO MS OF WIFE FURIOUSLY GRINDING AXE. (:01 sec.)

   Grind the axe,

7. CUT TO MS OF MAN RELAXED IN HAMMOCK. (:04 secs.)

   But take it easy, dear, relax!
   MALE VOCALIST: Oh, these women have a way,

8. CUT TO MS OF WIFE CARRYING TRAY WITH BEER GLASS AND CARLING BOTTLE. (:03 secs.)

   But maybe I forgot to say,

9. CUT TO MS OF MAN IN HAMMOCK AS WIFE ENTERS WITH TRAY. (:05 secs.)

   She always has my favorite brand,
   Carling's Black Label Beer in hand.

10. CUT TO MS OF BARTENDER. (:02 secs.)

    VOCAL CHORUS (V.O.): Want a happy thought? Hey, Mabel!

10A. MABEL ENTERS FRAME. (:01 sec.)

    A great idea?

11. CUT TO CU BARTENDER WITH MOUTH OPENED. POP ON REVERSE LOGO INSIDE MOUTH: "Black." (:0½ sec.)

    Black—

11A. POP OFF: "Black." POP ON: "Label." (:0½ sec.)	—Label!
12. CUT TO MS OF MABEL CARRYING SQUARE LABELED: "Black Label." SHE POURS IT INTO BEER GLASS. THE LABEL SHIFTS FROM SQUARE TO GLASS. (:04 secs.)	Nothing's too good for company; Carling's Black Label Beer.
12A. PAN RIGHT TO INCLUDE HAPPY MOUSTACHED MAN. (:05 secs.)	The quality brew at the popular price, Enjoy the best taste, our advice,
12B. PAN LEFT PAST MABEL TO ANOTHER HAPPY MAN TO WHOM SHE HANDS ANOTHER GLASS OF LABELED BEER. (:03 secs.)	Get Carling's Black Label,
13. CUT TO CARLING BOTTLE BOUNCING FORWARD FROM INFINITY TO CU. (:02 secs.)	Carling's Black Label Beer.
14. CUT TO CU OF MAN WITH WHISTLING FINGERS IN HIS MOUTH. MABEL ENTERS FRAME WITH CARLING BOTTLE. (:05 secs.)	(WHISTLE) Hey, Mabel! Black Label! (WHISTLE)
14A. ZOOM BOTTLE FORWARD TO FILL SCREEN WITH CARLING LABEL. (:05 secs.)	Carling's Black Label Beer!

* * *

That powerful radio jingle line, "Hey, Mabel! Black Label!"—the one that forever enshrined the Carling Beer-toting waitress in the minds and hearts of regional beer drinkers—was carried straight across to television in a long series of animated and live commercials, of which this was the first. The style is fresh and lively, busy but strictly post-Disney—again from the talented John Hubley.

The music track, like the original radio material, was the work of that old-line jingle professional, Phil Davis. The "Mabel" whistler . . . anonymous.

Scene 3   "Bert & Harry"

DETAILS

Black-and-white live action and animated film. 60 seconds. 174 words. Air
date 1955.
Piel Bros., *Advertiser.*
Young & Rubicam, Inc., *Agency.*
CBS/Terrytoons, *Producer.*

CREDITS

Pyrmen Smith, Loren Collard, John Blumenthal, *Creative.*
Victor Lukens, CBS/Terrytoons, *Production.*

"BERT & HARRY"

1. OPEN ON ANIMATED MCU OF BERT PIEL (THE AGRESSIVE LITTLE ONE) MIKE IN HAND, STANDING ON HOCKEY ICE. (:06½ secs.)

(SOUND: ROAR OF HOCKEY CROWD)
BERT (O.C.): This is Bert "Instant Refreshment" Piel, talking to you from ringside—

1A. ZOOM OUT TO FS THAT INCLUDES DUMB-LOOKING HOCKEY PLAYER AND HARRY PIEL. (:07 secs.)

—at New York's famous Madison Square Garden. Our guest is the famous hockey star Philippe Duprade.

1B. ZOOM BACK IN TO CU OF HARRY'S FACE AS BERT EXTENDS MIKE. (:04 secs.)

HARRY (O.C.): Bert thought you'd be interested in why Mr. Duprade prefers our refreshing beer. Unfortunately, he speaks no English.

1C. ZOOM OUT AND PAN LEFT TO MS OF BERT WITH DUPRADE. (:04½ secs.)

BERT: Never mind, Harry. I'll handle this. Monsewer Du-prade . . . why do you pre-fair Piel's Beer?

1D. ZOOM FURTHER OUT TO FS THAT INCLUDES HARRY. (:04 secs.)

DUPRADE (O.C.): Je ne comprend pas?
HARRY: See, Bert, he doesn't . . .
BERT: He said: "Because—

1E. BERT BENDS DOWN AND PICKS UP ROPE OF LITTLE SLED LABELED "INSTANT REFRESHMENT," LOADED WITH BEER AND GLASSES. HE PULLS IT INTO CENTER FRAME, OPENS CAN AND STARTS POURING. (:08 secs.)

—Piel's is just what he looks forward to after a long, hard night on the ice." He said . . .
HARRY: But Bert, he only said a few words.
BERT: Never mind, Harry!

2. MATCH CUT TO LIVE CU OF REAL SLED WITH PIEL'S CANS, GLASSES, AND POURING. (:07 secs.)

(V.O.) Let's whet a few appetites and show the viewers what Big Philippe means. Here it is, viewers! Instant refreshment from the first taste.

2A. ZOOM TO FILLED GLASSES AS HANDS ENTER FRAME AND RAISE THEM. TILT UP WITH HANDS. (:07 secs.)

HARRY (V.O.): Well, that's because our beer is cool-brewed—chilled as it's brewed and aged. That locks in that clean Piel's flavor.

3. CUT BACK TO ANIMATED MS OF BERT, DUPRADE AND HARRY. (:05 secs.)

DUPRADE (O.C.): Ah, messieurs! La bière Piels! Alors, comme ce rafraîchisant instantané! Comme ce magnifique!

3A. ZOOM TO MCU BERT AND HARRY. SUPER TITLE: "PIEL BROS./ BROOKLYN-STATEN ISLAND, N.Y." IN BOTTOM FRAME. (:07 secs.)

HARRY (O.C.): What's he saying now, Bert?
BERT (O.C.): I think he's trying to say "hello" to his mother in Montreal.

* * *

Although the product they peddled was never sold beyond a few hundred miles of New York City—and they never appeared on anything other than local New York television—Bert and Harry appear to have carved a secure niche for themselves in the history of American TV commercials.

The idea of using a pair of animated cartoon characters (personifying the "Piel Brothers") as beer spokesmen arose with Ed Graham at Young & Rubicam in the early '50's. For voices for soft-spoken, modest Harry, and loud overblown Bert, the agency chose Bob Elliott and Ray Goulding of the popular "Bob and Ray" NBC radio comedy team. A better choice could never have been made—Bob and Ray's voice *became* Harry and Bert (respectively).

UPA was picked as the original animation studio. The series became so successful and so long-lived that other studies also got their share of the Y & R animation contracts. The commercials were not only long-lived; they were long-*loved.* And thereby hangs a tale, famous throughout broadcast advertising. Because before long, Piel's was asking Young and Rubicam, "If everyone likes our TV spots so much, why aren't our beer sales going up?"

"Wait," said the agency. And everyone waited, for the longest time. And Bert and Harry kept right on making wonderful new friends—but too few new *customers.*

Thus Bert and Harry became the famous "object lesson" of TV advertising— entertaining TV commercials didn't necessarily sell product. The lesson became so famous that even the man in the street could eventually quote it to aspiring young TV copywriters: "Don't give me another Bert and Harry campaign! Give me 'hard sell'!"

For Piel's and Young & Rubicam, it was a costly experience. Presumably, by failing to include some adequate copy promises along with their somewhat long-winded fun, they blew a classic opportunity to shape a local product into a nationally-distributed one. "Why didn't Piel's just make a better beer?" ask the Monday-morning quarterbacks—and the Bert and Harry lovers. "Their beer was fine," answer the researchers.

The fight continues to rage. Bob and Ray have moved to greener fields, for General Motors and many other radio and TV advertisers, and even onto Broadway. But to anyone who watched television in the late '50's, Bob and Ray will always sound—isn't it funny?—just like Bert and Harry used to.

Scene 7   *"Was it Paris?"*

DETAILS

    Live action black-and-white film. 60 seconds. 138 words. Air date 1955.
    Schweppes USA, Ltd., *Advertiser.*
    Ogilvy & Mather, Inc., *Agency.*
    MPO Videotronics, Inc., *Producer.*

CREDITS

    Commander Edward Whitehead, David Ogilvy, *Creative.*
    Marvin Rothenberg, Michael Nebbia, *Production.*

"WAS IT PARIS?"

1. OPEN ON MS OF COMMANDER WHITEHEAD AT DIPLOMATIC RECEPTION. HE LEANS CASUALLY ON A MARBLE TABLE. FACING HIM, WITH HER BACK TO CAMERA, IS AN OBVIOUSLY STRIKING WOMAN. AS THEY SPEAK, OTHER GUESTS CROSS IN THE BACK-GROUND. (:16½ secs.)

(MUSIC: BACKGROUND)
WHITEHEAD (O. C.): Now wait, don't tell me. Was it Hong Kong? Beirut? Cairo, perhaps?
WOMAN: (LAUGHS GENTLY) Guess again, Commander Whitehead.
WHITEHEAD: London . . . it was London!
WOMAN: Well, I'll give you a hint. You were having a tonic, and you were warning the—

1A. WAITER'S HANDS ENTER LOWER LEFT FRAME TO PLACE TRAY WITH GLASS AND OPENED SCHWEPPES BOTTLE ON TABLE. (:04 secs.)

—waiter "to make jolly well sure" he mixed it with Schweppes.

2. CUT TO MCU OF WHITEHEAD'S FACE. HE RAISES GLASS INTO FRAME. (:06 secs.)

WHITEHEAD: But that might have been anywhere; Schweppes Quinine Water is famous all over the world.
WOMAN: In those days—

3. CUT TO MCU OF WHITEHEAD AND WOMAN'S BACK. (:03 secs.)

—you used to say it was impossible to mix tonic without Schweppes.

4. CUT BACK TO MCU OF WHITE-HEAD'S FACE AS HE LOOKS AT GLASS. (:07 secs.)

WHITEHEAD: Still is. No other mixer has Schweppes' bittersweet flavor and rare effervescence.

5. CUT BACK TO MCU OF WHITE-HEAD AND WOMAN'S BACK. SHE GENTLY TOUCHES HIS GLASS. (:05 secs.)

WOMAN: Effervescence? You used to call those little bubbles "Schweppervescence."

6. CUT BACK TO MCU OF WHITE-HEAD'S FACE. (:06 secs.)

WHITEHEAD: Schweppervescence! Of course! Those remarkable little bubbles, that last the whole drink through.

7. CUT TO MS OF WHITEHEAD AND WOMAN. SHE MOVES HER HAND TO WHITEHEAD'S ARM. (:06 secs.)

Did you know that Schweppes' Quinine Water is now bottled here in the States, from the imported elixir?

8. CUT TO CU OF HER GLOVED HAND MOVING OVER WHITE-HEAD'S, NEXT TO SCHWEPPES BOTTLE. (:06½ secs.)

Ah, but do tell me . . . where did we meet? Was it Paris . . . ?

Five years before Alain Resnais filmed *Last Year at Marienbad*—had he been watching American TV?—Schweppes (and David Ogilvy) introduced their quinine water product to the American market with this somewhat similar story of a bearded Britisher who couldn't remember where he last met a lovely lady. It is an interesting commercial, for many reasons.

First, Commander Edward Whitehead (with whom this writer worked for many years on the Schweppes account) is a very warm, real person who was also in charge of Schweppes distribution and bottling activity in North America. It took years for television viewers (and magazine readers) to believe he actually existed; he does, and he is also one of the world's great soft-drink marketers. He is also long-suffering; his bearded service in the malarial lagoons of the South Pacific in His Majesty's Navy during World War II prepared him well for some of the more hazardous locations to which David Ogilvy's art directors eventually dragged him in search of bizarre, memorable Schweppes advertising.

It was David Ogilvy himself who first convinced the Commander that the old advertising theorem, "keep the plant and the president out of the advertising," was not necessarily true. In appearance, style and dignity, Whitehead personified the Schweppes product—whose bubbles behave, of course, just like any other little CO_2 bubbles. But when Whitehead tells you they are *bubblier,* somehow you believe him.

His performances—this commercial is the earliest of all—were somewhat stiff at first, but he was patient, and so was his director, MPO's Marvin Rothenberg, who shot most of the Schweppes Saga. There are two bad jump-cuts in this spot (between Scenes 6 and 7, and 7 and 8), due mainly to Whitehead's lack of professional acting experience—but perhaps the director (or editor?) was looking ahead to *Marienbad.*

Other interesting aspects include Michael Nebbia's *single* camera position throughout; the lens tilts only for the hand close-up in the final scene! This puts the viewer deep into the situation far more adequately than any spastic contemporary cutting. It was dictated, of course, by the creative desire to keep the woman of mystery securely mysterious; Joan Alexander is never permitted to display her (lovely) face.

And of course, with this spot, Ogilvy cracked the problem of showing alcohol-drinking on TV. No one ever defines visually or orally what's in the glass Whitehead looks at so longingly, *and never sips.*

Now it can be told.

It's g-i-n.

Scene 12   "Beer Parade"

DETAILS

Black-and-white "stop-motion" film. 60 seconds. 116 words. Air date 1957.
Liebmann Breweries, Inc. (Rheingold Division), *Advertiser.*
Foote, Cone & Belding, Inc., *Agency.*
Sarra, Inc., *Producer.*

CREDITS

Marjorie Greenbaum, Howard Munce, Thomas M. McDonnell, *Creative.*
Thomas M. McDonnell, Robert Jenness, Ray Esposito, Jack Henderson, *Production.*

"BEER PARADE"

1. OPEN ON LS OF MINIATURE SET, LOOKING UP PAST LAMPPOST ("W. 42/TIMES SQ.") TO BILL-BOARD LOGO ("Rheingold/EXTRA DRY/Lager Beer"). (:06 secs.)

(MUSIC: MARCHING BAND)
CHORUS (V.O.): My beer is Rheingold, the dry beer!

2. CUT TO LOW MS OF LEFT-RIGHT PARADING "MARCHING BAND" OF RHEINGOLD BOTTLES AND CANS, BILLBOARD IN BACK-GROUND. (:09 secs.)

East Side, West Side,
And uptown and down,
Rheingold Extra Dry Beer
Is the beer of great renown.

3. CUT TO HIGH FS OF BEER CAN "CIRCUS WAGON." (:02 secs.)

Friendly, freshening Rheingold,

4. CUT TO LOW CU OF SCENE 3. (:02 secs.)

Always happily dry,

5. CUT BACK TO DOWN FS (SCENE 3) AS WAGON MOVES OUT LEFT-RIGHT AND PARADING BOTTLES ENTER FRAME. (:04 secs.)

The clean, clear taste
You want in beer
Is in Rheingold Extra Dry.

6. CUT TO LOW ECU OF BOTTLES. (:02 secs.)

SINGER (V.O.): From Lexington to Madison,

7. CUT TO LOW FS OF CANS AND BOTTLES WITH SKYLINE IN BACKGROUND. (:06 secs.)

And on both sides of Park,
CHORUS (V.O.): They ask for Rheingold Extra Dry
SINGER (V.O.): Before and after dark.

8. CUT TO FS OF BEER CAN AND BOTTLE "FREIGHT TRAIN" CROSSING MINIATURE SUSPENSION BRIDGE. DIRECTION SIGNS: "CONNECTICUT," "BROOKLYN," "NEW JERSEY," "LONG ISLAND" IN FORE-GROUND. (:05 secs.)

CHORUS (V.O.): From Coney to Connecticut,
Or Flatbush Avenue,

9. CUT TO ECU OF TRAIN ON BRIDGE. (:04 secs.)

From Jersey scenes, way out to Queens,
They sing as millions do:

91

10. CUT TO HIGH FS OF CANS, GLASS
     STEINS AND BOTTLES MARCHING
     LEFT-RIGHT PAST REVIEWING
     STAND FILLED WITH DOLL
     PEOPLE. (:04 secs.)

My beer is Rheingold, the dry beer,

11. CUT TO CU OF SCENE 10. STEINS
     FILL WITH BEER. DRUMMING
     BOTTLES ENTER FRAME. (:04
     secs.)

Friendly, freshening and happily dry
beer.

12. CUT BACK TO SCENE 10 AS
     PROPELLER-DRIVEN BEER KEG
     "BALLOON" SAILS IN FRAME
     WITH "Rheingold/EXTRA
     DRY/Lager Beer" LOGO ON ITS
     SIDE. (:02 secs.)

"Dry" means clean, and it's clear

12A. TILT UP WITH BALLOON AS IT
     CIRCLES TOWARD CAMERA AND
     STOPS, WITH ITS LOGO FILLING
     TOP FRAME. (:08 secs.)

"Dry" means thirst-quenching beer,
Join the millions who buy Rheingold Beer.
Extra Dry!

12B. FADE TO BLACK AS BALLOON
     STARTS MOVING LEFT-RIGHT
     OUT OF FRAME. (:02 secs.)

* * *

This commercial, photographed with miniatures for an East Coast brewery, was a *tour de force* of the "stop motion" film technique. (This unusual method of achieving apparent live movement of inanimate objects through single-frame-at-a-time photography was pioneered in France in 1860.) Before each frame of each scene in "Beer Parade" was exposed—individually—each of the "beer container" puppets were moved forward, or up, or down a *fraction of an inch*. This was done 1,440 times, for every frame in the commercial. *The photography of Scenes 10 and 11 alone required more than 10,000 different hand adjustments to the puppets involved!* Projection later at "sound speed" (24 frames per second) made the puppets "come alive."

"Beer Parade," produced to illustrate the advertiser's then-current theme song, is one of the more complicated American stop-motion commercials of the '50's. The musical track was completed first, to provide a basis for the camera choreography.

Since this is "movie trick" technique, it possessed a relatively low level of sophistication, fine for the earliest days of television viewing. Today this creative approach is no longer popular, and rising American labor costs have driven almost all of what is left of this kind of work overseas to specialists in Spain and to the Gesink Studios of Holland.

Scene 12C   "There's Bud"

DETAILS

    Live action black-and-white film. 60 seconds. 62 words. Air date 1957.
    Anheuser-Busch, Inc., *Advertiser.*
    D'Arcy, Inc. (St. Louis), *Agency.*
    MPO Videotronics, Inc., *Producer.*

CREDITS

    Bob Johnson, *Creative.*
    Marvin Rothenberg, Zoli Vidor, *Production.*

"THERE'S BUD"

1. OPEN ON CU OF GIRL'S FACE.   (MUSIC: FLUTE THEME)
   SHE HOLDS CONCH SHELL TO
   HER EAR. PULL BACK TO FRAME
   BACK OF MAN'S HEAD. (:04 secs.)

2. CUT TO CU MAN'S FINGERS
   PLAYING FLUTE. (:03 secs.)

3. CUT TO MS OF BREAKING SURF.   CHORUS (V.O.): (HUMS)
   (:03 secs.)

4. CUT TO CU FINGERS ON FLUTE,
   DIFFERENT ANGLE. (:03 secs.)

5. CUT TO (REVERSE-PRINTED) MS
   OF SURF ROLLING OFF BEACH.
   (:02 secs.)

6. CUT BACK TO CU GIRL'S FACE
   WITH SHELL TO EAR. (:02 secs.)

7. CUT TO ECU FINGERS ON FLUTE,
   DIFFERENT ANGLE. (:02 secs.)

8. CUT TO ECU BEER CAN OPENER   ANNOUNCER (V.O.): Open up Bud—
   CUTTING INTO CAN TOP. (:02
   secs.)

9. CUT TO ECU CAN LABEL,   —and pour yourself the most exciting glass
   FRAMING "Bud" AREA OF   of beer—
   "Budweiser" LOGO. ROTATE CAN
   AND ZOOM OUT TO CU OF FULL
   LABEL. (:02½ secs.)

10. CUT TO ECU OF TILTED CAN TOP   —you've ever tasted. Cold, golden
    POURING BEER. ZOOM BACK TO   Budweiser, with that good taste—
    MS OF BEACH PICNIC SCENE. (:06
    secs.)

11. CUT TO HIGH MS OF   —for good times. Well, go ahead! Live light.
    HAMBURGERS GRILLING NEXT
    TO COLD CHEST FILLED WITH
    ICED BUDWEISER CANS. HANDS
    PASS CAN. (:03 secs.)

12. CUT TO VARIOUS MOVING IMAGES MATTED INTO A MULTIPLE-SCREEN LAYOUT. SCENE OPENS WITH HAMBURGERS GRILLING IN UPPER LEFT FRAME. (:00½ sec.)	Every—
12A. ADD FS OF BREAKING SURF IN BOTTOM FRAME. (:00½ sec.)	—golden—
12B. ADD ECU OF BEER CAN BEING OPENED IN TOP RIGHT FRAME. (:02 secs.)	—minute of it. Enjoy—
12C. IN TOP RIGHT FRAME, CUT TO MCU OF BEER GLASS AND ZOOM IN TO GLASS. (:04 secs.)	—Budweiser. Every golden drop of it.
13. CUT TO MATCH ZOOM OF SAME BEER GLASS IMAGE FULL SCREEN. (:04 secs.)	CHORUS (V.O.): (SINGS) Budweiser is for folks who know
14. V-WIPE TO SURF WASHING AWAY FROM TITLE SCRATCHED IN SAND: "WHERE/THERE'S/LIFE/ THERE'S/BUD." (:04 secs.)	Where there's life . . .
15. CUT TO ECU OF TILTED CAN TOP POURING BEER. (:01½ secs.)	Where there's life . . . .
16. CUT TO ECU FINGERS ON FLUTE. (:02 secs.)	
17. CUT TO CU GIRL'S FACE. SHE TURNS AND ACCEPTS BEER GLASS FROM MAN'S HAND. (:02 secs.)	ANNOUNCER (V.O.): Go ahead. GIRL (O.C.): Sure.
18. CUT TO MS BREAKING SURF: SUPER TITLE CENTER FRAME IN SYNC WITH AUDIO: "Where there's life . . . /there's Bud." (:03 secs.)	CHORUS: Where there's life, there's Bud!
19. CUT TO MS GLASS BEAUTY SHOT OF TWO BUDWEISER CANS NEXT TO BOTTLE, WITH TITLE: "(logo) Budweiser/King of Beers/ANHEUSER-BUSCH, INC., ST. LOUIS, MO." (:04 secs.)	

Long before there was Expo '67, with its myriad arrangements of multiple motion picture scenes, there was Budweiser '57 . . . doing exactly the same thing with seawater, flutes and beer, all within the confines of a 19″ (diagonal) TV picture tube. In this pleasant beer-pouring commercial, scored both musically and visually with flutes, the multiple images in Scene 12 come and go as dramatically as anything produced for TV in the 70's, proving once again that Ecclesiastes was right.

Marvin Rothenberg's direction was simply handled; the actress has only one line, one word long. "Washing-on" the title in Scene 14 is an old camera trick even you can handle at the beach with an 8mm camera, writing backwards and holding the camera upside-down. It's effective.

Scene 19 is a "glass" shot, which doesn't mean a beer glass, but mounting all the props (cans, bottles) on a sheet of vertical glass, and photographing them against some visually interesting out-of-focus background.

All in all, a nice way to sell the suggested enjoyment of drinking beer.

Scene 12A   *"Ale Puppet"*

DETAILS

    Color "stop-motion" film. 60 seconds. 114 words. Air date 1957.
    P. Ballantine & Sons, *Advertiser.*
    William Esty, Inc., *Agency.*
    Joop Gesink (Holland), *Producer.*

CREDITS

    Joseph S. Forest, Hal Taylor, *Creative.*
    Joop Gesink, *Production.*

"ALE PUPPET"

1. OPEN ON MS PUPPET SET. TURN-OF-THE-CENTURY BARTENDER IS WORKING BEHIND BAR OF AN ALASKAN SALOON. (:06 secs.)

(MUSIC: HONKY TONK PIANO)
BARTENDER (O.C.): (SINGS) I'm Klondike Pete,
I tend the bar
For men both brave and bold,

1A. MINER ENTERS THROUGH SWINGING DOOR IN BACK-GROUND AND ORDERS GLASS OF ALE. PETE DRAWS IT. (:04 secs.)

It means a lot to serve them all
The ale that's "Brewer's Gold."

2. CUT TO FS OF PIANO, PLAYER, AND TWO MINERS SINGING. (:03 secs.)

CHORUS OF MINERS (O.C.): Enjoy that golden flavor,

3. CUT TO MS OF ABOVE. (:04 secs.)

Brewed-in flavor,
Oh, that Ballantine—

4. CUT TO MCU MOOSE HEAD ON WALL. ITS EYES ROLL AND ITS TONGUE WATERS. (:02 secs.)

5. CUT TO CU OF THREE HOISTED ALE GLASSES. SUPER TITLE: "brewed with/'Brewer's Gold'." (:03 secs.)

—Ale, with "Brewer's Gold."

6. CUT BACK TO PETE DRAWING MORE ALE AS THREE MINERS WALK PAST HIM TO BAR. (:04 secs.)

BARTENDER: True drinkers know
That "Brewer's Gold"
Is the best hops from the vine,

7. CUT TO MS OF END OF BAR WITH SIGN "BALLANTINE/ALE/(logo)." DOLLY BACK TO REVEAL PETE SERVING THREE MINERS. (:10 secs.)

They brew it into Ballantine
For flavor gen-u-ine.
CHORUS: It's got that golden flavor,
brewed-in flavor,
Oh, that Ballantine—

8. CUT TO CU OF PETE WIGGLING HIS EYEBROWS AND MOUSTACHE. (:02 secs.)

9. CUT TO THREE MINERS RAISING THEIR GLASSES. (:03 secs.)

—Ale, with "Brewer's Gold."

10. CUT TO MCU OF PETE AS HE DRAWS GLASS OF ALE. (:05½ secs.)	BARTENDER: Remember, friend, right to the end, Enjoy the gen-u-ine, For ale that's really light and gold—
10A. PETE MAKES "3-RING" CIRCLE SIGN WITH FINGERS. (:01½ secs.)	—just make the "3-Ring" sign.
11. CUT TO LIVE MS ALE GLASS BEING FILLED FROM SPIGOT. (:02½ secs.)	CHORUS: Enjoy that golden flavor,
12. CUT TO CU OF GLASS AS HEAD OVERFLOWS DOWN SIDES. (:05 secs.)	True ale flavor. Oh, that Ballantine—
12A. PETE ENTERS FROM RIGHT FRAME, MATTED AGAINST HUGE GLASS OF ALE. (:03 secs.)	BARTENDER: It's the gen-u-ine! CHORUS: Ale with—
13. CUT TO BEAUTY MS OF SPARK-LING ALE BOTTLE TOP, "3-RING" LOGO, AND TITLE: "P. BALLAN-TINE & SONS, NEWARK, N. J.". (:01½ secs.)	"Brewer's Gold"!

* * *

Beer advertisers in 1957 made much use of the half-real world of stop-motion film puppetry. Ballantine's long-running campaign for its Ale, based on Donald Devor's "Brewer's Gold" jingle, was filmed overseas at Joop Gesink's famous Dutch puppet studio "Dollywood." As with Rheingold's "Beer Parade," each of these 1,440 motion picture frames was exposed individually and the puppet(s) articulated a fraction of an inch at a time. These scenes averaged about four seconds per set-up, but a single error in either the camera move or puppet articulation in, for example, the 10-second scene (Scene 7) meant re-shooting 240 frames! In this exacting work, it was important to *eliminate* error—not just hold it to a minimum.

Although this commercial was photographed in color for uses other than television—sales meeting, promotion, etc.—in 1957 the TV medium was still monochrome. However, the use of color simplified the matting technique used in Scene 12A: The bartender puppet was photographed against a pure blue (clear) background and his figure was also inked-in on another negative for use as a "self-matte" over the separate beer glass footage.

Scene 5   *"Pour, Pour The Rosé"*

DETAILS

Live action black-and-white film. 60 seconds. 33 words. Air date 1958.
E. & J. Gallo Winery, Inc., *Advertiser.*
Doyle Dane Bernbach, Inc. (Los Angeles), *Agency.*
Robert Lawrence Productions, Inc., *Producer.*

CREDITS

Morris Flantzman, *Creative.*
Ben Norman, Jerry Schnitzer, Fred Gately, Ernst Fegte, *Production.*

"POUR, POUR THE ROSÉ"

1. OPEN ON ECU OF WINE POURING
    INTO GLASS. (:02 secs.)

    (MUSIC: JAZZ COMBO)

2. CUT TO MS POURING SHOWING
    NECK OF BOTTLE. (:01 sec.)

2A. ZOOM OUT TO REVEAL FORMAL
    PARTY SCENE WITH MOVING
    GUESTS. (:06 secs.)

3. CUT TO CU OF CANAPE TRAY
    WITH HANDS TAKING CANAPES.
    (:03 secs.)

3A. TRAY MOVES UP OUT OF RIGHT
    FRAME, REVEALING MS OF SIX
    FILLED WINE GLASSES ON
    SILVER SERVING TRAY. GUESTS'
    HANDS REMOVE ALL GLASSES.
    (:03 secs.)

4. CUT TO CU OF HOSTESS' SMILING
    FACE AS SHE RAISES WINE GLASS
    IN TOAST. (:01 secs.)

5. CUT TO MS OF HOSTESS SOFT
    FOCUS OVER MAN'S SHOULDER.
    HE HOLDS GLASS INTO WHICH
    WINE BOTTLE IS BEING EMPTIED.
    (:02 secs.)

6. CUT TO CU OF HAND PLACING
    EMPTY BOTTLE OF GALLO
    CALIFORNIA GRENACHE ROSÉ
    ON WINE TRAY CONTAINING 3
    FULL BOTTLES IN ICE BUCKET.
    (:01 sec.)

6A. PAN LEFT AS MAN'S HAND TAKES
    UNCORKED FULL BOTTLE AND
    POURS IT INTO EMPTY WINE
    GLASS. (:04 secs.)

7. CUT TO CU OF BOTTLE OF GALLO
WINE AND EMPTY TUMBLER ON
GRASS NEXT TO PICNIC BASKET.
MAN'S HANDS PICK THEM UP. (:01
sec.)

7A. ZOOM OUT AND TILT UP TO
REVEAL MS OF MAN AND WOMAN
ON PICNIC. (:05 secs.)

8. CUT TO ECU OF WINE BEING
POURED INTO TUMBLER. (:02
secs.)

9. CUT TO LOW MS OF MAN
ADMIRING WINE IN GLASS, AND
TURNING TO LOOK DOWN AT
BOTTLES. (:01 sec.)

10. CUT TO MS OF (HIS ANGLE ON)
TWO BOTTLES NEXT TO PICNIC
SPREAD. (:01 sec.)

11. CUT TO CU OF PATIO TABLE
WITH WINE BOTTLE AGAINST
FRUIT BACKGROUND. ZOOM IN
AND PAN RIGHT AS MAN'S HAND
PICKS UP BOTTLE AND POURS IT
INTO WINE GLASS. ZOOM OUT TO
REVEAL TWO COUPLES AROUND
PATIO TABLE. (:07 secs.)

12. CUT TO CU OF SALAD BOWL BEING
TOSSED. (:01 sec.)

13. CUT TO CU OF STEAKS BROILING
ON CHARCOAL GRILL. (:01 sec.)

14. CUT TO CU OF WINE GLASS   ANNOUNCER (V.O.): Gallo Grenache
BEING FILLED FROM BOTTLE.   Rosé.
(:02 secs.)

15. CUT TO ECU OF POURING WINE,   A fresh, bright, pink wine.
LOOKING INTO NECK OF BOTTLE.
(:02 secs.)

16. CUT TO HIGH ECU OF WINE   A party wine.
GLASS FILLING. (:02 secs.)

17. CUT TO CU OF WINE BOTTLE   A picnic wine. A beautiful dinner wine. Try
AGAINST FRUIT BASKET   Gallo Grenache Rosé chilled—
BACKGROUND. (:05 secs.)

18. CUT TO ECU OF BOTTLE LABEL: —or over ice. Discover just how refreshing
     "GALLO/CALIFORNIA/   wine can be.
     GRENACHE ROSÉ." (:07 secs.)

* * *

Much to vintners' dismay in the '50's, wine was still pretty much of a "special occasion" drink for most Americans. Even by 1970, when millions of dollars of advertising had inched U.S. adult wine consumption up to almost two gallons a year, it still hardly matched the 40 gallons a Frenchman is able to swallow.

This handsomely photographed black-and-white commercial tried to generate excitement for a new Gallo rosé wine with a simple (if somewhat studied) good food and drink, fun-'n'-games approach.

Happy young people party and picnic all over the stage, while Andre Previn and a few friends jazz away uncontestedly in the background. Even the voice-over announcer saves the 33 imperative wine-selling words for the final 16 seconds. By then, everyone has had a wonderful time becoming a wino. At least 19 beautifully bubbling glasses of Gallo California Grenache Rosé have been gaily poured or raised on high by the dozen members of the cast. But if anyone sneaked a sip, it was off-camera, to honor television's ban on visible consumption of alcoholic beverages. (All TV actors' incredulously admiring stares later dissolve to emptied glasses.)

Visually this commercial is marked by much cast and camera movement, including an in-and-out "ping pong" zoom that violates rules, but seems to work well. A man's back blocking the lens at the end of Scene 2A provides a handsome in-camera wipe. The view down the bottle neck presaged many more such camera angles, each getting tighter and tighter until the "snorkel" lens was actually inside the bottle! And the purposeful *cuts* instead of *dissolves,* between the party-picnic-patio sequences gave spontaneity in a true *"Nouvelle Vague"* manner at the moment that this French editing style was just being born, 6,000 miles away.

Tobacco

When the social historians of the 21st Century finally piece together the curious story of how their forefathers apparently poisoned themselves with tobacco and tobacco products, they can draw upon a wealth of U.S. cigarette commercials to illustrate two decades of misguided innocence.

From the earliest cute-sy dancing cigarettes to later images of super-masculinity, the tobacco industry's expenditures for broadcast advertising soared to a whopping $273 million per year by 1969, (8% of all network/station revenues, and a staggering exercise in the use of TV for brand-switching!). *Gotterdammerung* for this flood of spots came only after the institution of anti-smoking commercial counterparts by the American Cancer Society and the Tuberculosis and Heart Association, plus the aggressive legal efforts of such lonely individuals as John F. Banzhaf III and Warren Braren, who made even the mighty networks cry "uncle!"

By the summer of 1969, the Federal Communications Commission finally made it clear that it wanted cigarette advertising off the air—a step taken by the BBC in Britain many years back. Pussy-footing by both broadcasters and the tobacco industry, offering one palliative plan after another, exacerbated the situation.

It did small good for a president of the National Association of Broadcasters, Vincent Wasilewski, to argue in July, 1969 that the withdrawal of cigarette commercials (representing 60% of all tobacco advertising) would cause "substantial economic disruption and chaotic conditions in the broadcasting industry," and to offer instead a four-year phasing-out schedule. The proven health hazard was too great, replied the FCC, for anything other than prompt action—by January 2nd, 1971. They showed little interest in a proffered list of 85 U.S. cigarette brands, ranked by "tar" and nicotine content, and the tobacco industry's suggestion that the worst offenders go out first. Cigarette advertising finally went.

Yet it was so pervasive during the formative years of television that it seems hard to believe the false themes can ever die: American Tobacco's attempt to ease smoker anxiety by emphasizing the efficacy and smooth taste attributable to filters; Brown and Williamson's suggestion that *their* taste gave permanent relief from the physical discomfort of smoking other cigarettes; Liggett and Myers' flights of fancy from reality concerning the dangers of smoking; Lorillard's visceral smoker satisfaction; R. J. Reynolds' corny appeals to springtime, beauty and romance; etc., etc.

And from some far-off echo-ey commercial Nirvana still comes bouncing back Elmer Bernstein's haunting theme for Philip Morris' Marlboro Cigarettes— "Bum ... bum, bum ... bum, bum"—"Come to Marlboro Country!"

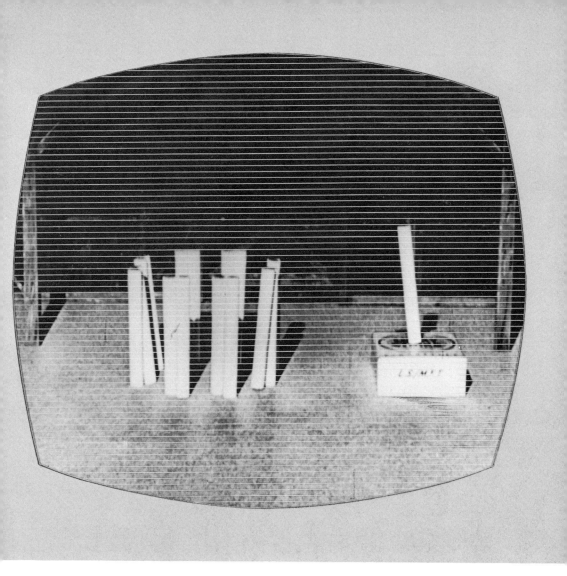

Scene 2   "Barn Dance"

DETAILS

    Black-and-white "stop motion" film. 60 seconds. 132 words. Air date 1948.
    The American Tobacco Co., *Advertiser.*
    N. W. Ayer & Son, *Agency.*
    Jam Handy Organization (Detroit), *Producer.*

CREDITS

    G. David Gudebrod, John Esau, *Creative.*
    Vince Herman, *Production.*

"BARN DANCE"

1. OPEN ON ANIMATED MS OF LUCKY STRIKE CIGARETTE PACK SUPERED OVER TOBACCO LEAF. ROTATE PACK; ZOOM FORWARD AND BACK. (:03½ secs.)	(MUSIC: SQUARE DANCE)
2. DISSOLVE TO HIGH STOP-MOTION FS OF 16 DANCING CIGARETTES NEXT TO "CALLER" CIGARETTE ATOP PACK END-LABELED "L.S./M.F.T." (:02 secs.)	CALLER (V.O.): Places all!
3. CUT TO HIGH CU OF CIGARETTES AS THEY FOLLOW CALLER'S INSTRUCTIONS. (:11 secs.)	(SINGING) All join hands and circle left. Now circle right and listen to me, L.S., L.S., M.F.T. Allemand your corner like swinging on a gate. A right to your honey, to your right and left mate.
4. CUT TO LOW CU OF DANCING CIGARETTES. (:08½ secs.)	Grand right and left around you go, Lucky Strike means fine tobacc-o!
5. CUT BACK TO HIGH MS OF DANCING CIGARETTES. (:04 secs.)	Meet your honey and give her a whirl, All swing around in the midst of a barrel.
6. CUT TO OVERHEAD MS OF DANCING CIGARETTES. SUPER LOGO OVER CENTER FRAME: "L.S./M.F.T." (:07 secs.)	Smoke 'em, smoke 'em; then you'll see: L.S., L.S., M.F.T.!
7. CUT TO LOW FS OF DANCING CIGARETTES. PAN RIGHT TO FRAME CALLER ATOP PACK. CIGARETTES START CIRCLING PACK. (:12½ secs.)	Promenade, and don't you fall, Promenade around the hall. Lucky Strike is first again, First again with tobacco men. Promenade, straight down the pike, It's time right now for a Lucky Strike.
7A. "CALLER" CIGARETTE STARTS TO SMOKE. OTHER CIGARETTES MARCH OFF TO RIGHT. (:04½ secs.)	
8. CUT TO CU OF SMOKING "CALLER." (:02 secs.)	Yes, for smoking that you're bound to like,

9. TILT UP AND DISSOLVE TO FS OF   You just can't beat a Lucky Strike.
   LUCKY STRIKE PACK IN BLACK
   LIMBO. CIGARETTES POP UP AS IT
   ROTATES AND ZOOMS FORWARD
   TO CU. (:05 secs.)

* * *

In 1860, the Frenchman Pierre Devignes nailed a still camera to a table, trained it on the flywheel of a stationary steam engine, and exposed sixteen identical photographic plates. After each exposure, he rotated the flywheel 22½°. The prints that resulted were mounted inside a slitted viewing disc (a device invented—simultaneously—in Vienna and Brussels thirty years previous) and what Devignes was then able to show friends was a perfect "moving" picture of the steam engine—taken with a *still* camera.

Ninety-two years later marked an equally historic invention time for TV commercials; Devignes' live-giving idea was traded for a pack of smokes. Sixteen cigarettes were moved ever so slightly between each frame-at-a-time motion picture camera exposure—and appeared to dance. Before long, the airwaves were filled with dancing cigarettes, marching cigarettes, parading cigarettes, even flying cigarettes.

Competitive brands went so far as to put real live people inside dancing cigarette packs—a startling idea for which even M. Devignes cannot take credit. The American cigarette developed an entirely new and charming personality—its size and scale was exactly right for such TV high-jinks—and all the successful campaigns helped bring a great number of viewers a little closer to lung cancer.

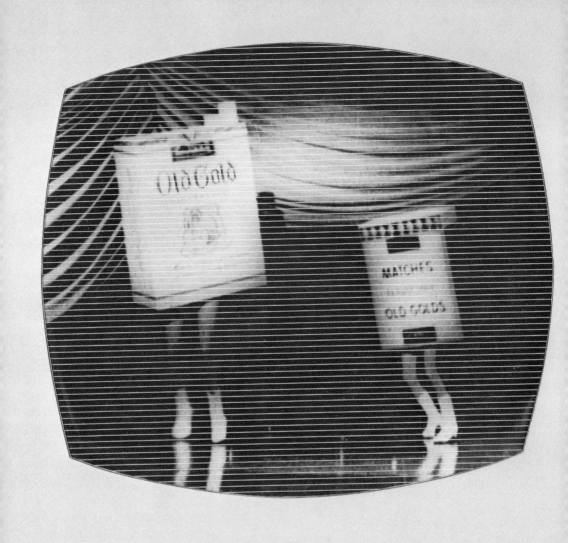

Scene 7   "Dancing Butts"

DETAILS

    Live black-and-white kinescope film. 60 seconds. 107 words. Air date 1950.
    P. Lorillard Co., *Advertiser.*
    Lennen & Newell, Inc., *Agency.*
    CBS-TV Network (N.Y.), *Producer.*

CREDITS

    Nicholas Keesely, Peter Keverson, *Creative*

"DANCING BUTTS"

1. OPEN ON MS OF DENNIS JAMES IN LIVING ROOM ARMCHAIR. HE PUFFS ON CIGARETTE AND EXHALES. (:10 secs.)

DENNIS JAMES (O.C.): Well, howdy, folks. This is Dennis James with the finest smoke in the world, Old Gold Cigarettes.

2. DISSOLVE TO SMOKY LIMBO. (:01 sec.)

3. DISSOLVE TO FS OF (TAP-DANCING GIRL INSIDE) HUGE OLD GOLD CIGARETTE PACK. (:06 secs.)

(MUSIC: "DAISY, DAISY . . . ")
JAMES (V.O.): Yes, Old Golds, the cigarette—

4. CUT TO CU OF DANCING PACK. (:06 secs.)

—with nearly two hundred years of tobacco know-how behind it. Made by tobacco men, not medicine men.

5. CUT BACK TO FS OF DANCING PACK AS IT IS JOINED BY A DANCING MATCHBOX LABELED: "MATCHES/TO LIGHT YOUR/ OLD GOLD." (:06 secs.)

Smoother, milder, tastier Old Gold cigarettes.

6. CUT TO CU OF PACK'S DANCING FEET. (:04 secs.)

7. CUT TO FS OF PACK AND BOX, DANCING TOGETHER. (:06 secs.)

Just you try an Old Gold. Old Gold, the cigarette that treats you—

8. CUT TO CU OF TWIRLING PACK. (:05 secs.)

—better in every way, because in every way, it's a better—

9. CUT TO FS OF PACK AND BOX. (:02 secs.)

—cigarette.

10. CUT TO CU OF TWIRLING PACK. (:02 secs.)

11. CUT TO FS OF PACK AND BOX AS THEY STOP DANCING. CIGARETTE POPS UP OUT OF PACK. (:04 secs.)

(MUSIC: ENDS)

12. DISSOLVE TO SMOKY LIMBO. (:01 sec.)

13. DISSOLVE TO MS OF DENNIS JAMES   JAMES (O.C.): Well, it's like I keep saying
    IN ARMCHAIR. (:07 secs.)   all the time, "If you want a treat, instead of
                                     a treatment, get a pack or a carton of Old
                                     Gold Cigarettes." You'll love 'em as much as
                                     I do.

* * *

Who can ever forget those wonderful dancing cigarette packs? Or Dennis James—TV's original Wednesday night boxing commissioner—leaning back in his overstuffed living room, pursing a puff of Old Gold tars and nicotines right into our set . . . and off we drifted through clouds of smoke to a fantasy world where birds swim, fish fly, and a pack of cigarettes (with a matchbox lady-in-waiting) waltz their way through one hundred and seven words of dulcet voice-over, to the strains of ". . . Give me your answer true."

A great mnemonic device—Old Golds, *the pack that danced!* Beyond that concept, the live cameras had little to do except cut spastically from full shot to closeup until James and the music are finished. Then, the cigarette finally pops up out of the pack. What an ending!

At little expense, comparatively, this commercial was shot with TV cameras; then transferred to film for later playbacks by the process known as *kinescoping:* a special film camera photographed the face of a special TV tube. Complicated shutter circuitry transferred the 1/30 sec. TV sweep to the 1/24 film frame. The film results, however, were always poor; a *record* of advertising rather than advertising itself. But it was better than nothing, and it served, somehow, until only today has a satisfactory television picture-to-film "flying spot" scanning technique been developed.

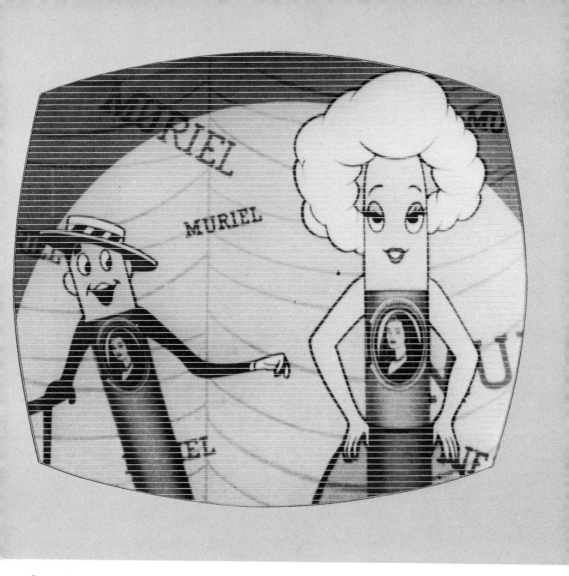

Scene 1B   "Sexy Cigar"

DETAILS

    Black-and-white animated film. 60 seconds. 114 words. Air date 1951.
    P. Lorillard Co., *Advertiser*.
    Lennen & Newell, Inc., *Agency*.
    Shamus Culhane, Inc., *Producer*.

CREDITS

    Nicholas Keesely, *Creative*.
    Clark Agnew, Shamus Culhane, *Production*.

"SEXY CIGAR"

1. OPEN ON ANIMATED MS OF CLOSED MURIEL CIGAR BOX. (:03½ secs.)

CHORUS (V.O.): (SINGING) Muriel—

1A. BOX LID OPENS AND TWO CIGARS POP OUT IN FRONT. (:03 secs.)

—Muriel, Muriel!

1B. CIGARS METAMORPHOSE INTO A MAE WEST-TYPE BLONDE IN A DIAPHANOUS SKIRT, AND A MAN WITH A CANE AND STRAW HAT. CURTAIN LABELED "MURIEL" DROPS BEHIND THEM. PAN RIGHT AS THEY BEGIN TO DANCE AND SING. (:11 sec.)

MAN AND WOMAN (O.C.): We're today's new Muriel, the fine cigar,
The pleasure that we give is really better by far.
WOMAN: I'm today's new Muriel—

1C. DANCING STOPS. PUSH IN TO CU OF BLONDE CIGAR. (:03 secs.)

MAN: Only a dime.

2. CUT TO ECU OF BLONDE CIGAR AS SHE FLICKS HER HAIR. (:03½ secs.)

WOMAN: Why don't you pick me up and smoke me some time?

3. CUT TO CU OF MALE CIGAR AS HE BALANCES HAT ON CANE. PAN LEFT AS HE DANCES BEHIND BLONDE AND OFF. HOLD ON BLONDE. (:14 secs.)

MAN: Everybody likes the wrapper, really they do,
It's luxury-light, and it's better for you.
She's today's new Muriel, mellow and ripe.
WOMAN: You're gonna' like me, friend, I'm just your type.

4. CUT TO ECU OF MALE CIGAR. PULL BACK TO MS THAT ALSO FRAMES BLONDE. (:10 secs.)

MAN: Everywhere we go they seem to like her shape,
Firm and trim and handsome, so easy to take.
WOMAN: I'm today's new Muriel.
MAN: Only a dime.

5. CUT TO ECU OF BLONDE. (:04 secs.)

WOMAN: Why don't you pick me up and smoke me some time?

6. CUT TO FS OF BOTH CIGARS IN FRONT OF CURTAIN. CURTAIN RISES OUT OF FRAME. CIGARS WHIRL AND CLOTHING DIS-APPEARS. THEY POP BACK INTO BOX. ZOOM TO BOX. (:08 secs.)

MAN AND WOMAN: Muriel, a Muriel cigar.
CHORUS (V.O.): Smoke Muriel, the fine cigar.

It certainly was not a very far cry from tap-dancing Old Gold cigarette packs to vamping Muriel cigars. It took Lorillard's agency less than a year to dope out (with Shamus Culhane, dean of early TV commercial cartooning) a lady cigar that looked and purred a little like Mae West—but not enough to be legally actionable. Even the line, "Why don't you pick me up and smoke me some time?" was just, well—close.

The animation itself was safe and uninspired; sad, because by 1951, Hollywood's Storyboard and UPA creative geniuses were already shattering the hoary Disney tradition with bold new (and inexpensive to ink and paint) graphic techniques.

The agency must have come to Shamus (who also did very imaginative and exciting work) and said, "Now this is what we want, and we have a very cute jingle by Ed Flynn to go with it." And so they did. And so this is what they got. And of course, like in the fairy stories, it was also exactly what the TV viewer knew and loved, titillation and all; it really registered.

If you have doubts, ask anyone over 30, in a sexy voice: "What cigar says (*says,* not *said*), 'Why don't you pick me up and smoke me some time?' " You'll get the right answer—even in 1984.

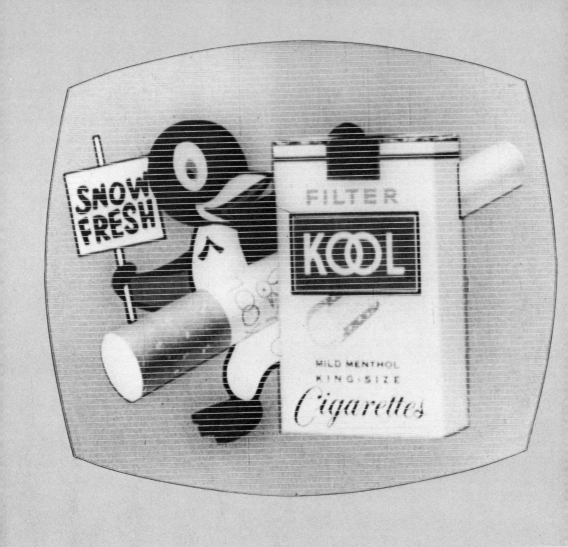

Scene 7A   *"Smoking Penguin"*

DETAILS

Black-and-white live action and animated film. 60 seconds. 98 words. Air date
1954.
Brown & Williamson Tobacco Corp., *Advertiser.*
Ted Bates, Inc., *Agency.*
Chad Associates, *Producer.*

"SMOKING PENGUIN"

1. OPEN ON ANIMATED PENGUIN
   INSIDE UPPER LEFT FRAME IRIS.
   (:01 sec.)

1A. IRIS OUT TO REVEAL FS PENGUIN
    IN TURBAN, WALKING ON BED OF
    HOT COALS. HE LEAPS OUT OF
    FRAME. (:03 secs.)

(SOUND: FEET CRUNCHING ON COALS)
ANNOUNCER (V.O.): Switch from hots
to—

2. VERTICAL FLIP WIPE TO ICY
   LAKE. PENGUIN LEAPS INTO
   FRAME AND SKATES AROUND,
   ZOOMING A KOOL CIGARETTE
   PACK TOWARD CAMERA WITH HIS
   SKATE BLADES. (:06 secs.)

—snow-fresh Filter—
PENGUIN (O.C.)—Kools!
(MUSIC: CHIME)
FEMALE VOCALIST (V.O.):
Kools, snow-fresh Kools,
Taste so clean, so refreshing,

3. IRIS WIPE TO LIVE FS OF ICY
   MOUNTAIN BROOK. (:09 secs.)

Smoke cool—
ANNOUNCER: As cool and as clean
VOCALIST: —cool—
ANNOUNCER: As a breath of fresh air.
VOCALIST:—cool!
ANNOUNCER: That's snow-fresh Filter
Kools.

4. ZOOM IN CIGARETTE-SHAPE
   MATTE WIPE, AND DISSOLVE TO
   CU LIVE CIGARETTE IN
   ANNOUNCER'S FINGERS. (:01 sec.)

VOCALIST: Smoke cool, cool, cool.

5. ZOOM BACK TO MCU ANNOUNCER.
   HE PUFFS ON CIGARETTE AND
   TURNS TO CAMERA. (:12 secs.)

ANNOUNCER (O.C.): Your mouth feels
clean, your throat refreshed. The finest leaf
tobacco, mild refreshing menthol, and—

5A. HE HOLDS UP CIGARETTE. (:07
    secs.)

—the world's most thoroughly tested filter.
That's snow-fresh Filter Kools. Why don't
you switch from hots, to—

5B. HE HOLDS UP KOOL PACK. (:03
    secs.)

—the snow-fresh coolness of Kools?

6. IRIS OUT TO LIVE ICY BROOK. (:09
   secs.)

VOCALIST: Smoke cool—
ANNOUNCER (V.O.): As cool and as
clean . . .
VOCALIST: —cool—
ANNOUNCER: As a breath of fresh air.

7. ZOOM IN CIGARETTE-SHAPE
   MATTE WIPE TO CU OF ANIMATED
   CIGARETTE. (:04 secs.)

VOCALIST:–cool!
ANNOUNCER: America's most refreshing cigarette.

7A. CIGARETTE TURNS. POP ON KOOL
    PACK IN RIGHT FRAME. PENGUIN
    APPEARS FROM BEHIND PACK
    WITH SIGN: "SNOW FRESH." (:05
    secs.)

Snow-fresh Filter–
PENGUIN (O.C.):–Kools!

* * *

Sometime in the 1940's–long before television–the Brown & Williamson Tobacco people somehow decided that the unusual menthol taste of their Kool Brand cigarettes was best personified by a penguin, who eventually became known as "Willie." It was not surprising that Willie jumped into the TV medium as Kool's spokesman; in this commercial, he walks on hot coals and skates on ice. He also gurgles "K-o-o-l-s" on cue.

The opticals are fairly complicated. The shape of a cigarette is used as a matte wipe twice, there are two irises, and the action shifts from animation to live and back again. Despite all this effort, the spot remains reasonably dull, while its promises of smoking delight are typical of the period.

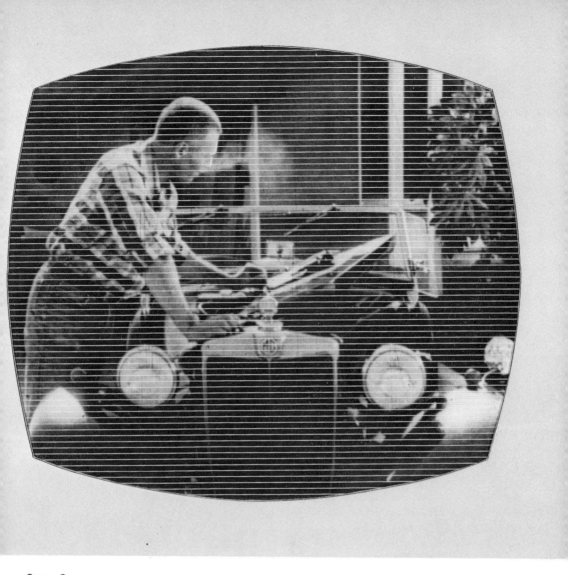

Scene 2   "Smoker"

DETAILS

Live action black-and-white film. 60 seconds. 140 words. Air date 1955.
Philip Morris, Inc., *Advertiser.*
Leo Burnett, Inc., *Agency.*
Hal Roach, Inc. (L.A.), *Producer.*

CREDITS

Draper Daniels, Gordon Minter, Don Tennant, *Creative.*
Jack Reynolds, Guy Roe, *Production.*

"SMOKER"

1. OPEN ON CU MAN'S FACE SMOKING CIGARETTE. (:04 secs.)

ANNOUNCER (V.O.): This is a man who smokes Marlboro Cigarettes. What kind of a man is he?

2. CUT TO MS OF MAN WORKING OVER SPORTS CAR ENGINE. (:10 secs.)

MAN (V.O.): I'm a guy who likes to work on my car. I like to take it apart, and put it back together. I get to working on it, and I forget where I am . . . what time it is.

3. CUT TO LOW MCU OF MAN LEANING OVER ENGINE. (:04½ secs.)

I even forget to eat.
ANNOUNCER: You don't forget to smoke, though.

4. CUT TO HIGH REVERSE ANGLE MS. (:06 secs.)

MAN: I always smoke when I work. They go together.
ANNOUNCER: Why Marlboro?

5. CUT TO HIGH MCU OF MARLBORO PACK ON ENGINE FIREWALL. (:05 secs.)

MAN: Well, it's a combination of things. When I draw on a—

6. CUT TO CU MAN'S FACE, SMOKING. (:07 secs.)

—cigarette, I want to taste something. With Marlboro, I do. And it's got a filter that works.

7. CUT BACK TO HIGH MCU OF MARLBORO PACK. HAND ENTERS FRAME, PICKS UP BOX, FLIPS TOP. (:08 secs.)

Then there's this Flip-Top box. I like things that are well-designed. This box is interesting and practical.

8. CUT BACK TO CU MAN'S FACE, SMOKING. (:04 secs.)

ANNOUNCER: Would you recommend Marlboro to your friends?
MAN: I already have.

9. CUT TO ECU OF MARLBORO PACK. (:11½ secs.)

ANNOUNCER: New Marlboro. Filter. Flavor. Flip-Top box. Popular filter price.

* * *

This was the first of a vast group of competitive cigarette commercials that succeeded in equating masculine virility with puffing, and probably did as much for U.S. lung cancer specialists as it did for U.S. tobacco companies. The "Marlboro

118

Man" epitomized this glamorous, independent approach—male actors swathed in a heavy dose of reality and documentary lighting. It was certainly a change-of-pace campaign for what had once been considered "a woman's cigarette."

Curiously in this commercial, the "stream-of-consciousness" voice-over technique for the principal actor (and of course for the announcer) heightens the realistic effect, instead of detracting from it. Perhaps the actor delivering pat answers directly into camera would have created the usual phony never-never-land feeling. Here it was skillfully avoided.

One interesting note about this commercial—and the stream of "Marlboro Men" spots it engendered: 25 years later, Draper Daniels could be found writing copy for Compassion, Inc., a public service group dedicated to eradicating smoking—and urging smokers to use cigarette money to assist needy overseas children.

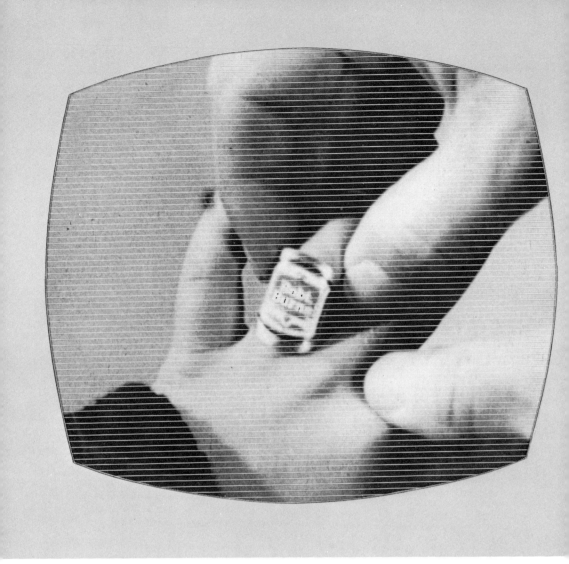

Scene 3   "Here's A Band"

DETAILS

    Live action black-and-white film. 60 seconds. 155 words. Air date 1956.
    General Cigar Co., Inc., *Advertiser.*
    Young & Rubicam, Inc., *Agency.*
    Republic Films, Inc. (L.A.), *Producer.*

CREDITS

    W. Thompson, Hanno Fuchs, *Creative.*

"HERE'S A BAND"

1. OPEN ON FS OF OCEAN BEACH WITH FIGURES OF BOY AND MAN IN DISTANCE. (:11 secs.)

(MUSIC: GENTLE BACKGROUND) NARRATOR (V.O.): I remember an uncle of mine whom I loved very much. He lived by the sea, and I often spent all day on the beach with him, just walking along.

2. CUT TO MS OF MAN. BOY RUNS TOWARD HIM FROM SURF. HE TAKES OUT CIGAR, UNWRAPS IT, AND REACHES FOR BOY'S HAND. (:10 secs.)

He liked to smoke cigars, and each time he took one out, he asked the same question: "Do you like music" "Yes," I said. "Well, then—

3. CUT TO ECU CIGAR BAND BEING SLIPPED ON BOY'S FINGER. (:04 secs.)

—here's a band for you." He put the Robert Burns band on my finger.

4. CUT TO MS MAN LIGHTING CIGAR AND WALKING WITH BOY. (:03½ secs.)

And we'd go on walking in the sun.

5. DISSOLVE TO MS LIVING ROOM WITH NARRATOR SEATED IN EASY CHAIR, SMOKING CIGAR. (:12 secs.)

(O.C.) Years later, that memory made me start smoking Robert Burns. This is the Robert Burns Panatela. An especially wonderful cigar, with the rich and comfortable taste—

6. CUT TO CU BEAUTY SHOT PANATELA BOX. SUPER TITLES: "Robt. Burns," "Nature-Filtered." (:04½ secs.)

—because the tobaccos are nature-filtered for mildness and better taste,

7. DISSOLVE TO LOW CU OF TOBACCO LEAVES ON CURING RACK. (:08 secs.)

No artificial quick curing for Robert Burns. Every leaf is cured in clean air.

8. DISSOLVE TO MS BEAUTY SHOT OF FIVE OPENED CIGAR BOXES. ZOOM TO CENTER (PANATELA) BOX. (:07 secs.)

Why don't you smoke a Robert Burns Cigar soon? They come in five different shapes— from two for a quarter, to twenty-five cents.

* * *

Certainly one of the more charming of the early location commercials, but it hardly encouraged a man to leap from his easy chair and rush out to the nearest tobacconist. Perhaps it foretold that cigar manufacturers, once huge TV advertisers, would eventually cut back on their use of the medium. Which they did.

Scene 1C   *"Winston Tastes Good"*

DETAILS

     Black-and-white animated film. 30 seconds. 40 words. Air date 1956.
     R. J. Reynolds Tobacco Company Inc., *Advertiser.*
     William Esty, Inc., *Agency.*
     Grantray-Lawrence, Inc. (L.A.), *Producer.*

CREDITS

     Walter King, Grant Simmons, *Creative.*

"WINSTON TASTES GOOD"

1. OPEN ON ANIMATED LINE
    FORMING CLEF CU IN CENTER
    FRAME. (:01½ secs.)

1A. CLEF MOVES TO LEFT FRAME AND   CHORUS (V.O.): (WHISTLES THEME)
    EMITS 7 MUSICAL NOTES. (:02½
    secs.)

1B. NOTES METAMORPHOSE INTO
    LETTERS: "W-i-n-s-t-o-n." (:02 secs.)

1C. WAVING MUSICAL BAR FORMS   (SINGS) Winston tastes good
    BEHIND LETTERS. (:03½ secs.)   Like a cigarette should,

2. LOSE CLEF. BAR METAMOR-   Winston tastes good, like a . . .
    PHOSES INTO WINSTON PACKAGE.
    ZOOM TO CU PACKAGE. (:02½ secs.)

2A. FADE OFF "Winston" LOGO IN   (SOUND: CLAP, CLAP)
    CENTER OF PACKAGE. TOP AND   . . .cigarette should.
    BOTTOM OF PACKAGE COME
    TOGETHER TWICE IN SYNC WITH
    AUDIO CLAPS, OPEN TO REVEAL
    TITLE: "tastes good/like a/cigarette/
    should." (:01 sec.)

2B. ZOOM TITLE FORWARD OUT OF
    FRAME AND DISSOLVE TO BLACK.
    (:01 sec.)

3. SLIDE "Winston" TITLE INTO   Winston gives you real flavor,
    FRAME FROM RIGHT. SPIN IT AND   Full, rich tobacco flavor.
    METAMORPHOSE INTO VERTICAL
    TITLE: "FLAVOR." LETTERS
    REARRANGE HORIZONTALLY. (:04
    secs.)

4. POP ON "FILTER" TITLE UNDER-   Winston's easy drawing, too,
    NEATH. SLIDE "FLAVOR" BEHIND   The filter lets the flavor through.
    "FILTER" AND ZOOM IT FORWARD
    THROUGH "FILTER" OUT OF
    FRAME. (:03½ secs.)

5. DISSOLVE TO CU PACKAGE.   Winston tastes good, like a . . .
   REPEAT SCENE 2A. (03½ secs.)   (SOUND: CLAP, CLAP)
                                          . . .cigarette should.

6. REPEAT SCENES 1A & 1B. (:04 secs.)   (WHISTLES THEME)

7. LETTERS METAMORPHOSE INTO
   LOGO. PACKAGE FORMS AROUND
   THEM. (:01 sec.)

                              *   *   *

    This 30-second spot was a complicated animation interpretation of Gene
Hazelton's ubiquitous Winston Cigarette jingle, originally written for radio. It is
designed with some charm; the letters and shapes metamorphose pleasantly against
the flowing choral background, and the solid bands at the top and bottom of the
Winston package design serve percussively to score the clapping on the soundtrack.
However, after two and a half decades of the same soundtrack, "Sedulus' " com-
ment in the *Introduction* was not out of order.

Scene 12   "Smoking Cowboys"

DETAILS

    Live action black-and-white film. 60 seconds. 119 words. Air date 1957.
    Liggett & Myers Tobacco Co., Inc.*Advertiser.*
    McCann-Erickson, Inc., *Agency.*
    Filmways, Inc., *Producer.*

CREDITS

    Robert Nathe, James Manilla, David Lippincott, *Creative.*
    Richard Bagley, *Production.*

"SMOKING COWBOYS"

1. OPEN ON ARTWORK OF TRI-
COLOR RIBBON WITH TITLE:
"MEN OF/AMERICA." HOLD ART,
TILT DOWN TO BACKGROUND FS
OF CATTLE DRIVE. (:04 secs.)

CHORUS (V.O.): (SINGS) Chesterfield!

2. CUT TO CU OF MILLING CATTLE.
(:02 secs.)

BARITONE (V.O.): (SINGS) Driving cattle,

3. CUT TO MS OF MILLING CATTLE.
(:02 secs.)

Desert sun ablaze,

4. CUT TO MS OF COWBOY ON
HORSE. (:03 secs.)

Pounding leather, rounding up the strays.

5. DISSOLVE TO MS OF TWO
COWBOYS RIDING TOWARDS
EACH OTHER. (:03 secs.)

Herding steers across the range, you'll find a
a man,

6. CUT TO CU FIRST COWBOY'S
FACE WITH CIGARETTE IN
MOUTH. (:02 secs.)

Stops and takes big pleasure

7. CUT TO MS OF FIRST COWBOY
REACHING INSIDE HIS JACKET
FOR CIGARETTE PACK, AND
OFFERING IT TO SECOND
COWBOY. (:02 secs.)

When and where he can.

8. CUT TO CU OF SECOND COW-
BOY'S HAND EXTRACTING
CIGARETTE FROM CHESTER-
FIELD "KING" PACK. (:03 secs.)

CHORUS: Chesterfield!
ANNOUNCER (V.O.): Join the men who
know.

9. CUT BACK TO SCENE 7, BOTH
COWBOYS SMOKING. (:02 secs.)

Nothing satisfies like the big, clean taste—

10. CUT TO CU SECOND COWBOY'S
FACE, SMOKING. (:03 secs.)

—of top tobacco in Chesterfield Kings.

11. CUT TO CU OF FIRST COWBOY'S
FACE, SMOKING. (:03 secs.)

BARITONE: Sun-drenched top tobacco's
gonna' mean

12. CUT TO MS OF BOTH COWBOYS,
SMOKING. (:04 secs.)

That you're smoking smoother and you're
smoking clean.

13. DISSOLVE TO MCU OF SECOND COWBOY RIDING. (:02 secs.)	Only top tobacco,
14. CUT TO MCU OF FIRST COWBOY SWINGING ROPE. (:02 secs.)	Full king-size,
15. CUT TO HIGH MS OF COWBOYS HERDING CATTLE. (:02 secs.)	Gives the big clean taste
16. CUT TO FS OF CATTLE DRIVE. (:03 secs.)	That always satisfies. CHORUS: Chesterfield!
17. DISSOLVE TO CU OF FIRST COWBOY, SMOKING. (:02 secs.)	ANNOUNCER: The taste you've been missing—
18. CUT BACK TO SCENE 8. (:04 secs.)	—in the length you've learned to like. Full king-size.
19. DISSOLVE TO MS OF TOBACCO FARMER CRITICALLY EXAMINING A TOBACCO LEAF. (:01 sec.)	Top tobacco all the way—
19A. SUPER TITLE FULL FRAME: "TOP-TOBACCO/FILTER ACTION." (:02 secs.)	—for top tobacco filter action.
19B. REPLACE TITLE WITH: "TOPS/IN FRIENDLY/SATISFACTION." (:02 secs.)	Tops in friendly satisfaction.
20. DISSOLVE TO FARMER'S FACE, SMOKING. (:03 secs.)	Join the big swing to Chesterfield King, new choice of Men of America.
21. DISSOLVE TO LOW FS OF SKY WITH TOBACCO PLANTS IN FOREGROUND BOTTOM FRAME. CHESTERFIELD KING PACK COMES TUMBLING INTO RIGHT FRAME FROM INFINITY. POP ON FOUR MORE PACKS ALONGSIDE FIRST PACK IN SYNC WITH TIMPANI. METAMORPHOSE FIVE PACK LINE-UP INTO CHESTER-FIELD CARTON. SUPER TITLE: "KING" IN LOWER LEFT FRAME; CHANGE POLARITY TWICE. (:04 secs.)	CHORUS: Chesterfield! (MUSIC: TIMPANI FLOURISH)

Another candidate for top honors in delineating cigarette smoking as a mark of real masculinity was the Chesterfield "Men of America" series. The subjects were economically downscale from the usual cigarette men of distinction gracing competitive TV commercials: they were cowboys (as here), mill hands, steel-workers, policemen, etc. But all of them smoked like smoking was going out of style on TV, which it has finally done.

Chester Gierlach's jingle could just as easily have been used on radio—the cinematography merely scored his lines. And Jackson Beck's deep, booming voice tolled the virtues of manhood and Chesterfield smoking with deliberately misleading copy such as (Scene 19A) "top tobacco filter action," suggesting there was some kind of a tar and nicotine "filtering" action in a longer, *non-filter* cigarette. Perhaps dreams like this sustained the habit for a lot of people who might otherwise be watching TV commercials today.

The closing effect (Scene 20) was used for years to end all Chesterfield spots. It was highly complicated and equally effective, and probably ranks next to the Hertz man dropping into the driver's seat as a well-remembered TV commercial optical effect.

Household Products

An absolutely unending flow of television commercials for products designed to help the harried American housewife poured out of TV film production houses during the '50's. The "Classics" that follow represent only a tiny flick of foam from this fantastic flood. It should be no surprise that more than half of the spots in this section sold cleaners and detergents. Their manufacturers were the multi-million-dollar sponsors of the traditional radio "soap operas"; high product profit margins made it easy for them to make a quick switch to TV wild spot and network commercials and programming.

By 1970, Procter & Gamble's, Colgate's and Lever Brothers' TV investments were around $400 million, with P & G's expenditures in that year running over $200 million! Note, however, that the soap industry's startling diversification now included many food items; Procter & Gamble's TV-advertised products ranged from enzyme detergents to peanut butter, and helped that giant corporation maintain its virtually unchallenged position as the biggest spender on U.S. television.

Creative background for almost every commercial in this category was—and is—"problem + solution"; the "Classics" are no exception, whether the problem was dirty bathtubs, greasy pots, nasty bugs, messy kids, rusty golf clubs (rusty golf clubs!), or unclean wash. With such a formidable array of visually disgusting situations to conquer, one can understand a certain commercial tendency towards animation. Throughout the '50's, the animated Ajax pixies and the hermaphroditic Mr. Clean (both shown here) continued jollying untold millions of female daytime viewers, getting them to make their own little part of America cleaner and purer than anyone ever dreamed possible.

Part of the unavoidable net result was a paradoxical water pollution problem—only partially overcome in the mid-'60's by the introduction of biodegradable detergents—as American women hit 404 million washloads a week. And by then we'd developed a brand-new threat: possible lung damage from detergent enzyme dust—the returns on which won't be in for a decade or two.

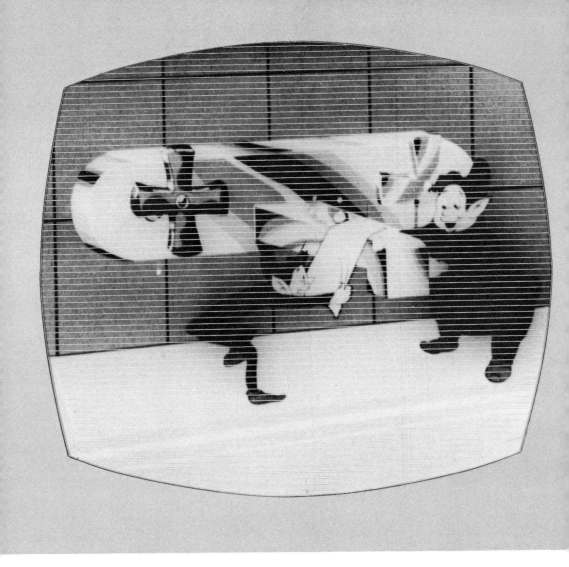

Scene 6   "Bathroom Pixies"

DETAILS

    Black-and-white animated film. 60 seconds. 107 words. Air date 1948.
    Colgate-Palmolive-Peet Co., Inc., *Advertiser.*
    Sherman & Marquette, Inc., *Agency.*
    Shamus Culhane, Inc., *Producer.*

CREDITS

    Carl Brown, *Creative.*
    Shamus Culhane, Art Heinneman, *Production.*

"BATHROOM PIXIES"

1. OPEN ON CU OF THREE TINY
   ANIMATED PIXIES AROUND AJAX
   CLEANSER CAN. PULL BACK TO
   MS. (:03 secs.)

   PIXIES (O.C.): (SINGING)
   Use Ajax!
   Bum, bum.

2. DISSOLVE TO MS OF BATHROOM.
   PAN RIGHT FROM DIRTY TOILET
   TO DIRTY TUB. (:05½ secs.)

   PIXIE (V.O.): Colgate's new Ajax cleans all
   bathroom surfaces up to fifty per cent
   faster!

3. CUT TO FULL SHOT OF SINGLE
   PIXIE SHAKING AJAX CAN INTO
   TUB. (:02 secs.)

   PIXIES (SINGING):
   Use Ajax,
   Bum, bum,

4. CUT TO FS OF ANOTHER PIXIE
   TURNING ON TUB FAUCET. (:01
   sec.)

   The Foaming Cleanser,
   Bum, bum, bum, bum, bum, bum,

5. CUT TO FS OF THIRD PIXIE
   SWINGING ON TUB STOPPER AND
   POLISHING DIRTY TUB. HE
   TEMPORARILY REVEALS THE
   WORD "AJAX" IN DIRT. (:07½
   secs.)

   Gets things clean,
   Just like a whiz.
   Bum, bum, bum, bum, bum, bum,
     bum, bum, bum.
   You'll stop paying
   The elbow tax

6. CUT TO FS OF TWO PIXIES
   POLISHING TUB FAUCET. (:04
   secs.)

   When you start cleaning
   With Ajax.
   So use Ajax,
   Bum, bum,

7. CUT TO MS OF PIXIE SWINGING
   ON TUB STOPPER, POLISHING. HE
   FALLS INTO DRAIN. (:05 secs.)

   The Foaming Cleanser,
   Bum, bum, bum, bum, bum, bum,
     bum,
   Floats the dirt
   Right down the drain,
   Bum, bum, bum, bum, bum, bum,
     bum.

8. CUT TO CU OF FALLEN PIXIE IN
   DRAIN. (:06 secs.)

   PIXIE (O.C.):
   Ajax leaves no gritty cleanser scum in
   tub or sink.
   PIXIES (SINGING): So use Ajax,
   Bum, bum,
   The Foaming Cleanser,
   Bum, bum, bum, bum, bum, bum,
     bum,

9. CUT BACK TO MS OF BATHROOM. PAN RIGHT FROM CLEAN TOILET TO CLEAN TUB. (:05 secs.)	Floats the dirt Right down the drain, Bum, bum, bum, bum, bum, bum, bum.
10. CUT TO FS OF PIXIE ON TUB RIM NEXT TO AJAX CAN WITH PLACARD: "FOAMS/AS IT/CLEANS." (:05 secs.)	PIXIE (O.C.): Ajax, the new scouring cleanser, foams as it cleans!
10A. SECOND PIXIE APPEARS FROM BEHIND CAN WITH PLACARD: "CUTS/GREASE/FASTER." (:04 secs.)	SECOND PIXIE (O.C.): Ajax cuts grease faster than any other leading cleanser!
10B. THIRD PIXIE APPEARS OVER CAN WITH PLACARD: "POLISHES/WITH HALF/THE EFFORT." (:01 sec.)	THIRD PIXIE (O.C.): Ajax—
11. CUT TO CU OF THIRD PIXIE AS HE SNIFFS CAN. (:06 secs.)	—polishes with half the effort! Ummmmmmm! And it smells good, too!
12. CUT BACK TO FS OF ALL THREE PIXIES WITH PLACARDS AROUND CAN. ZOOM TO CU OF CAN. (:05 secs.)	PIXIES (SINGING): So use Ajaxxxxx!

* * *

pix.y (pik'sē) n. pl. *pix.ies* A fairy or elf:
also spelled *pyxie.* Also *pix'ie* (−dial. E.
pixey, pisky−Scand.Cf. dial. Sw. *pysk,
pyske* a small fairy, dwarf.)

Who remembers when a copywriter's/animator's mnemonic little dream of three pixies first made the tube scene? It was the year my daughter was born, and until she was eight years old, those three caroling dwarfs kept floating their TV dirt right down the drain—to Joe Rines' bouncy "bum, bum, bum, bum" music.

By the time the pixies were finally retired by Colgate, they must have sold a whole mountain range of cleanser. And by then things were changing. Colgate-Palmolive was dropping their "Peet"; Sherman & Marquette, their agency, was being swallowed up in mergers. Even Shamus Culhane, the animation firm that did so much early (and excellent) TV animation work, was going out of business . . . temporarily.

But *ars longa est*—and the memory of those three dirt-chasing little pixies, pure Mickey Mouse in style and technique, lingers on. Show a clip of this commercial to anyone over 20 today and their eyes light up. Be careful: if it's a "professional" audience, they may even applaud!

Scene 1C   "Soap Opera"

DETAILS

    Live black-and-white kinescope film. 148 seconds. 269 words. Air date 1955.
    S.O.S., Inc., *Advertiser.*
    McCann-Erickson, Inc. (San Francisco), *Agency.*
    CBS-TV Network (N.Y.), *Producer.*

CREDITS

    Sanford Wolin, Bill Nye, John Magnuson, *Creative.*
    CBS-TV, *Production.*

"SOAP OPERA"

1. OPEN ON FS OF TABLE FILLED WITH DIRTY POTS AND PANS IN FRONT OF STAGE CURTAIN. DURWARD KIRBY AND DENISE LOR ENTER THROUGH CURTAIN, DRESSED IN WAGNERIAN COSTUMES. (:36 secs.)

LOR (O.C.): Achtung! And so vy haven't you finished cleaning the pots and the pans here?
KIRBY (O.C.): Vyn't I?
LOR: Vy?
KIRBY: Hilda, listen to me. Listen to me! Because it's such a mess, that's vy it is. Look, ve got here . . . ve got the burned-on sauerkraut dere. Und ve got the scorched vienerschnitzel. All of it's a mess.
LOR: Stupid fool. But dere's a easy way to clean up the pots and the pans.

1A. LOR PULLS TWO S.O.S. BOXES OUT FROM UNDER HER ROBE. (:04 secs.)

KIRBY: Vot is that you giff here?
LOR: S.O.S.!
KIRBY: Ah? S.O.S.?

1B. THEY WALK OUT FROM BEHIND THE TABLE, AND START TO "MOUTH" SINGING (AGAINST A PRE-RECORDED TRACK). (:47 secs.)

LOR: Ja!
KIRBY: (SINGING) When you have pots and pans to do . . .
LOR: (SINGING, MALE VOICE) S.O.S.!
KIRBY: No need to get into a stew . . .
LOR: S.O.S.!
KIRBY: These magic pads will help you star . . .
LOR: At cleaning pans and stains and grease, they're wunderbar!
KIRBY: These fibers strong . . .
LOR: Are what you need.
KIRBY: They're filled with soap . . .
LOR: They clean with speed.
KIRBY: And if you find things, tough to clean,
LOR: You just ain't using the right, stuff to clean.
KIRBY: These magic pads are simply grand.
LOR: S.O.S.!
KIRBY: Like finding that you've got three hands.
LOR: S.O.S.!
KIRBY: They'll make your pots and pans shine like mad.

1C. WIDEN TO INCLUDE GARRY
MOORE, ENTERING DRESSED IN A
BLONDE WIG. (:16 secs.)

MOORE: (SINGING) Because there's soap right in each magic scouring pad!

KIRBY & LOR: Because there's soap right in each magic scouring pad . . . Because there's soap right in each magic scouring pad . . . It makes those pots and pans just shine like mad!

1D. CUT TO CU OF GARRY MOORE'S
FACE AS HE HOLDS UP S.O.S.
CARTON (:11 secs.)

MOORE: S.O.S., S.O.S., S.O.S., S.O.S., Magic Scouring Pads!

1E. MOORE BOWS TO APPLAUSE,
STRIPS OFF HIS WIG AND RE-
TURNS TO HIS DESK AND
MICROPHONE (:34 secs.)

(MUSIC: PLAYOFF)
MOORE: S.O.S.! S.O.S. Magic Scouring Pads. I would like to take a half a second to send my heartfelt thanks to the McCann-Erickson Advertising Agency out in San Francisco, who wrote that thing for us. We had nothing to do with it; it was all their idea, and boy, I would sure like to see more fun commercials like that on television.

* * *

Breathing hot down Arthur Godfrey's popularity neck throughout much of his TV career was another CBS star, Garry Moore. Far from having Godfrey's "wised-up" image, Moore—a former NBC page—played (and *was*) the pleasant, crew-cut, all-American boy. His persuasive selling powers never quite matched those of the Ol' Redhead, but they were still pretty good.

In this commercial, a film transfer from Moore's live daytime show that used Durward Kirby as announcer-sidekick and Denise Lor as singer-sidekick, the three plug the powers of S.O.S. Scouring Pads in Wagnerian style to a pre-recorded singing track. The effect of Denise Lor singing in a deep bass voice may even have been hilarious back in 1955; the kinescope audience certainly laughs loudly enough!

Later, in the '60's, Moore apparently ran afoul of the later-defrocked CBS programming czar, James Aubrey; like A. A. Milne's sad little hero, he hasn't much "been heard from since." It's a pity; as you can see, he liked to do *different* things.

Scene 12   "Killer Raid"

DETAILS

    Black-and-white live action and animated film. 60 seconds. 113 words. Air
date 1956.
S. C. Johnson & Co., Inc., *Advertiser.*
Foote, Cone & Belding, Inc. (Chicago), *Agency.*
Cascade Pictures, Inc. (L.A.), *Producer.*

CREDITS

    W.G.T. Hyer, Charles Shank, *Creative.*
Barney Carr, Hal Mason, *Production.*

"KILLER RAID"

1. OPEN ON ANIMATED MS OF TORN WINDOW SCREEN. ZOOM TO CU AS INSECT APPEARS IN OPENING, SCREAMING. (:02 secs.)

   INSECT (O.C.): Raid's here!

2. CUT TO FS OF INSECT POPPING UP OUT OF SUGAR BOWL. (:01 sec.)

   INSECT (O.C.): Raid!

3. CUT TO MS OF INSECT HITTING CEILING IN TERROR. (:01 sec.)

   INSECT (O.C.): Raid!

4. CUT TO FS OF SIX INSECTS POPPING UP OUT OF BUREAU DRAWER IN TERROR. (:01 sec.)

   INSECTS (O.C.): Raid!

5. CUT TO CU TERRIFIED INSECT. (:01 sec.)

   INSECT (O.C.): Raid!

6. EXPLOSION WIPE TO MS OF HUMANIZED RAID CAN WITH FLASHING LOGO. HE FLEXES HIS MUSCLES. (:01 sec.)

   ANNOUNCER (V.O.): Yes, Raid—

6A. SUPER TITLES AROUND CAN: "NEW/DISCOVERY," "from/ JOHNSON'S WAX." (:02 secs.)

   —new bug-killer from Johnson's Wax!

7. CUT TO CU OF RAID CAN AS IT REMOVES CAP AND PUSHES BUTTON. PAN RIGHT WITH SPRAY CLOUD. (:03 secs.)

   Raid contacts and kills all kinds of bugs indoors.

7A. RADAR-LIKE ARC LINES EMANATE FROM CLOUD. (:02 secs.)

   Raid hunts them like radar.

8. CUT TO MS OF RUNNING BUG HITTING FIRST RADAR LINE. IT TRAPS HIM IN BOX-LIKE SHAPE, BURIES HIM UNDERGROUND. FLOWER POPS ON. (:03 secs.)

   (SOUND: CRASH. SEALING AND BURYING EFFECT)

9. CUT TO PANNING MS OF MOSQUITO SWARM. THEY FLY INTO RAID CLOUD, OUT OF THE OTHER SIDE, AND DROP OUT OF FRAME, DEAD. (:05 secs.)

   (SOUND: BUZZING)
   Sweeps bugs from the air.
   (SOUND: FALLING EFFECT)

10. CUT TO FS OF GALLOPING HERD OF INSECTS. CLOUD PASSES OVER THEM, LEAVING OPEN GRAVES. (:05 secs.)	Attacks them as they crawl. And kills them dead.
11. CUT TO MS OF INSECT HIDING IN CORNER. AS HE PEEKS OUT, A TINY CLOUD KILLS HIM. (:05 secs.)	A little goes a long way. Kills bugs even where they hide. (SOUND: DEATHBLOW)
12. CUT BACK TO CU TOP OF RAID CAN AS HE SPRAYS CLOUD. TITLES APPEAR IN CLOUD IN SYNC WITH AUDIO, DISINTE-GRATE AND FALL OUT. (:04 secs.)	Yes, Raid kills flies . . . mosquitoes . . . roaches . . . ants—
12A. ZOOM TO CLOUD WITH TITLE: "ALL KINDS OF/BUGS INDOORS." (:02 secs.)	—all kinds of bugs indoors.
13. DISSOLVE TO LIVE MS OF WOMAN SPRAYING RAID CAN ON ROSEBUSHES IN GARDEN. (:03 secs.)	Outdoors, Raid protects your garden, too.
14. CUT TO CU HAND SPRAYING ROSES. (:04 secs.)	A little kills insects that attack flowering plants, evergreens—
15. DISSOLVE TO CU HAND SPRAY-ING TOMATOES (:04 secs.)	—vegetables. Caution! Ordinary household sprays kill plants.
16. CUT TO MS WOMAN SPRAYING EVERGREENS. (:04 secs.)	Raid saves plants. So don't buy several bug-killers. Get—
17. DISSOLVE TO RAID CAN ZOOM-ING FORWARD TO MS FROM INFINITY. (:03 secs.)	—Raid, first bug killer for—
17A. ZOOM SUPER TITLES AND SYMBOLS OFF CAN: "House & Garden" AND BACK ON, AGAIN. ZOOM TO CAN LABEL. (:04 secs.)	—house and garden. Raid . . . house and garden bug killer.

* * *

By the mid-'50's, a new creative trend in "busier" animation had set in, confined primarily to West Coast studios. This commercial, introducing a new brand of insecticide, is a good example of the way this technique took what was essentially radio copy, and made fair television advertising out of it. The cartooned visuals were done imaginatively, and contained enough action to hold the viewer's eyes while the announcer hammered away in his ears.

This animation approach was as much default as design, since it was difficult and not a little unpleasant to show live bugs being killed on the living-room TV screen. Where there *was* something pleasant to show—roses, evergreens, tomatoes—the commercial quickly switched to live action.

Scene 1   *"Good Manners"*

DETAILS

    Live action black-and-white film. 60 seconds. 123 words. Air date 1957.
    Kimberly-Clark Corp., *Advertiser.*
    Foote, Cone & Belding, Inc. (Chicago), *Agency.*
    Cascade Pictures, Inc. (L.A.), *Producer.*

CREDITS

    Thomas Brennan, John Rand, *Creative.*
    George Sertz, Steve Goosoon, Roy Seawright, *Production.*

"GOOD MANNERS"

1. OPEN ON MS OF KITCHEN DOOR
   SWINGING OPEN TO REVEAL
   ¼-SIZE BUTLER IN DOORWAY.
   (:06 secs.)

   MOTHER (V.O.): Oh, Timmy! What a mess!

2. CUT TO FS OF KITCHEN WITH
   MOTHER, YOUNG DAUGHTER AND
   BABY BOY IN FOREGROUND;
   BUTLER (MATTED) IN BACK-
   GROUND. (:05 secs.)

   (O.C.) Mary Ann! What are you doing?
   DAUGHTER (O.C.): My napkin fell off.
   There it goes again.

3. CUT TO MS OF IRRITATED
   MOTHER. (:04 secs.)

   MOTHER: Oh, I'll get it. Honestly, I hate
   the way these paper napkins—

4. CUT TO DIFFERENT ANGLE MS OF
   KITCHEN AS MOTHER KNEELS TO
   PICK UP NAPKIN. BUTLER ENTERS
   AND PUTS (NORMAL-SIZED) BOX
   OF KLEENIX PAPER NAPKINS ON
   STOOL. (:06 secs.)

   —keep sliding off your lap.
   BUTLER (O.C.): Madam . . .
   MOTHER: Gracious! Now I'm seeing
   things!

5. CUT TO HIGH MS OF BUTLER. HE
   REMOVES HIS BOWLER HAT,
   TAKES A NAPKIN FROM BOX, AND
   HANDS IT OFF LEFT FRAME. (:05
   secs.)

   BUTLER: Oh, no. I'm Manners, the Butler.
   And I wish you'd try Kleenex Table
   Napkins.

6. CUT TO MS OF KITCHEN AS
   MOTHER (OPTICALLY) TAKES
   NAPKIN FROM BUTLER AND PUTS
   IT IN HER LAP (:03 secs.)

   They won't slide off your lap.
   MOTHER: Really?

7. CUT TO CU OF OPENED NAPKIN
   ON MOTHER'S LAP, AS SHE
   BOUNCES HER KNEES. NAPKIN
   STAYS IN PLACE. (:05 secs.)

   (V.O.) Why, it's true! Why, they cling like
   cloth!

8. CUT TO HIGH FS OF BIG MOTHER
   AND TINY BUTLER AS HE HANDS
   NAPKIN OFF RIGHT FRAME.
   (:03 secs.)

   BUTLER: And Kleenex Table Napkins are
   strong enough—

9. CUT TO MS OF DAUGHTER TAKING
   NAPKIN AND TUGGING ON IT. (:03½
   secs.)

   —to last through the whole meal without
   shredding.

10. CUT TO LOW MS OF MOTHER AND BABY. SHE PUTS NAPKIN ON BABY AS BIB. (:07 secs.)

MOTHER (O.C.): Oh, they're so soft. None of that stiff, paper-y feel. And just the right size.

11. CUT BACK TO HIGH MS OF BUTLER NEXT TO STOOL WITH NAPKIN BOX. HE PUTS HIS BOWLER BACK ON. (:05 secs.)

BUTLER: Yes, they're perfect for every member of the family. Remember—

12. CUT BACK TO MS OF DAUGHTER TRYING UNSUCCESSFULLY TO BOUNCE NAPKIN OFF HER LAP. (:03 secs.)

—Kleenex Table Napkins won't slide off your lap.

13. CUT BACK TO HIGH MS OF BUTLER WITH TITLE: "cling like cloth" IN BOTTOM FRAME. (:04½ secs.)

They cling like cloth. Thank you.

* * *

It was George Méliès who first imagined the possibility—by "matteing" (exposing only half the emulsion of his motion picture frame at one time)—of having an actor meet and talk to himself. It wasn't long before he also found that by shifting his camera field, he could even make a giant talk to a midget.

This half-frame device was quickly replaced by ingenious "travelling" mattes, laboriously hand-drawn solid outlines of live actors that either put Fay Wray in King Kong's paw or Kong himself on the Empire State Building. By the 1950's, Hollywood had devised much more efficient ways of matteing midgets into giant pictures (or vice-versa) by using special color filters. So when Foote, Cone & Belding decided to launch a new brand of paper napkin in 1957, they turned West.

The result was a highly successful series of Kleenex Napkin commercials featuring Richard Cutting as "Manners," the tiny quarter-sized butler with perfect entree into anyone's kitchen. He was the essence of politeness, always removing his hat before he spoke, and usually ending his sales pitch with a quiet, "Thank you." This first commercial was simply and dramatically produced; a series of thirteen cuts from simple camera angles, planned so as not to detract from the pleasant surprise of the optical matteing. As the series progressed however, it (inevitably?) became more complicated and somewhat less effective.

Scene 12   "Meet Mr. Clean"

DETAILS

Black-and-white animated film. 60 seconds. 154 words. Air date 1958.
Procter & Gamble, Inc., *Advertiser.*
Tatham-Laird, Inc. (Chicago), *Agency.*
Cascade Pictures, Inc. (L.A.), *Producer.*

CREDITS

Hal Mason, *Creative.*
Hal Mason, Grace Baughman, *Production.*

"MEET MR. CLEAN"

1. OPEN ON ANIMATED MS OF DIRTY
WINDOW GLASS AS MR. CLEAN
SCRATCHES ON TITLE: "Mr./Clean,"
THEN WIPES CIRCLE TO REVEAL
HIMSELF. (:05 secs.)

ANNOUNCER (V.O.): Meet Mr. Clean,
Procter & Gamble's new—

2. HE IS ZOOMED BACK (ONTO
LABEL) AS DIRTY WINDOW
GLASS DISSOLVES INTO FS OF
MR. CLEAN BOTTLE. (:02 secs.)

—all purpose liquid cleaner.

3. DISSOLVE TO MS OF MR. CLEAN
IN LEFT FRAME HOLDING
BOTTLE IN LEFT HAND. IN RIGHT
FRAME ARE THREE PANELS OF
SYMBOLIC DIRT LABELED:
"DIRT," "GRIME," "GREASE." MR.
CLEAN MOVES BOTTLE ACCROSS
ALL THREE. THEY DISAPPEAR.
(:04 secs.)

4. HE IS ZOOMED BACK AND FS OF
HOUSE OUTLINE MATERIALIZES
AROUND HIM. (:02 secs.)

FEMALE SINGER (V.O.):
Mr. Clean will clean your whole house,

4A. POP ON MAJOR APPLIANCES
INSIDE HOUSE. (:01 sec.)

And everything that's in it,

4B. TILT DOWN TO MS AS TILE FLOOR
SLIDES OUT UNDER HOUSE AND
MR. CLEAN. (:01 sec.)

MALE SINGER (V.O.):
Floors, doors,

4C. WALL DROPS IN FRONT OF HIM,
HE OPENS DOOR IN WALL. (:01
secs)

Walls, halls,

5. WHITEWALL TIRE ROLLS
LEFT-RIGHT TO WIPE SCENE,
FOLLOWED BY BOUNCING GOLF
BALL. (:01 sec.)

White sidewall tires
And old golf balls.

5A. EACH BALL BOUNCE MATERIALIZES
A MAJOR APPLIANCE. (:02 sec.)

FEMALE:
Sinks, stoves, golf clubs he'll do;

6. CUT TO MS OF MR. CLEAN
DIAPERING BABY. (:02 secs.)

He'll even help clean laundry, too.

143

7. CUT BACK TO FS OF DIRTY WINDOW GLASS AS MR. CLEAN BOTTLE WIPES IT CLEAN, REVEALING HAPPY HOUSEWIFE. (:03 secs.)	MALE: Mr. Clean gets rid of dirt and grime And grease in just a minute,
7A. BOTTLE FLIES BACK TO HOUSE-WIFE'S HAND. (:01 sec.)	
8. HOUSE OUTLINE MATERIALIZES AROUND HER. (:01 sec.)	FEMALE: Mr. Clean will clean your–
8A. HOUSE EXPANDS. (:01 sec.)	–whole house,
9. REPLACE HOUSEWIFE WITH MAJOR APPLIANCES. (:01 sec.)	And everything that's in it.
10. CUT TO ADMIRING HOUSEWIFE AND MR. CLEAN NEXT TO DIRTY SINK. (:02 secs.)	Can he clean a kitchen sink?
10A. MR. CLEAN POINTS AT SINK AND IT BECOMES CLEAN. (:02 secs.)	MALE: Quicker than a wink.
10B. DIRTY WINDOW SLIDES DOWN FROM TOP FRAME. (:02 secs.)	FEMALE: Can he clean a window sash?
10C. MR. CLEAN POINTS AT WINDOW AND IT BECOMES CLEAN. (:02 secs.)	MALE: Faster than a flash.
11. CUT TO CU OF REFLECTION OF HOUSEWIFE'S FACE IN DIRTY MIRROR. (:02 secs.)	FEMALE: Can he clean a dirty mirror?
11A. THE MIRROR BECOMES CLEAN. ZOOM OUT TO MS REVEALING HAPPY HOUSEWIFE. (:02 secs.)	MALE: He'll make it bright and clearer.
11B. MIRROR FADES OUT. HOUSEWIFE HOLDS UP HER HAND WITH DIAMOND RING. (:02 secs.)	FEMALE: Can he clean a diamond ring?
11C. SHE REACHES DOWN OUT OF FRAME AND LIFTS UP DOG AND FISHBOWL. (:02 secs.)	MALE: Mr. Clean cleans anything.
12. DISSOLVE TO MR. CLEAN AND HOUSEWIFE (HOLDING BOTTLE AND SPONGE) FLANKING "DIRT," "GRIME," "GREASE" PANELS, SHE WIPES THEM AWAY WITH SPONGE. (:04 secs.)	DUET (V.O.): Mr. Clean gets rid of dirt and grime And grease in just a minute,

12A. ZOOM BACK TO REVEAL THEM IN FS OF OUTLINE HOUSE. POP ON APPLIANCES AROUND THEM. (:04 secs.)	Mr. Clean will clean your whole house And everything that's in it.
13. CUT TO MS OF MR. CLEAN. (:01 sec.)	Mr. Clean,
14. BOTTLE MATERIALIZES IN LEFT FRAME, AND HE IS ZOOMED BACK ONTO LABEL. (:01 sec.)	Mr. Clean,
14A. POP ON SUPER TITLE IN UPPER RIGHT FRAME: "PROCTER & GAMBLE'S/MR. CLEAN." SPARKLES ANIMATE ON LABEL. (:06 secs.)	Mr. Clean.

* * *

Some people back in the '50's still doubted the efficacy of television as a marketing medium. All such speculation ended with the astounding sales success of the liquid cleanser commercials. The route to the bank was shown by Lestoil, very first of the liquid cleansers, produced by an absolutely unknown firm in Holyoke, Massachusetts. By relying exclusively on television as it moved into market after market, Lestoil became a landmark in the history of American advertising. Its original (and highly unimaginative) live action commercial was produced in 1954 for less than $5,000—but by 1958 it was running in more than $12,000,000 worth of television spot advertising time.

That was enough for the soap majors. If there was that kind of money to be made from nationally-marketed liquid cleansers, they could outspend Lestoil. Research and development departments all over the country cranked up to get a competitive product on supermarket shelves as quickly as possible. And instead of Lestoil's "slice-of-life" commercial approach showing a woman wiping crayon marks off a wall, experts on psychological motivation of the American housewife were called on to provide a catchier name—and a sexier product image.

Procter and Gamble won the race on August 11, 1958. Television made their liquid cleanser a household word in one great big brawny, bald-headed wink—"Mr. Clean." Don Cherry and Betty Bryan sang the praises of the smug new giant with his single earring in a bright little "Billy Boy"-type duet, written by Tatham-Laird and arranged by Bill Walker.

The result was more liquid cleanser sales history. Within weeks, viewers all over America were humming, "Mr. Clean, Mr. Clean, Mr. Clean . . . " By 1960, Mr. Clean had caught up with Lestoil, and remained #1 until 1962, when it was finally pushed from first place by Colgate's Ajax and its "white Tornado" concept—which sold 35 million bottles in nine months, and of course left America cleaner (and probably more polluted) than ever.

Scene 2A   *"Cleanest Clean"*

DETAILS

Live action black-and-white film. 60 seconds. 90 words. Air date 1958.
Procter & Gamble, Inc., *Advertiser.*
Benton & Bowles, Inc., *Agency.*
Filmways, Inc., *Producer.*

CREDITS

Frank Stephan, Joan Lipton, Bob Lelle, *Creative.*
Ben Gradus, Boris Kaufman, Bernie Friend, *Production.*

"CLEANEST CLEAN"

1. OPEN ON FS OF SUNLIT SEASHORE. (:03 secs.)

1A. ZOOM OUT SUPER TITLE: "CLEANEST CLEAN" FROM INFINITY TO TOP FRAME. (:03 secs.)

(MUSIC: INTRODUCTION)
CHORUS (V.O.): (SINGING) The cleanest clean—

1B. LITTLE GIRL RUNS OUT FROM BEHIND DUNE AS ADDITIVE SUPER TITLE: "UNDER THE SUN" ZOOMS OUT FROM INFINITY TO CENTER FRAME UNDER PREVIOUS TITLE. (:02 secs.)

—under the sun is—

2. VERTICAL WIPE (1. to r.) TO MS OF WOMAN WITH TOWEL RUNNING ALONG WASH-HUNG CLOTHESLINE STRETCHING DOWN DUNE. SUPER TITLE: "Tide CLEAN" IN TOP FRAME. ZOOM IT DOWN TO FILL BOTTOM FRAME. (:05 secs.)

—Tide clean, New Tide clean!
(MUSIC: BRIDGE)

2A. LOSE SUPER TITLE. PAN RIGHT FOR CU OF WOMAN AS SHE HANGS TOWEL ON LINE. (:03 secs.)

3. CUT TO FS OF GIRL RUNNING ACROSS DUNE TOWARD CAMERA. (:03 secs.)

ANNOUNCER (V.O.):
Clean and bright as the sun on the sand.

3A. PAN AND TILT TO MS OF GIRL AS MOTHER DRAPES TOWEL OVER GIRL'S HEAD. (:02 secs.)

The kind of clean you—

4. CUT TO CU OF MOTHER'S HANDS RUBBING GIRL'S HAIR DRY. (:06 secs.)

—like best, next to those you love.

5. CUT TO CU OF OPENED TIDE PACKAGE ON BEACH TABLE, NEXT TO LAUNDRY BASKET. (:05 secs.)

That's because new Tide has extra cleaning power. With Tide—

6. CUT TO MS OF MOTHER ON PORCH   —things always come out fresh and clean as
    AS WIND HOLDS CURTAIN   a sea breeze. More than white, more than
    AGAINST HER FACE. TILT DOWN   bright, really clean!
    AS SHE FOLDS CURTAIN, KNEELS   CHORUS (V.O.): (SINGING) Clean!
    AND PUTS IT IN BASKET. (:12 secs.)

7. DISSOLVE TO SUNBURST. ZOOM   ANNOUNCER (V.O.): The cleanest clean
    SUPER TITLE: "CLEANEST   under the sun!
    CLEAN/UNDER THE SUN" FROM
    INFINITY TO FRAME EDGES AND
    BEYOND. (:04 secs.)

8. TILT DOWN TO MS OF CLOTHES-   CHORUS (V.O.): (SINGING)
    LINE ON DUNE (SCENE 2). PAN   What a wonderful sight when your wash
    LEFT ALONG SUNLIT WASH. (:08   is done,
    secs.)   The cleanest clean under the sun,
                                   Is—

9. DISSOLVE TO MS OF TIDE BOX ON —Tide clean, new Tide clean!
    DUNE. ZOOM IN SLOWLY TO CU OF (MUSIC: STING)
    BOX. (:04 secs.)

* * *

Sand dunes, a deserted littoral, gentle surf (Tide should pardon the expression) and a harp arpeggio introduces one of the least expensive and certainly one of the most pleasant commercials ever produced for Procter & Gamble's highly successful laundry detergent.

This Tide spot—somewhat obviously choreographed but simply and expertly photographed—psychologically captured much of the sunlit brightness and whiteness of the Tide "promise"—the "cleanest clean under the sun!"

A mother/daughter combination (they never speak a word), a hank of clothesline draped with washday props, the inevitably heavily-retouched box of the product, and a free million-dollar seashore set make it all happen. Tony Faillace composed a pleasantly lilting background score . . . and Tide was in, again.

But wait! What's that off-screen, thudding through the shallows up the beach: A *white knight* . . . on a *horse*! Good Lord!

Medical Products

This is a field in which U.S. television commercials have turned out their most successful—and also sorriest—performance. Astronomical sums of money have been spent each year since the late '40's, convincing American viewers that they are in dire need of a wide assortment of pills, tablets and capsules if they are to continue to survive as happier, healthier and far less offensive human beings. "Please, Mother," screams the mad TV housewife, "I'd rather cure my own headache!", and headache tablets are currently being swallowed at the astronomical rate of 519 million *per week.*

A half-dozen major manufacturers operate in this area; most of them sell cosmetics and toiletries as well. Total expenditures on TV drug advertising in 1970 ran over a *quarter of a billion dollars!* The rate of profit return on items like analgesics—discussed in an early footnote above—is amazing, and suggests that this type of TV drug advertising will be with Americans for a long, long time.

The creative approach to selling drugs on TV has, in recent years, begun to eschew extravagant claims in favor of more cautious representation. To avoid citation by a grossly-irritated FTC or Pure Food and Drug Administration—under "go back ten spaces" cease-and-desist orders—agency copywriters now lean heavily on manufacturers' "clinicals"—research reports based on specific product experience by (often deceptively limited) groups of medical "guinea pigs."

It is not to the writers' credit that the truth in these clinicals is then stretched to the farthest boundary short of willful misinterpretation.

The author was agency producer on over a hundred Bufferin commercials, and knows from experience the way in which agency and client lawyers could spend weeks arguing the "intended meaning" of a single adjective in an arthritis commercial.

Occasionally, one of these commercials pushes too far—and is cited ten months after the fact by a laggard government agency, and ordered off the air. But by then it has been off the air for a half a year already, replaced by some different version of the same thing (which must now be cited again.)

In the Fall of 1970, the Code Authority of the National Association of Broadcasters—a professed self-regulatory unit—finally published a thirty-paragraph set of "formal Guidelines" dealing with TV drug advertising . . . but limited it to stimulants, calmatives and sleeping aids *only!* By then the horse had been stolen, and the youthful viewers of America were deep into our "pop-a-pill" culture, many conditioned by the great $289 million annual TV race that began when the "B's" first beat out the "A's."

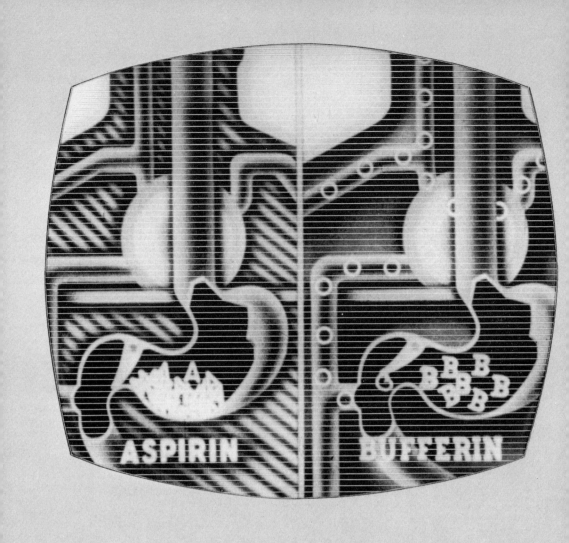

Scene 6A   "The Great A & B Race"

DETAILS

    Live action black-and-white film. 60 seconds. 135 words. Air date 1952.
    Bristol-Myers Co., Inc., *Advertiser.* *
    Young & Rubicam, Inc., *Agency.*
    Caravel Films, Inc., *Producer.*

CREDITS

    Tom Ford, Harry Hartwick, Richard Zellner, *Creative.*
    Jack Semple, Thelma Allen, *Production.*

---

* Bristol-Myers was quick to grab the brass ring of broadcast advertising. It was the fourth
national radio advertiser to sign with the AT&T Red Network, long before that 12-station
hookup was sold to the National Broadcasting Company in 1926.

"THE GREAT A & B RACE"

1. OPEN ON ANIMATED MS OF DRUMSTICK BEATING ON BASS DRUM. (:05 secs.)

(SOUND: DRUM BEATS)
ANNOUNCER (V.O.): (RHYTHMICALLY)
Headache throbbing like a drum?

1A. SUPERIMPOSE LIVE MAN'S PAINED FACE INTO CENTER OF DRUM. (:05 secs.)

Don't let it last and last!
Get quick relief with Bufferin,
It's fast . . . fast . . . fast!

2. DISSOLVE TO MS OF BUFFERIN CARTON ON GRAY BACK-GROUND. ZOOM TO CU. (:07 secs.)

(SOUND: OUT)
Yes, Bufferin relieves the pain of headahce, neuralgia or ordinary muscular aches and pains—

3. ZOOM BUFFERIN LOGO UP OFF CARTON TO FILL TOP FRAME. SUPER TITLE: "Twice as fast" IN MIDDLE FRAME. (:02 secs.)

—twice as fast—

4. ADDITIVE TITLE: "as aspirin" IN BOTTOM FRAME. (:01 sec.)

—as aspirin.

5. DISSOLVE TO TWIN SYMBOLIC CUTAWAY HUMAN TORSOS. TORSO AT LEFT IS LABELED "ASPIRIN"; "BUFFERIN" IS AT RIGHT. (:06 secs.)

These two diagrams will show you why. As you see, both Bufferin and aspirin—

6. DISSOLVE TO MS OF STOMACH AREAS. "A" AND "B" TABLETS DROP INTO EACH STOMACH. (:07 secs.)

—take exactly the same time to get through the stomach. But for a pain reliever to do its best and quickest work—

6A. THE ACTION STARTS. EACH TABLET METAMORPHOSES INTO A GROUP OF TINY LETTERS WHICH KEEP REGENERATING THEMSELVES, EITHER LEAVING THE STOMACH THROUGH A FLAPPY TRAPDOOR OR PILING UP, INSIDE. BY THE END OF THIS SCENE, 36 "B's" HAVE EASILY MADE THE GRADE, TURNING INTO "O's" AS THEY BUBBLE ALONG THROUGH THE BLOOD-STREAM'S PIPES. ONLY 4 "A's" HAVE ESCAPED. ZOOM TO THE "BUFFERIN" STOMACH. (:12 secs.)

—it must get out of the stomach into the bloodstream. Now Bufferin's formula combines aspirin with two special antiacid ingredients which get the pain reliever out of the stomach into the bloodstream—

151

7. DISSOLVE TO WIDER DEPICTION   —twice as fast as aspirin. That's why
   OF "BUFFERIN" TORSO, "O's"   Bufferin acts twice as fast as aspirin.
   BUBBLING WILDLY THROUGH
   EVERY ARTERY. (:05 secs.)

8. DISSOLVE TO MS OF LIVE LIMBO   What's more, Bufferin doesn't upset—
   HAND TILTING BUFFERIN
   BOTTLE TO SHAKE OUT
   TABLETS. (:02 secs.)

9. CUT TO CU MAN'S PALM. TWO   —your stomach—
   TABLETS DROP INTO PALM (:01
   sec.)

10. DISSOLVE TO CU OF MAN   —as aspirin often does.
    DRINKING GLASS OF WATER. (:03
    secs.)

11. DISSOLVE TO MS OF BATHROOM   So get Bufferin today. Bufferin.
    SHELF WITH BUFFERIN BOTTLE
    AND CARTON. (:04 secs.)

                              *   *   *

"Aspirin may cause gastric irritation," says the *Encyclopædia Britannica* about man's most common wonder drug. So buffered aspirin was invented, to minimize gastric problems and allow people to swallow more tablets without necessarily developing the *Encyclopædia's* overdose symptoms: ". . . ringing of the ears, headache, dizziness, dimness of vision, mental confusion, nausea and vomiting."

Description of the complicated stomach chemistry of this "buffering"—the balance between the acetylsalicylic acid and the acetylsalicylates, etc.—was hardly an exciting story for a one-minute television commercial; the *promise* was much more important—"Bufferin goes to work faster!"

The mock-up body-machines in this historic commercial were one of television's earliest attempts to demonstrate an otherwise invisible promise.

The commercial itself is a potpourri of styles that laid the groundwork for much future analgesic advertising—by many other brands. There is animation, zooming titles, drums in the head, copy that says "fast . . . fast . . . fast," and the greatest fixed race of the century—night after night, "B's" always beat the "A's" out of the stomach (something the FTC might look dimly at today).

Bufferin sales zoomed. The commercial seemed to run forever, until viewers could almost swear it was causing "ringing of the ears, headache, dizziness, dimness of vision, etc."

Scene 2   "Speedy"

DETAILS

Black-and-white "stop motion" and live action film. 60 seconds. 134 words.
Air date 1953.
Miles Laboratories, Inc., *Advertiser.*
Wade Advertising, Inc. (Chicago), *Agency.*
Swift-Chaplin, Inc. (Los Angeles), *Producer.*

CREDITS

Booth Luck, *Creative.*
Charles Chaplin, John Abbott, Miles Pike, Howard Swift, *Production.*

"SPEEDY"

1. OPEN ON STOP-MOTION MS OF ALKA-SELTZER PUPPET "SPEEDY," READY TO LEAD A MARCH OF ALKA-SELTZER CARTONS. (:06 secs.)

SPEEDY (O.C.): All over America for fast relief, it's "Speedy Alka-Seltzer!"

2. CUT TO FS AS MARCH BEGINS, REVEALING U.S. CAPITOL GROUNDS IN BACKGROUND. (:08 secs.)

(SINGS) It's Speedy Alka-Seltzer,
On that most folks agree.
The choice of every party,
In Washington, D. C.

3. CUT TO MS AS MARCH STOPS AND CARTONS FAN OUT BEHIND SPEEDY. (:02 secs.)

(SPEAKS) Washington, D.C.:

4. CUT TO LIVE MS OF LEGISLATOR AT LIMBO PODIUM, DELIVERING SPEECH. (:03 secs.)

(RECITES) When Congressmen debate a bill,
Headaches are a common ill.

5. CUT TO MS OF LEGISLATOR IN BATHROOM, DRINKING GLASS OF WATER. (:02 secs.)

But they take Alka-Seltzer, too,

6. CUT TO CU OF LEGISLATOR'S FACE. (:02 secs.)

LEGISLATOR (O.C.): What's good for me is good for you!

7. CUT TO SIDE STOP-MOTION MS OF SPEEDY LEADING MARCHING CARTONS THROUGH COTTON FIELD. (:06 secs.)

SPEEDY: (SINGS) The South has fields of cotton
And choice tobacco leaf.
And when they have a headache,

8. CUT TO FRONT FS AS MARCH STOPS AND CARTONS PILE UP FLAT BEHIND SPEEDY. (:04 secs.)

Alka-Seltzer brings relief.

9. CUT TO MCU OF SPEEDY. (:02 secs.)

(SPEAKS) New Orleans:

10. CUT TO LIVE STOCK NIGHT FS OF MARDI GRAS. (:02 secs.)

(RECITES) Mardi Gras, you dance and sing,

11. CUT TO MCU OF WOMAN IN LIMBO NIGHT CLUB. (:02 secs.)

And Basin Street, where jazz is king.

12. CUT TO MS OF WOMAN IN LIMBO, DRINKING GLASS OF WATER. (:02 secs.)

The morning after when you wake,

12A. "Alka-Seltzer" LOGO APPEARS
ABOVE HER HEAD, REAR
PROJECTION. (:02 secs.)

Alka-Seltzer's what you take.

13. CUT TO SIDE STOP-MOTION CU OF
SPEEDY LEADING MARCHING
CARTONS OVER MAP OF U.S.A.
ZOOM BACK TO REVEAL "FAST
RELIEF" DIRECTION SIGN AND
BUILDING WITH "ALKA-
SELTZER" SIGN ON TOP. (:08 secs.)

(SINGS) It's Speedy Alka-Seltzer,
For fast relief, you know.
It's Speedy Alka-Seltzer,
No matter where you go.

14. CUT TO FRONT CU OF MARCH.
(:04 secs.)

If you have got a headache,
Or your stomach is upset,

15. CUT TO FS AS MARCH STOPS AND
CARTONS FAN OUT IN A ROW
BEHIND SPEEDY. (:02 secs.)

Get Speedy Alka-Seltzer,
For—

15A. SPEEDY METAMORPHOSES INTO
A BUBBLING GLASS OF ALKA-
SELTZER. SUPER TITLE "FAST
RELIEF" IN BOTTOM FRAME. (:03
secs.)

—fast re-lief, you bet!

* * *

On the opposite side of the coin from the dead-serious, almost threatening analgesic advertising sponsored by Bufferin, was Speedy, Alka-Seltzer's rotund little puppet with his tablet hat. This cheerful, ubiquitous, squeaky-voiced monster led his ranked Alka-Seltzer cartons up and down the TV screen for many years to Country Washburn's perfect 4/4 march time.

Speedy was shot in stop-motion—the puppet's head and limbs were moved (or exchanged) in every frame, to simulate movement. The cartons, too, were adjusted from side to side. Because there was not too much apparent movement, this technique was relatively simple to execute, and was certainly effective. Speedy remained on the air for years; he was dropped only when the account switched agencies.

When the account *did* move, it is interesting to note that the creative TV commercial approach shifted from this Never-Never-Land of stop-motion puppets (and live limbo Congressman, right out of *Finian's Rainbow*), to the most *verité* of all the *cinema verité* approaches . . . focussing the live camera directly into people's upset stomachs.

Even later, the stomach was extracted from the person and sat in a chair, having an animated conversation with him.

And even later, manifestations of gigantic dumplings and marshmallow meatballs. Not too far from Bufferin's "A's" and "B's," after all.

And the account moved again. And again. And . . .

Scene 7   *"Boil An Egg"*

DETAILS

    Live action black-and-white film. 60 seconds. 163 words. Air date 1956.
    Johnson & Johnson, Inc., *Advertiser.*
    Young & Rubicam, Inc., *Agency.*
    Robert Lawrence, Inc., *Producer.*

CREDITS

    Warren Schloat, Pat Grew, Claude Gillingwater, *Creative.*
    Robert Lawrence, *Production.*

"BOIL AN EGG"

1. OPEN ON SPOTLIT HIGH CU OF BAND-AID CAN. (:03 secs.)

ANNOUNCER (V.O.): Look! Here is a new Band-Aid Plastic Strip—

1A. SUPER TITLE: "with/SUPER-STICK" IN TOP FRAME. (:01½ secs.)

—with new Super-Stick. It—

1B. ADDITIVE SUPER TITLE: "STICKS BETTER THAN/ANY OTHER BANDAGE" IN BOTTOM FRAME. (:03 secs.)

—sticks better than other bandage.

2. DISSOLVE TO SPOTLIT MCU OF HAND PLACING EGG ON TALL GOLF TEE. (:04 secs.)

The proof? Take a dry egg at room temperature. Touch the egg—

2A. HAND REENTERS FRAME WITH DANGLING BANDAGE AND DRAGS ADHESIVE TAB ACROSS EGG. SUPER TITLE: "BRAND X" IN BOTTOM FRAME. (:01 sec.)

—with any other bandage. Brand X.

3. HAND REPEATS ACTION WITH SECOND BANDAGE. DISSOLVE TITLE TO: "BRAND Y." (:01 sec.)

Brand Y.

4. HAND REPEATS ACTION WITH THIRD BANDAGE. DISSOLVE TITLE TO: "BRAND Z." (:01 sec.)

Brand Z. Not one sticks.

5. DISSOLVE TITLE TO: "BAND-AID PLASTIC STRIP." HAND REPEATS ACTION WITH BAND-AID STRIP. IT PICKS UP THE EGG. (:04 secs.)

But a Band-Aid Plastic Strip with new Super-Stick sticks tight instantly.

6. CUT TO SLOW-MOTION CU OF ACTION IN SCENE 5. (:07½ secs.)

Watch it again in slow motion. No pressure, yet we could lift the egg.

7. CUT TO HIGH MS OF GLASS SAUCEPAN WITH BOILING WATER ON STOVE. HAND LOWERS EGG ON STRIP INTO PAN. (:01½ secs.)

(SOUND: BOILING WATER) Even boil it!

8. CUT TO CU OF EGG ENTERING BOILING WATER. (:03 secs.)

And the Band-Aid Plastic Strip never comes loose.

9.	CUT TO MS OF KITCHEN AS WOMAN REMOVES BAND-AIDED EGG FROM SAUCEPAN AND COMES TOWARD CAMERA. (:08 secs.)	WOMAN (O.C.): Maybe you don't like to boil eggs this way, but you do want the extra protection of Band-Aid Plastic Strips.
10.	CUT TO ECU OF BAND-AID STRIP BEING WRAPPED AROUND WOMAN'S FINGER. (:05 secs.)	(V.O.) They take better care of little cuts and scratches. They stay put. ANNOUNCER (V.O.): Yes, even in—
11.	CUT TO UNDERWATER MCU OF HAND WITH BAND-AID ENTERING GLASS DISHPAN. (:04 secs.)	—hot, soapy dishwater. Neat, flesh-colored, almost invisible.
12.	CUT TO HIGH BEAUTY CU OF BAND-AID CAN. (:01 sec.)	Band-Aid Plastic Strips—
12A.	SUPER TITLE: "with/SUPER-STICK" IN TOP FRAME. (:01 sec.)	—with new Super-Stick.
12B.	ADDITIVE TITLE: "STICKS BETTER THAN/ANY OTHER BANDAGE" IN BOTTOM FRAME. (:03 secs.)	Stick better than any other bandage. Made only by—
12C.	REPLACE TITLING WITH: "(logo) Johnson & Johnson" IN TOP FRAME, "THE MOST TRUSTED NAME/IN SURGICAL DRESSINGS" IN BOTTOM FRAME. (:04 secs.)	—Johnson & Johnson, the most trusted name in surgical dressings.
12D.	LOSE ALL TITLING. (:03½ secs.)	Be sure you get Band-Aid Plastic Strips.

* * *

This simple, straightforward commercial is notable for three reasons. The handsome shape of the egg in close-up photography gave the spot a very graphic "feel." The dramatic demonstration, one of the earliest true demonstrations in television advertising, was also one of the medium's most memorable ones. And this commercial marks one of the earliest uses of comparative "Brand X" labeling. Add to this the very pretty shot of the egg under bubbling boiling water, and it is clear why this Johnson & Johnson spot ran on-air for a long time.

And sold a lot of bandages, too.

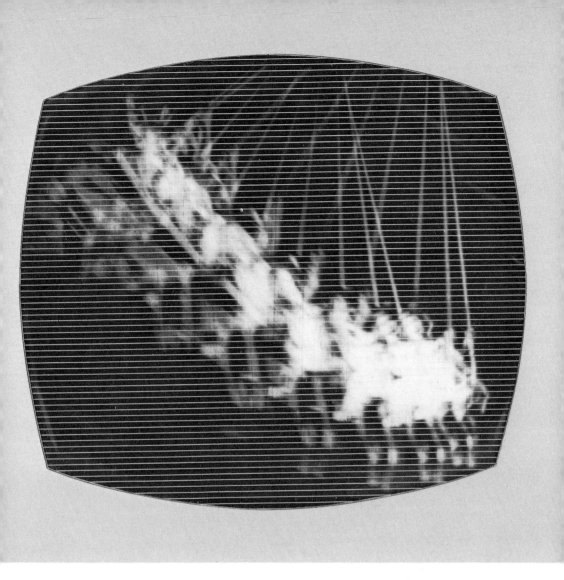

Scene 2   *"Funny Bandages"*

DETAILS

    Live-action black-and-white film. 60 seconds. 54 words. Air date 1957.
    Johnson & Johnson, Inc., *Advertiser.*
    Young & Rubicam, Inc., *Agency.*
    Elbee et Cie., (Paris), *Producer.*

CREDITS

    Stephen Frankfurt, William Schnurr, *Creative.*
    M. Lemoine-Boussac, *Production.*

"FUNNY BANDAGES"

1. OPEN ON FS OF CHILDREN PLAY-
    ING IN WHITE LIMBO, SEEN
    THROUGH CHAIN LINK FENCE.
    (:04 secs.)

    (MUSIC: PLAYFUL)

1A. VERTICAL BLACK WIPE FROM
    SIDES TO CENTER WITH FENCE
    LINK SHAPES. (:01 secs.)

2. DISSOLVE IN STROBOSCOPIC
    EFFECT OF GIRL IN SWING
    AGAINST BLACK LIMBO. (:05 secs.)

    BOY (V.O.) Hurt finger!
    CHORUS (V.O.): Oooooooooh!

2A. FREEZE GIRL IN SINGLE FRAME.
    POP ON HEART-SHAPED BAND-
    AID BANDAGE, ZOOM IN TO
    INFINITY. (:02 secs.)

    BOY: Band-Aid Plastic Bandages, in color!

2B. UNFREEZE FOR MORE STROBE.
    (:01½ secs.)

    CHORUS: Ahhhhhhhhhh!

3. DISSOLVE IN AND OUT OF BLACK
    TO STROBE EFFECT OF BOY ON
    POGO STICK AGAINST BLACK
    LIMBO. (:07 secs.)

    BOY: Hurt elbows!
    CHORUS: Oooooooooh!

3A. FREEZE BOY IN SINGLE FRAME.
    POP ON "EYE" BAND-AID
    BANDAGE, SPIN AND ZOOM IN TO
    INFINITY. (:03 secs.)

    BOY: Band-Aid Bandage. It's blue!

3B. UNFREEZE FOR MORE STROBE.
    (:03 secs.)

    CHORUS: Ahhhhhhh!

4. DISSOLVE IN AND OUT OF BLACK
    TO STROBE EFFECT OF GIRL
    SKIPPING ROPE AGAINST BLACK
    LIMBO. (:04 secs.)

    BOY: Hurt ankles!
    CHORUS: Oooooooooh!

4A. FREEZE GIRL IN SINGLE FRAME.
    POP ON "HORSE" BAND-AID
    BANDAGE, SPIN AND ZOOM IN TO
    INFINITY. (:02 secs.)

    BOY: Band-Aid Bandage. It's yellow!

5. UNFREEZE FOR MORE STROBE.
    (:02 secs.)

6. DISSOLVE IN AND OUT OF BLACK TO BOY ON ROLLER SKATES AGAINST BLACK LIMBO. (:07 secs.)	BOY: Hurt knees! CHORUS: Oooooooooooh!
6A. FREEZE BOY IN SINGLE FRAME. POP ON "STAR" BAND-AID BANDAGE, SPIN AND ZOOM IN TO INFINITY. (:02 secs.)	BOY: Band-Aid Bandage. It's red! CHORUS: Wow!
6B. UNFREEZE FOR MORE STROBE. (:03 secs.)	
7. CUT TO MCU OF BAND-AID "STARS AND STRIPS" CONTAINER AGAINST BLACK LIMBO. (:02½ secs.)	BOY: Band-Aid "Stars and Strips"!
8. WIPE WITH SLID-ON BLACK CARD WITH ASSORTED BAND-AID STRIPS CU. (:02 secs.)	CHORUS: Oooooooooh!
9. SLIDE OFF CARD TO REVEAL MCU OF BAND-AID "CHARMER" CONTAINER AGAINST BLACK LIMBO. (:03 secs.)	BOY: Band-Aid "Stars and Strips Charmers"!
10. CUT TO CU OF POPPED-ON BAND-AIDS OF DIFFERENT DESIGNS. THEY ROTATE. (:06 secs.)	CHORUS: New! BOY: In color! CHORUS: (LAUGHS) BOY: Get them! CHORUS: Wooooooo!

* * *

Television commercial creators are always searching for some unusual new graphic or photographic technique to set their advertising message apart from all their other visual competition on the face of the tube. Often these new developments come from Europe. This Band-Aid commercial is a good example of a step-printing method of photography originally developed in French laboratories as an art-film effect. An alert Young & Rubicam art director named Stephen Frankfurt thought it could be pressed into the service of selling more Band-Aids.

The film was shot in Paris—children playing on a limbo stage—and the negative was completed there with repetitive printing techniques that closely resemble the multiple-image prints of *still* stroboscopic flash photography.

This effect however, is most effective when shot against a dead-black background, so the overall tone of this visually-arresting commercial is therefore a bit gloomy. Steve Frankfurt is hardly gloomy. Today, he's president of Y & R.*

---

*Since the above was written, *The New York Times* reported (November 26, 1970) without explanation that Mr. Frankfurt had resigned from Young & Rubicam. Life and death in American advertising is somewhat reminiscent of the French Revolution.

Toiletries

Vanity of appearance, oldest of the human emotions, offered a made-to-order selling area for the new television medium. From those earliest of late late evenings, when video pitchman Sid Hassman tugged at his unusually healthy head of hair (and ascribed its condition completely to the wonders of bottled lanolin), scripts have called for more and more male and female "head shots," showing razor blades scraping "cleaner than ever," electric razors shaving "closer, more comfortably," and deodorants making you *seem* prettier. And the right brand of toothpaste attracting all the boys.

Short of obvious misrepresentation (where the FTC might step in today), the commercials produced for this category may be characterized as generally pleasant, and relatively harmless. For men, they have moved beyond the shaving baseball players shown here to the sex-oriented area of incredibly georgeous Scandanavian women who coo throatily, "Take it off! Take it *all* off!"

For the ladies, beautiful models and husky-voiced announcers extol the virtues of hair color and conditioning products and makeup. Although educational television has long since penetrated the myth that night creams selling for several dollars really contain something more than several *cents* of emollient and perfume, women still don't seem to care.

After all, if you *feel* you are as beautiful as the most beautiful girl on TV—should someone in this best of all possible worlds tell you otherwise? *Quo vadis* women's lib?

162

Scene 1F   *"How'R'Ya Fixed"*

DETAILS

    Black-and-white (negative) animated film. 30 seconds. 54 words. Air date 1952.
    Gillette Safety Razor Co., *Advertiser.*
    Maxon, Inc., *Agency.*
    TV Spots, Inc. (L.A.), *Producer.*

CREDITS

    Allen Z. Hodshire, *Creative.*
    Allen Z. Hodshire, Sam Nicholson, *Production.*

"HOW'R'YA FIXED?"

1. OPEN ON TINY ANIMATED MUSICAL
    NOTE IN UPPER LEFT FRAME. (:01½
    secs.)

1A. ZOOM NOTE FORWARD TO MS
    AND POP ON TITLE "LOOK/
    SHARP" IN CENTER. POP ON
    SECOND TINY NOTE UNDER-
    NEATH. (:01 sec.)

<u>MALE VOCALIST (V.O.)</u>: Look sharp!

1B. LOSE FIRST NOTE. ZOOM SECOND
    NOTE FORWARD TO MS AND POP
    ON "FEEL/SHARP" IN CENTER. POP
    ON THIRD TINY NOTE UNDER-
    NEATH. (:01 sec.)

Feel sharp!

1C. LOSE SECOND NOTE. ZOOM THIRD
    NOTE FORWARD TO MS AND POP
    ON "BE/SHARP" IN CENTER. (:01
    sec.)

<u>Be</u> sharp!

1D. METAMORPHOSE THIRD NOTE
    INTO DRUM WITH BEATING
    STICKS. A PARROT HOLDING A
    GUITAR DROPS DOWN INTO
    FRAME. PAN RIGHT WITH PARROT
    AS HE LEAPS OFF DRUM. (:01 sec.)

And listen, mister—

1E. VOCAL WORDS APPEAR IN TINY
    NOTES OVER PARROT'S HEAD. (:04½
    secs.)

How'r'ya fixed for blades? You bet,
blades.

1F. PARROT SPINS GUITAR. IT
    METAMORPHOSES INTO DIS-
    PENSER OF GILLETTE BLUE
    BLADES. (:07 secs.)

How are you fixed for blades? You betcha'.
Please make sure you have enough,
'Cause a—

1G. PARROT SPINS DISPENSER. IT
    METAMORPHOSES INTO A STRING
    BASS. (:04½ secs.)

—worn-out blade makes shavin' mighty
tough!

1H. PARROT SPINS BASS AND IS
    HIMSELF CAUGHT UP IN SPIN.
    (:04½ secs.)

How are you fixed for blades? Better look.

1J. SPIN METAMORPHOSES INTO   Gillette Blue Blades, I mean!
    GILLETTE BLUE BLADES PACKAGE.
    (:04 secs.)

                                    *   *   *

The Gillette Safety Razor Co., traditional radio baseball sponsor, faced the problem of neatly inserting a TV commercial message for razor blades in the brief moments between innings without significantly interrupting the visual flow and excitement of the ball game.

They came up with a simply-drawn *negative* cartoon parrot—more than vaguely reminiscent of José Carioca from Walt Disney's "Brazil"—surrounded by musical instruments and a couple of over-detailed razor blade packages.

The ball game never left the home screen—Sam Nicholson's parrot and props were "burned-in" over the live camera image off the diamond, while the audio was wholly given over to that famous echo-y question by Scott-Textor's vocalist. Later improvements in TV matteing amplifiers permitted the parrot animation to be superimposed, instead of burned-in, for a clearer picture.

The parrot and his pregnant one-scene question were introduced in 1952. His 30-second turn, no matter how repetitious, was so successful that you may even see him doing his thing in *this year's* World Series. If baseball outlasts television.

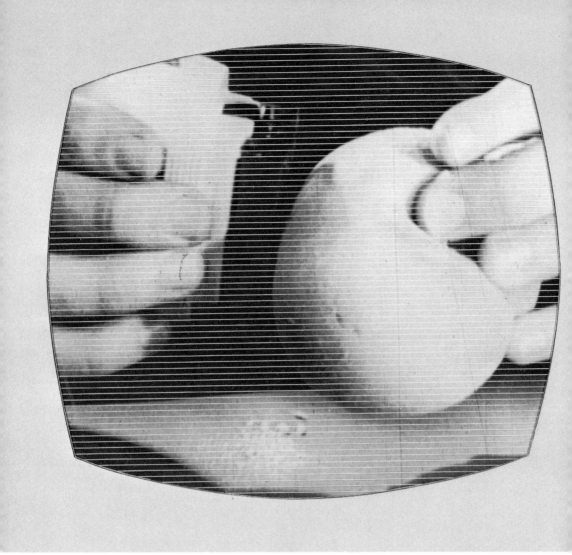

Scene 5   "Peach of a Shave"

DETAILS

    Live action black-and-white film. 60 seconds. 125 words. Air date 1954.
    Remington-Rand, Inc., *Advertiser*.
    Young & Rubicam, Inc., *Agency*.
    Peter Elgar, Inc., *Producer*.

CREDITS

    Pyrmen Smith, Hanley Norins, Dick Zellner, *Creative*.
    Peter Elgar, *Production*.

"PEACH OF A SHAVE"

1. OPEN ON MCU OF PEACH BASKET. HAND REACHES INTO FRAME AND LIFTS PEACH. (:02 secs.)

ANNOUNCER V.O.): We're going—

1A. TILT UP WITH HAND AND PEACH. (:05 secs.)

—to use an ordinary garden-variety peach, with its short, close fuzz and tender skin—

2. MATCH DISSOLVE TO CU OF HAIRBRUSH WITH HAND STROKING BRISTLES. (:04 secs.)

—and a regular regimental hairbrush, with its rough tough bristles—

3. DISSOLVE TO MCU BEAUTY SHOT OF REMINGTON "60" ELECTRIC SHAVER IN CASE. DOLLY IN SLOWLY. (:04 secs.)

—to prove to you that the man-sized Remington Electric Shaver—

4. DISSOLVE TO CU MAN SHAVING WITH ELECTRIC SHAVER. (:06 secs.)

—will give you a close, comfortable shave, no matter how tender your skin, no matter how tough your beard.

5. DISSOLVE TO CU OF HANDS SHAVING PEACH WITH REMINGTON SHAVER. FUZZ FALLING ON TABLE. (:09 secs.)

Look at this amazing demonstration! The Remington is so gentle that it can shave the short, close fuzz of a peach without harming its tender skin.

6. DISSOLVE TO CU OF HANDS SHAVING HAIRBRUSH WITH REMINGTON SHAVER. BRISTLES FALLING ON TABLE. (:06 secs.)

And the Remington is so powerful, it can shave the bristles off a brush, bristles tougher than any beard!

7. DISSOLVE TO MCU OF HANDS HOLDING UP BRUSH AND PEACH. (:04 secs.)

Remember the amazing demonstration of the peach and brush! For the—

8. DISSOLVE TO MCU BEAUTY SHOT OF REMINGTON SHAVER IN CASE. (:02 secs.)

—close, comfortable shave you've always wanted—

8A. HAND ENTERS FRAME AND LIFTS SHAVER FROM CASE. (:08 secs.)

—reach for the Remington Electric Shaver.

8B. SUPER LOCAL DEALER I.D. (:10 secs.)

"Look at this amazing demonstration!" says the disembodied announcer, and it really was—one of the most memorable moments from the days when television commercials first began to *demonstrate* product superiority. Looking back, we can recognize that the peach-and-brush shaving demonstration was a "natural"—it was brief, it worked, it was germane and easily understood. Later demonstrations became more difficult; advertisers tried to squeeze "realistic" presentations within the narrow confines of the one-minute form. Inevitably, they cheated.

The most famous cheat was another shaving demonstration—non-electric—involving Palmolive Shave Cream applied to sandpaper. The FTC came down hard on Ted Bates, the offending agency, in a landmark decision now known throughout the commercial industry as the "Sandpaper Case." The event succeeded in introducing a level of reform into the field, and also switched many TV copywriters from somewhat bizarre realistic demonstrations to an area of *total unreality* which could never be called deception by any stretch of the imagination—unless you could conceive of an Alka-Seltzer tablet forty feet high being dropped into an eighty foot glass of water.

Scene 4   *"Sporting Shaves"*

DETAILS

Live action black-and-white film. 55 seconds. 154 words. Air date 1955.
Gillette Safety Razor Co., *Advertiser.*
Maxon, Inc., *Agency.*
Van Praag, Inc., *Producer.*

CREDITS

Hugh S. Hole, Joe Nixon, *Creative.*
William Van Praag, *Production.*

"SPORTING SHAVES"

1. OPEN ON HIGH MS OF PEE WEE REESE IN DODGER UNIFORM, SHOWING ROOKIE PLAYER HIS BATTING GRIP. (:04 secs.)

AL HELFER (V.O.) Pee Wee Reese has a way with Dodger rookies or sandlot youngsters.

1A. PAN RIGHT TO INCLUDE AL HELFER, AS REESE TURNS. (:18 secs.)

(O.C.) Pee Wee, you do a lot of work with boys.
PEE WEE REESE (O.C.): Hot work, Al. I like baseball and kids. I enjoy helping teenagers start right.
HELFER: That's around shaving age. Do you give 'em pointers on personal appearance, too?
REESE: Yes, a boy has more self-respect when he's clean-shaved. I tell 'em to use a Gillette Razor.

2. DIAGONAL DOWNWARD WIPE TO CU MIRROR SHOT OF ROY CAMPANELLA SHAVING. SUPER TITLE: "ROY CAMPANELLA" IN BOTTOM FRAME. (:05 secs.)

HELFER (V.O.): You said it: The Gillette Super Speed Razor. And today, there are three.

2A. ZOOM OUT WHITE LINE REVERSE SUPER OF GILLETTE "LIGHT" SUPER SPEED RAZOR CASE FROM INFINITY TO CENTER FRAME. OPEN COVER. (:02 secs.)

Light . . . for sensitive skin and most younger men.

3. DIAGONAL UPWARD WIPE TO CU MIRROR SHOT OF DON ZIMMER SHAVING. SUPER TITLE: "DON ZIMMER" IN BOTTOM FRAME. ZOOM OUT WHITE LINE REVERSE SUPER OF GILLETTE "REGULAR" RAZOR CASE FROM INFINITY TO CENTER FRAME. OPEN COVER. (:02 secs.)

Regular . . . for average skin and beard.

4. DIAGONAL DOWNWARD WIPE TO CU OF PEE WEE REESE SHAVING. SUPER TITLE "PEE WEE REESE" IN BOTTOM FRAME. ZOOM OUT WHITE LINE REVERSE SUPER OF "HEAVY" GILLETTE RAZOR CASE FROM INFINITY TO CENTER FRAME. OPEN COVER. (:03 secs.)

Heavy . . . for men who like the heft and feel of a heavier razor.

5. DISSOLVE TO CU TOP OF GILLETTE SUPER SPEED RAZOR. BLADE FLOATS OUT AND DROPS INTO PLACE ON RAZOR, WHICH CLOSES. (:03 secs.)

Each is different . . . precisely engineered.

6. CUT TO ECU PHOTO OF RAZOR TOP, BLADE EDGE SHOWING. CALIPERS AND RULER SLIDE IN TO "MEASURE" BLADE AND ANGLE. (:04 secs.)

One has the right blade edge exposure and edge angle to shave you, in a breeze.

7. VERTICAL WIPE OUT FROM CENTER TO MS OF SMILING PEE WEE REESE RUBBING SHAVED CHIN. (:04 secs.)

Comfortable, good-looking shaves you may never have had before.

8. SOFT IRIS OUT TO CU OF HAND CHANGING BLADE FROM DISPENSER. (:02 secs.)

And convenient! You change blades—

9. BARN DOOR WIPE TO MS OF HAND RINSING RAZOR UNDER FAUCET AND SHAKING DRY. (:02 secs.)

—and rinse clean . . . so.

10. WING WIPE UP FROM CENTER TO CU GILLETTE SUPER SPEED RAZOR DISPLAY. (:02 secs.)

Choose your Gillette Super Speed Razor.

10A. ZOOM SUPER TITLE: "$1.29" OFF DISPLAY TO FILL CENTER FRAME. (:04 secs.)

A dollar twenty-nine, with Gillette Blue Blade Dispenser and handy Travel Case.

* * *

Pudovkin once observed that a "dissolve"—or any optical effect for that matter—was a poor excuse for a good film *cut*. Certainly the New Wave of directors has "re-discovered" the cut, and even put it to uses Pudovkin never dreamed of. But for the World Series in 1955, the editor of this pedestrian little commercial for razor blades still glued it all together with so many busy opticals that it's hard to tell what you're looking at.

There are supers of titles and product, wipes up, wipes down, wipes across, wipes around, barn-door wipes (where the whole screen flips around), irises and dissolves. And just to keep things complicated, there are magical special effects where razor blades float into razors that close by themselves.

However, it's nice to see Pee Wee, Roy and Don in their prime—when the Dodgers were still in Brooklyn. Ebbets where?

Scene 10   *"Mum's the Word"*

DETAILS

  Live action black-and-white film. 60 seconds. 54 words. Air date 1955.
  Bristol-Myers, Inc., *Advertiser.*
  Doherty, Clifford, Steers & Shenfield, Inc., *Agency.*
  MPO Videotronics, Inc., *Producer.*

CREDITS

  Robert Dall'Acqua, Barbara Holbrook, Richard Strome, *Creative.*
  Marvin Rothenberg, Howard Magwood, *Production.*

"MUM'S THE WORD"

1. OPEN ON MS OF SINISTER WOMAN IN BLACK IN DIMLY-LIT CAFE. SHE REMOVES PHOTO FROM PURSE. (:08 secs.)

   (<u>MUSIC</u>: OMINOUS ZITHER)

2. CUT TO CU OF PHOTO OF BACK OF MAN'S HEAD IN HER HANDS. (:02 secs.)

3. CUT BACK TO MS OF WOMAN AS SHE TURNS AND COMPARES PHOTO. (:02 secs.)

4. CUT TO MS OF SINISTER MAN (MATCHING PHOTO) AT NEARBY TABLE. HE TURNS AND BECKONS WOMAN WITH HIS HEAD. (:06 secs.)

5. CUT TO HIGH PANNING CU OF CAFE FLOOR AS WOMAN'S FEET MOVE TO MAN'S TABLE. SHE DROPS FOLDED MESSAGE, WALKS OUT OF FRAME. HIS HAND PICKS UP MESSAGE. (:05 secs.)

6. CUT TO MS OF WOMAN COMING THROUGH BEAD CURTAIN TO WALL PHONE. (:04 secs.)

7. CUT TO CU OF MAN'S HANDS UNFOLDING MESSAGE: "new MUM/(jar photo)/now has/secret/ weapon." (:04 secs.)

8. CUT BACK TO MS OF WOMAN SPEAKING ON PHONE. SHE TURNS A PAGE IN PHONE DIRECTORY. (:06 secs.)

   <u>WOMAN (O.C.)</u>: I delivered the message. Mum.
   <u>MAN (V.O.)</u>: (ON PHONE) Now let's check the second message.

9. CUT TO ECU DIRECTORY PAGE WITH LEGEND: "MUM/doctor's/ deodorant/discovery." (:04 secs.)

   <u>WOMAN (V.O.)</u>: Ready.
   <u>MAN (V.O.)</u>: (ON PHONE) Mum. The doctor's deodorant discovery—

9A. PAN RIGHT TO LEGEND ON NEXT   —now contains M-3. Got that? M-3, to stop
    PAGE. "now contains/M-3/to   odor twenty-four hours a day. Remember
    stop/odor 24 hours/a day." (:06 secs.)   now . . .

10. CUT BACK TO MS OF WOMAN ON   WOMAN (O.C.): I know . . . for security
    PHONE. (:05 secs.)   reasons, Mum's the word.

11. CUT TO BEAUTY CU OF MUM   (V.O.) New Mum Cream Deodorant, now
    JAR ON LIMBO VELVET. (:03 secs.)   with M-3.

12. CUT TO MCU WOMAN PUSHING   (O.C.) Got the message?
    ASIDE BEAD CURTAIN AND
    ADDRESSING CAMERA. (:05 secs.)

* * *

Playing off the product name in the style of a standard Hollywood thriller, this little spy spoof—directed by versatile Marvin Rothenberg (who also staged Charley-the-washing-machine-repair-man and Josephine-the-lady-plumber)—was a very literal, no-nonsense but gently-worded message about a cream underarm deodorant. All cuts, no dissolves or opticals, bang-bang-bang—with very shadowy cinematography to set the mood. A far cry from the bouncy teen-age approach to other deodorant products that soon supplanted spies and secret agents on TV screens—and left Mum standing at the post, wondering which way the exploding market had gone as 86 million Americans each day began to cream, roll-on, or spray themselves.

This creative idea has now come full circle. Commercials are once again imitating many of the old Warner stars, but the put-on Greenstreets and Lorres and Boyers are camp-y spoofs indeed, and played strictly for laughs.

Scene 10B   *"The Yellow Went"*

DETAILS

    Black-and-white animated film. 60 seconds. 151 words. Air date 1956.
    Lever Brothers, Inc., *Advertiser.*
    Foote, Cone & Belding, Inc., *Agency.*
    Cascade Pictures, Inc. (L.A.), *Producer.*

CREDITS

    Roger Pryor, Catherine H. O'Brien, Don Williams, Terry Macri, *Creative.*
    Tex Avery, *Production.*

"THE YELLOW WENT"

1. OPEN ON ANIMATED MS OF TEENAGE GIRL WALKING PAST DOORWAY. TWO BOYS' HEADS APPEAR IN DOORWAY AS SHE PASSES OUT OF FRAME. (:04 secs.)

BOY (O.C.): (WHISTLES)
BOY (O.C.): Hey, hey, Suzie Q,

2. CUT TO PANNING MS OF SUZIE AS BOYS RUSH INTO FRAME. PAN STOPS. ONE BOY HANGS FROM TOP FRAME. (:05 secs.)

What's cookin' with you?
BOY: Your teeth look whiter than new, new, new.
SUZIE (O.C.): My teeth aren't new,

3. CUT TO CU OF SUZIE AS SHE RAISES PEPSODENT CARTON INTO FRAME. (:02 secs.)

But my toothpaste is . . . new—

4. LOSE SUZIE AS CARTON ZOOMS FORWARD AND BACK AGAIN. (:02 secs.)

—(V.O.) Pepsodent,
Get with it, kids!

4A. SUPER TITLE: "NEW/PACKAGE." (:01 sec.)

New package,

4B. REPLACE TITLE WITH: "NEW/FLAVOR. (:01 sec.)

New flavor,

4C. REPLACE TITLE WITH: "NEW/ FORMULA." (:01 sec.)

New formula, too,

4D. ZOOM IN AND OUT TO ECU's OF ILLUSTRATIONS ON BOTH ENDS OF CARTON. (:03 secs.)

Means brighter teeth for me and you.

5. CUT TO ANIMATED MCU SKETCH OF ANOTHER GIRL'S FACE. SHE HOLDS TOOTHBRUSH AND PEPSODENT TUBE. TITLE: "YELLOW" IS ON HER TEETH. AS SHE BEGINS BRUSHING, TITLE ZOOMS FORWARD TO COVER HER FACE AND THEN FLIES OFF RIGHT FRAME. (:02 secs.)

CHORUS (V.O.): (SINGS) You'll wonder where the "yellow" went,

5A. HER TEETH TURN PURE WHITE. (:02 secs.)

When you brush your teeth with—

6. ZOOM TO ECU PEPSODENT TUBE. (:03 secs.)

—Pepsodent! (CHANTS) The new formula with—

7. "PEPSODENT" LETTERING ON TUBE METAMORPHOSES INTO FULL-FRAME TITLE: "I.M.P." (:04 secs.)

—"I.M.P.",
Gets teeth much whiter, you can see.

8. TOOTHPASTE TUBE METAMORPHOSES INTO ARROW SHAPE WHICH FLIES ACROSS TARGET WITH DULL MOUTH IN CENTER. AS IT PASSES, IT WIPES MOUTH PURE WHITE AND SMILING. (:02 secs.)

It cleans the stains and film away,

8A. TITLE: "IRIUM" FLIES IN FROM TOP FRAME AND ZOOMS BACK TO COVER SMILING MOUTH. (:03 secs.)

While "Irium" fights tooth decay.

9. REPEAT SCENE 5 & 5A. (:04 secs.)

(SINGS) You'll wonder where the "yellow" went,
When you brush your teeth with Pepsodent!

10. CUT TO CU OF SUZIE'S HAPPY FACE. PULL BACK TO MCU AS SUPERED CLOCKFACE, HANDS WHIRLING, PASSES ACROSS FRAME L-R. SUZIE'S TEETH SPARKLE. (:05 secs.)

(CHANTS) The taste is new, so fresh and clean,
That new taste really lasts, it's keen.
And while it makes your—

10A. BOY'S FACE ENTERS FRAME, BOW TIE SPINNING. HE KISSES SUZIE. (:06 secs.)

—smile the rave,
It also makes your breath behave.
So start goin' steady, right away—

10B. BOTH RAISE PEPSODENT CARTON INTO FRAME. IT ZOOMS FORWARD TO CU. (:02 secs.)

—with Pepsodent,
Get some today!

11. "PEPSODENT" LOGO ON CARTON METAMORPHOSES INTO SCENES 5 & 5A. (:04 secs.)

(SINGS) You'll wonder where the "yellow" went,
When you brush your teeth with—

12. ZOOM PEPSODENT TUBE FORWARD. IT METAMORPHOSES INTO CARTON. "PEPSODENT" LOGO BOUNCES ON AND OFF CARTON IN SYNC WITH AUDIO WHILE TITLE: "NEW" FLASHES ON AND OFF IN UPPER RIGHT FRAME. (:04 secs.)

—Pepsodent . . . Pepsodent . . . Pepsodent!

This bouncy commercial from the late '50's contributed the memorable "You'll wonder where the 'yellow' went . . ." to American culture.

It was one of the earliest TV spots deliberately aimed at the teenage market—destined to be the great selling-ground of the '60's and '70's. While it is far from unpleasant, it was also one of the earliest commercials to utilize the advertising impact of repetition: "Tell 'em. Tell 'em you told 'em. Tell 'em you told 'em you told 'em." And so it does, repeating its flying "yellow" device three times.

It is optical-heavy, using zooms, titles, metamorphoses, etc., in all but two or three scenes. Some are so swift and brief they hardly have enough time to register on the eye—but perhaps just enough! A fact that moved the theory of TV visuals forward toward the flickering, spastic 30- and 20-second spots of the late '60's.

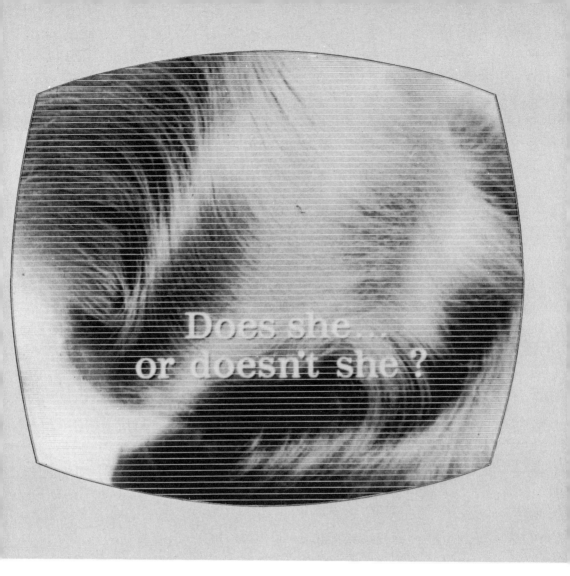

Scene 4A   "Does She . . . or Doesn't She?"

DETAILS

    Live action black-and-white film. 60 seconds. 113 words. Air date 1957.
    Clairol, Inc., *Advertiser.*
    Foote, Cone & Belding, Inc., *Agency.*

CREDITS

    Shirley Polykoff, Ray Betuel, *Creative*
    Roger Pryor, *Production.*

"DOES SHE . . . OR DOESN'T SHE?"

1. OPEN ON LS OF SPRING HILL-SIDE. FATHER IS PLAYING BALL WITH SON AT BOTTOM OF HILL. SLOW ZOOM TO FS OF MOTHER PLAYING WITH INFANT ON BLANKET IN FOREGROUND. (:07 secs.)

WOMAN ANNOUNCER (V.O.):
Every season, every age, has its own special beauty.

2. DISSOLVE TO MS OF MOTHER/BABY. ZOOM IN TO ECU OF MOTHER'S HAIR. (:04 secs.)

BABY (O.C.): COOS.
But the quality of freshness never loses its appeal. Her hair—

3. DISSOLVE TO HIGH CU ON MOTHER/BABY. (:04 secs.)

—so soft and shiny . . . the color fresh, sparkling.

4. DISSOLVE TO ECU OF MOTHER'S HAIR. (:01 sec.)

4A. SCRATCH ON SUPERIMPOSED TITLE: "Does she . . . /or doesn't she?" IN BOTTOM FRAME. (:02 secs.)

Does she . . . or doesn't she?

4B. FADE OUT TITLE. FADE IN "MISS CLAIROL" CROWN LOGO IN TOP FRAME. (:02 secs.)

Miss Clairol Hair Color looks so natural—

4C. FADE IN SUPERIMPOSED TITLE: "only her hairdresser/knows for sure" UNDER LOGO. (:03 secs.)

—only her hairdresser know for sure!

5. RIPPLE FLASHBACK DISSOLVE TO MOUSY-HAIRED MOTHER TURNING AWAY FROM CRIB IN CHILD'S BEDROOM. (:01 sec.)

Yet just after the baby was born—

5A. PAN LEFT WITH MOTHER AS SHE PAUSES IN FRONT OF WALL MIRROR. (:04 secs.)

—she caught a glimpse of herself.

5B. ZOOM IN TO CU OF HER UNEASY FACE. SHE FEELS HER HAIR. (:04 secs.)

Her hair seemed lifeless, so faded.

6. RIPPLE DISSOLVE BACK TO (SCENE 2) ECU OF MOTHER/BABY ON HILLSIDE. SLOW ZOOM BACK TO MS. (:09 secs.)	BABY (O.C.): COOS. Then she tried Miss Clairol. Now she looks as wonderful as she feels. Miss Clairol really covers gray, keeps hair young, radiant—
7. DISSOLVE TO (SCENE 3) HIGH CU ON MOTHER/BABY AS BABY TUGS MOTHER'S HAIR. (:04 secs.)	—sparkling with life. So beautiful, soft and silky.
8. CUT TO CU OF MOTHER'S HAIR WITH BABY TUGGING. TILT UP AS MOTHER LAUGHS. (:08 secs.)	BABY (O.C.): COOS.
9. DISSOLVE TO ECU OF MOTHER'S HAIR. ZOOM UP SUPERIMPOSED MISS CLAIROL PACKAGE FROM INFINITY TO FULL FRAME. (:05 secs.)	MOTHER (O.C.): LAUGHS. Miss Clairol Hair Color Bath, the natural-looking hair coloring.
9A. ZOOM UP SUPERIMPOSED GOOD HOUSEKEEPING SEAL OFF PACKAGE TO FILL FRAME. (:02 secs.)	So quick and easy, you'll love it. BABY (V.O.): COOS.

* * *

This simple black-and-white outdoor film commercial with its long dissolves (and *single* cut) seems a little dull by today's TV *go-go* hair product standards. However, in 1957 it initiated a long and successful series of television executions for Shirley Polykoff's famous and still-running Miss Clairol creative campaign—and American women continue to color their hair over 200 million times a year.

Perhaps because several production houses worked on this particular "Does She . . ." footage, it set a style of its own for much lovely television close-up hair photography that followed. (Of course, when the camera moves indoors for the "pre-Clairol" flashback, all the beautiful sun-glints in the mother's hair disappear. Current Federal Trade Commission practice theoretically requires such before-and-after scenes to be photographed under comparable lighting conditions.)

Music would have augmented the romantic mood of this spot, but was not used. The soft female voice-over announcer is rare in television; tradition uses her—as here—for women's personal products.

Scene 1B   "Look, Ma!"

DETAILS

     Black-and-white film. 60 seconds. 129 words. Air date 1958.
     Procter & Gamble Co., *Advertiser.*
     Benton & Bowles, Inc., *Agency.*
     Warner Brothers Pictures, Inc. (L.A.), *Producer.*

CREDITS

     Bob Colodzin, Paul Walsh, Caesar Cirigliano, *Creative.*
     Dave Monahan, P. Manlay, Walter Bien, *Production.*

"LOOK, MA!"

1. OPEN ON FS OF DAUGHTER JUMP-
ING OUT OF CAR IN SUBURBAN
DRIVEWAY. (:02 secs.)

1A. PAN AND TILT WITH DAUGHTER
AND DOG AS THEY RACE ACROSS
LAWN. (:04 secs.)

DAUGHTER (O.C.): Mama!

1B. HOLD ON DAUGHTER CU AS SHE
HOLDS UP HER CAVITY "REPORT
CARD." (:01 sec.)

Look, Ma! No cavities!

2. CUT TO REVERSE MS OF
DAUGHTER. MOTHER KNEELS
DOWN TO EMBRACE HER AND
READ CARD. (:06 secs.)

MOTHER (O.C.): Oh, Debbie, really? The
dentist says, "no new cavities." Golly, what
a difference—

2A. SUPER TUBE OF CREST OVER
BOTTOM FRAME. (:05 secs.)

—that Crest Toothpaste has made.
ANNOUNCER (V.O.): Yes, Crest is the
toothpaste that works—

3. HOLD TUBE. DISSOLVE OUT
MOTHER AND DAUGHTER TO
GRAY BACKGROUND. (:02 secs.)

—because Crest is the toothpaste with—

3A. "fluoristan" TITLE POPS UP
BEHIND TUBE AND ZOOMS UP TO
FILL TOP FRAME. (:01½ secs.)

—Fluoristan, a special—

3B. "fluoristan" TITLE BUNCHES UP,
SPREADS OUT AGAIN AS
"fluoride." (:01 sec.)

—fluoride formula.

4. MATCH DISSOLVE "fluoride"
TITLE INTO "FLUORIDE" LABEL
ON GLASS MEDICAL JAR. LOSE
TUBE AND GRAY BACKGROUND.
(:01 sec.)

Fluoride, you know, is—

4A. PULL BACK TO REVEAL
DENTIST'S OFFICE. DENTIST IS
TREATING BOY WITH SWAB
DIPPED IN MEDICAL JAR. (:03
secs.)

—the decay fighter dentists use; the decay
fighter that dentists—

4B. FADE ON JIGGLING "fluoride" TITLE IN BOTTOM LEFT FRAME AS DENTIST STARTS TO SWAB BOY'S TEETH. (:05 secs.)	—put right on the teeth, just as you see it here. Now—
5. IRIS WIPE IN AND OUT OF BLACK, TO REVEAL SAME BOY BRUSH-ING TEETH AT BATHROOM SINK. (:02 secs.)	—with Crest, you can put the same—
5A. FADE ON JIGGLING "fluoride" TITLE IN BOTTOM CENTER FRAME. (:03 secs.)	—fluoride on your teeth at home, too—
5B. FADE OFF TITLE AS MOTHER'S HAND PICKS UP CREST TUBE ON SINK. (:02½ secs.)	—every time you brush. That's—
6. CUT TO MS OF MOTHER AND BOY AS SHE SQUEEZES TUBE ONTO HER TOOTHBRUSH. (:03 secs.)	—how Crest stops cavities for all the family.
7. CLOCKWISE WIPE TO MS OF MOTHER IN DRUGSTORE. DOLLY IN SLOWLY TO HER PUZZLED FACE AS SHE PICKS UP WRONG TOOTHPASTE CARTON. (:05 secs.)	Next time you buy toothpaste, think; Simply by switching from ordinary toothpaste—
8. CUT TO REVERSE MS OF MOTHER EXCHANGING WRONG CARTON FOR ONE FROM CREST DISPLAY. (:02 secs.)	—to Crest with fluoride—
9. CUT TO ECU OF CREST CARTON. (:01 sec.)	—you can cut—
9A. SUPER TITLE: "Cuts Cavities Almost in Half." (:04 secs.)	—your family's cavity rate almost in half. You, too, may hear—
10. CUT BACK TO REPRISE SCENES 1, 1A, 1B. (:06 secs.)	DAUGHTER (O.C.): Mama! Look, Ma! No cavities!

* * *

The car door flies open, a six-year old in pigtails dances across the suburban lawn clutching her dental "report card"—and suddenly, with the immortal "Look, Ma! No cavities!", the fluoride toothpaste era was born. This copy-heavy, optical-heavy and rather unspectacular Warner backlot commercial is of interest only because it was the first of an absolutely unending series of different freckle-faced kid creative approaches that Procter & Gamble has used since 1958 to keep Crest Toothpaste way out in front as the biggest-selling fluoridated product.

This little playlet was soon superseded by a series of documentary demonstrations of half-classes—"Half my class used Crest (and brushed like mad); the other half brushed with ordinary toothpaste." Then the American Dental Association's Council on Dental Therapeutics came to the creative man's rescue, with the immortal line: "Crest has been shown to be an effective decay-preventing dentifrice that can be of significant value, etc.", which became an essential part of the audio and video of every Crest commercial for almost a decade and a half.

But will it ever replace: "Look, Ma! No cavities!" in the minds and hearts of the first TV Generation?

Apparel

Commercials in this field have been an amazing force in shifting the American viewing public's traditional custom from the small downtown local haberdasher to mass clothing retail operations all over the country.

The earliest of these commercials—for the highway clothing chain Robert Hall (the "plain pipe rack" people)—made simple and verifiable claims of lower overhead, ergo: greater merchandise value. American affluence grew during the '50's, so commercial emphasis inevitably shifted from price to style and fashion. By the late '60's, clothing spots for such giant retailing outlets as Sears were providing viewers with flashing kaleidoscopes of TV color not unworthy of a *Vogue* film presentation.

* * *

In addition to the large clothing retailers, fiber manufacturers found a valuable promotional medium in television. As new "wonder fabrics" were developed in the laboratory and slowly came onto the market, their introductory praises were sung all across the land by waves of "hang-tag" commercials, featuring clothing, rugs, stockings, etc.

But always the message to America was the same: consume . . . consume . . . consume! It consumed.

Scene 1B   *"Watch the Birdies"*

DETAILS

Black-and-white animated film. 20 seconds. 26 words (and whines). Air date
1954.
Robert Hall Corp., *Advertiser.*
Arkwright Advertising Co., Inc., *Agency.*
Pelican Films, Inc., *Producer.*

CREDITS

Jack Wilcher, *Creative.*
Jack Zander, *Production.*

"WATCH THE BIRDIES"

1. OPEN ON ANIMATED MS OF THREE BIRDS ON A PHONE WIRE: MAN, WOMAN AND CHILD. (:06 secs.)

(MUSIC: INTRODUCTION)
LADYBIRD (O.C.): (SINGS)
Clothing values are high . . .
CHILDBIRD (O.C.): (WHINES)
MANBIRD (O.C.): High!

1A. DOLLY BACK TO FS AS LADYBIRD SWINGS DOWN UNDER WIRE AND THE OTHERS FOLLOW SUIT. (:04 secs.)

LADYBIRD: And the prices are low . . .
CHILDBIRD: Low!
MANBIRD: Low!

1B. PAN RIGHT AS THEY WALK UPSIDE DOWN ALONG WIRE. TITLE: "Robert Hall" COMES INTO RIGHT FRAME ABOVE WIRE. (:03 secs.)

LADYBIRD: That's why at Robert Hall . . .

1C. BIRDS AND TITLE SPIN AROUND WIRE. BIRDS END UP ON TOP, TITLE AT BOTTOM, UPSIDE DOWN. (:02 secs.)

CHILDBIRD: (WHINES)
MANBIRD: Yeah!

1D. BIRDS WALK OUT OF LEFT FRAME ALONG WIRE AS NEW TITLE "Family Clothes" COMES IN FROM RIGHT FRAME, UPSIDE-DOWN. (:03 secs.)

LADYBIRD: You save on family clothes.

1E. TITLES SPIN UPRIGHT. CHILDBIRD AND MANBIRD REAPPEAR FROM BEHIND TITLES. (:02 secs.)

CHILDBIRD: (WHINES)
MANBIRD: Clothes!

* * *

This brief little attempt at traditional animation meets the qualifications of a classic only because it was one of the first spots in the quickly popular 20-second station break length, and perhaps because the advertiser never seemed to get tired of running it over and over. The bird family itself was rather scroungy-looking, with overtones of Moran & Mack, the early "black" radio duo.

It was also an early effort of Jack Zander, the animation designer, who since then has done a whole lot better.

Scene 11   *"Kedso the Clown"*

DETAILS

Black-and-white live action and animated film. 60 seconds. 138 words. Air
date 1958.
United States Rubber Company, Keds Division, *Advertiser.*
Fletcher Richards, Calkins & Holden, Inc., *Agency.*
Paul Fennell, Inc. (L.A.), *Producer.*

CREDITS

S. J. Frolick, Vic Miranda, *Creative.*
S. J. Frolick, Paul Fennell, Burt Glennon, *Production.*

"KEDSO THE CLOWN"

1. OPEN ON ANIMATED FS OF
SNEAKER AGAINST SKY BACK-
GROUND. (:01 sec.)

(MUSIC: CALLIOPE)

1A. ANIMATED CLOWN (KEDSO) WITH
UMBRELLA POPS UP FROM
INSIDE SNEAKER. (:02 secs.)

1B. BLACK "KEDSO" POPS INTO
EMPTY GRAY OVAL OF KEDSO'S
SUIT. (:01 sec.)

1C. "KEDSO" LETTERING TURNS
WHITE. KEDSO TAKES OFF HIS
HAT. (:01 sec.)

1D. LETTERING BECOMES BLACK
AGAIN. ZOOM TO CU OF KEDSO.
HE LEAPS OUT OF SNEAKER. (:05
secs.)

KEDSO (O.C.): Hi, kids!
KIDS (V.O.): Hi, Kedso!
KEDSO: Kids, let's all sing the Keds' Song!

2. CUT TO FS OF LETTERED TITLE:
"IF/YOU WANT/SHOES" IN RIGHT
FRAME. KEDSO DROPS DOWN
INTO LEFT FRAME. (:02 secs.)

(SINGS) If you want shoes—

2A. REPLACE TITLE WITH: "WITH/
LOTS OF/PEP" AS KEDSO
DANCES. (:01 sec.)

—with lots of pep,

3. CUT TO CU OF CIRCULAR
"U.S./KEDS" LOGO ON SIDE OF
ANIMATED SNEAKER. (:01 sec.)

KIDS (SINGING) (V.O.): Get Keds—

3A. LOGO MOMENTARILY BECOMES
BOY'S GRINNING FACE. (:01 sec.)

—Kids' Keds!

4. CUT BACK TO FS OF KEDSO
DANCING (SCENE 2A) WITH NEW
TITLE: "FOR/BOUNCE/AND/
ZOOM." (:01 sec.)

KEDSO (O.C.): For bounce and zoom—

4A. REPLACE TITLE WITH: "IN/
EVERY/STEP". (:01 sec.)

—in every step;

5. CUT BACK TO CU OF SNEAKER   KIDS (V.O.): Get Keds. Kids' Keds!
    LOGO (SCENE 3). PUSH IN TO ECU
    AS LOGO MOMENTARILY
    BECOMES BOY'S GRINNING FACE.
    (:02 secs.)

6. CUT TO FS OF KEDSO WITH BAT.   KEDSO (O.C.): You'll be a champ-i-on with
    HE HITS BALL AND RUNS OUT OF   style,
    RIGHT FRAME. (:04 secs.)   (MUSIC: BAT SOUND)
                                       KIDS (V.O.): You'll hit that ball a half a
                                       mile.

7. CUT TO CU OF FLYING BASE-   (MUSIC: SLIDE WHISTLE)
    BALL. (:01 sec.)

8. CUT BACK TO FS OF FIELD AS   They're tough; they last a long, long while!
    KEDSO RUNS INTO FRAME AND
    CATCHES BALL (:03 secs.)

8A. ZOOM TO ECU OF BALL. IT   Keds—
    BECOMES CIRCULAR "U.S./KEDS"
    LOGO. (:01 sec.)

8B. LOGO MOMENTARILY BECOMES   —Kids' Keds!
    BOY'S GRINNING FACE. (:01 sec.)

9. CUT TO KEDSO (ANIMATED)   KEDSO (O.C.): There's a pair of smart
    LEANING AGAINST (LIVE) WATER   youngsters.
    PAIL. HE POINTS OFF FRAME. (:03
    secs.)

10. CUT TO LIVE FS OF TWO BOYS   KEDSO (V.O.): Hi, kids!
    (WEARING KEDS) WALKING   KIDS (O.C.): Hi, Kedso!
    ACROSS FIELD. (:03 secs.)

11. CUT TO LIVE/ANIMATION CU AS   KEDSO (O.C.): Say! Why do you kids wear
    THEY LEAN INTO FRAME   Keds?
    TOWARDS KEDSO. (:06 secs.)   FIRST KID (O.C.): So I can run faster and
                                       jump faster!
                                       SECOND KID (O.C.): So I can win more
                                       often!

12. CUT TO ANIMATED MS OF KEDSO.   KEDSO (O.C.): Right! (SINGS) Always
    (:02 secs.)   look for—

13. CUT TO LIVE CU OF SNEAKER   KEDSO (V.O.): —the—
    BACK WITH KEDS LOGO AND
    TITLE: "The Shoe of Champions."
    (:01 sec.)

13A. POP ON WHITE OUTLINE ARROW   —label—
     POINTING TO LOGO. (:01 sec.)

13B. ZOOM TO ECU OF LOGO.   —big and blue.
     REVERSE BLACK AND WHITE   KIDS (V.O.): Keds. Kids' Keds!
     VALUES THREE TIMES. (:02 secs.)

13C. FADE LOGO TO GRAY. POP BACK   KEDSO: That spells out "U.S. Keds" for
     "U.S. Keds" ONE LETTER AT A   you.
     TIME. FLASH GRAY BACK-   KIDS: Keds. Kids' Keds!
     GROUND TWICE. (:04 secs.)

14. CUT TO LIVE MS OF SNEAKER.   Those shockproof arches sure are neat,
     TILT TO REVEAL INSOLE. (:02
     secs.)

15. CUT TO LIVE ECU OF INSOLE   The right support for growing feet. So be—
     LABEL: "CUSHIONED INSOLE/
     SHOCK-PROOF ARCH CUSHION."
     (:02 secs.)

16. CUT TO LIVE MS OF TWO BOYS   —a champion ath-lete! Keds. Kids' Keds!
     WEARING "CHAMP" BADGES.
     THEY HOLD UP SNEAKERS. (:03
     secs.)

17. CUT TO ANIMATED MS OF KEDSO   KEDSO (O.C.): Product of United States
     NEXT TO CIRCULAR "U.S.   Rubber.
     RUBBER" LOGO. HE TIPS HIS
     HAT. (:02 secs.)

* * *

Film animation styles may change, but the form will never lose its appeal—particularly for young audiences. If you doubt this, get up early next Saturday or Sunday morning and look at the tube.

Here was Kedso the Clown, serving the U.S. Rubber Company's sneaker division in print for more than a decade. "Why not transfer him to TV?" "Wow!" "And add a couple of *live* kids!" "Wow, wow!"

So with rotoscoping—an optical printing technique using cartoon "cels" and their opaque mattes—Kedso and the kids started selling sneakers to youngsters all over the country. No technical breakthrough here—the cinematographic procedures were all pioneered by George Méliès (the father of everyone) in his *"Twenty Thousand Leagues Under The Sea"* at the turn of the century.

The appropriate "ricky-tick" score by Ben Ludlow was probably memorized by a million kids—some of whom may even now be junior executives in rubber companies.

Scene 28A   "A Lady Isn't Dressed"

DETAILS

Limited animation color film. 60 seconds. 95 words. Air date 1958.
The Chemstrand Corporation, *Advertiser.*
Doyle Dane Bernbach, Inc., *Agency.*
Transfilm, Inc., *Producer.*

CREDITS

Don Tremor, Robert Gage, Phyllis Robinson, *Creative.*
William Helburn, Bob Bergman, Eli Levitan, *Production.*

"A LADY ISN'T DRESSED"

1. OPEN ON STILL MS OF FASHION MODEL, EYES CLOSED, LIPS PUCKERED. ZOOM IN TO CU. (:03 secs.)

   FEMALE SINGER (V.O.): Some girls think summer—

2. DISSOLVE TO STILL CU TO MODEL'S HAND WITH STOCKING. ZOOM IN TO ECU. (:01½ secs.)

   —means stockings—

3. CUT TO STILL CU OF OPEN HAND. STOCKING HAS BEEN DROPPED. (:02 secs.)

   —goodbye!

4. CUT TO STILL MS OF MODEL WITH FINGER RAISED. (:02 secs.)

   If that's your trick—

5. CUT TO STILL MS OF MODEL WITH HANDS OVER HEAD. (:00½ sec.)

   —you're an—

6. CUT TO STILL MS OF MODEL WITH HANDS NEAR FOREHEAD. (:00½ sec.)

   —un—

7. CUT TO STILL MS OF MODEL WITH HANDS NEAR CHIN, HALF-VIGNETTED IN SOLID OUTLINE. (:01 sec.)

   —hip—

8. CUT TO STILL MS OF MODEL'S FACE IN SOLID VIGNETTE. (:01 sec.)

   —chick!

9. CUT TO STILL FS OF MODEL'S PROFILE. (:00½ sec.)

   Here's—

10. CUT TO STILL FS OF MODEL WITH HANDS TO HER MOUTH. ZOOM IN AND TILT DOWN TO CU OF HER LEGS. (:03 secs.)

    —why!

11. CUT TO STILL CU OF MODEL'S DANCING LEGS. (:00½ sec.)

12. CUT TO STILL FS OF DRESSY SHOE. (:01 sec.)	She may have spent a—
13. CUT TO STILL FS OF ANOTHER SHOE, WITH TITLE: "fortune." (:01 sec.)	—fortune on the—
14. CUT TO STILL FS OF ANOTHER SHOE, WITH TITLE: "newest." (:01 sec.)	—newest—
15. CUT TO STILL FS OF ANOTHER SHOE, WITH TITLE: "newest/shoe." (:01 sec.)	—shoe,
16. CUT TO STILL FS OF DRESSES ON HANGERS. REVEAL WITH VERTICAL (l. to r.) SOLID WIPE. (:02½ secs.)	Have twice as many dresses as the others do,
17. CUT TO STILL CU OF MODEL'S HAND. PAN RIGHT TO REVEAL MANY BRACELETS ON HER ARM, WITH TITLE: "bracelets to here." (:03½ secs.)	Though she wears bracelets to <u>here</u>,
18. CUT TO STILL CU OF MINK-WRAPPED MODEL, WITH TITLE: "mink." TILT UP. (:03 secs.)	Mink up to her ear,
19. CUT TO STILL FS OF MODEL WITH TITLE: "a lady." (:01 sec.)	A lady—
19A. ADDITIVE TITLE: "isn't dressed." SOLID RECTANGLE DROPS INTO FRAME TO COVER ALL OF MODEL BUT HER LEGS. (:01 sec.)	—isn't dressed—
20. CUT TO STILL CU OF MODEL'S LEGS WITH TITLE: "unless her legs/are." (:01½ secs.)	—unless her legs are—
20A. ADDITIVE TITLE: "too!" (:02½ secs.)	—too! (<u>MUSIC</u>: BRIDGE)
21. CUT TO STILL CU OF MODEL YAWNING UNDER HAIR DRYER. (:02 secs.)	She may have had her hair done in the—
22. CUT TO STILL CU OF MODEL'S HAIRDO WITH TITLE: "latest/do." (:02 secs.)	—latest "do,"

23. CUT TO STILL FS OF MODEL. (:01   The magazines—
     sec.)

24. CUT TO DIFFERENT STILL FS OF   —may say her shape is—
     MODEL. (:01 sec.)

25. CUT TO DIFFERENT STILL FS OF   —"madly new,"
     MODEL WITH TITLE: "madly new."
     (:01½ secs.)

26. CUT TO REAR STILL FS OF   Though she's sporting a—
     MODEL. ZOOM IN TO MS. (:02
     secs.)

26A. SUPER TITLE: "tan." (:03½ secs.)   —tan,

27. CUT TO DIFFERENT STILL MS OF   That can—
     MODEL (:01 sec.)

27A. SUPER TITLE: "dazzle/a man."   —dazzle a man,
     (:02½ secs.)

28. CUT TO STILL FS OF SEATED   A lady—
     MODEL WITH TITLE: "a lady."
     (:00½ sec.)

28A. ADDITIVE TITLE: "isn't dressed."   —isn't dressed—
     SOLID RECTANGLE DROPS INTO
     FRAME TO COVER ALL OF
     MODEL BUT HER LEGS. (:01 sec.)

29. CUT TO STILL CU OF MODEL'S   —unless her legs—
     LEGS WITH TITLE: "unless her
     legs." (:01 sec.)

29A. ADDITIVE TITLE: "are." (:01 sec.)   —are—

30. HOLD TITLING IN PLACE. CUT TO   —too!
     DIFFERENT STILL CU OF
     MODEL'S LEGS WITH FINGER
     POINTING TO STOCKING.
     ADDITIVE TITLE: "too!" (:02 secs.)

30A. DROP ALL TITLING. SUPER TITLE   (MUSIC: PLAYOFF)
     ACROSS LEGS: "THE CHEM-
     STRAND/CORPORATION." (:00½
     sec.)

30B. ADDITIVE TITLE: "makers of." (:01
     sec.)

30C. ADDITIVE TITLE: "fine nylon yarn."
     (:02 secs.)

It was in *Ars Magna Lucis et Umbrae* that Athanasius Kircher first outlined the principle of using a light source and lenses to project enlarged images of still pictures onto a flat surface. Thus, in 1646, the magic lantern was born.

Two hundred and twelve years later, Chemstrand took a significant leap forward in applied TV graphics by returning, so to speak, to Father Kircher's magic lantern. Fashion photographer Bill Helburn was commissioned to shoot hundreds of stills of model Dovima. From these, thirty-odd blowups were chosen for the "animation stand," a vertically-mounted motion picture camera that exposes—if desired—only one frame of film at a time.

But first Mitch Leigh (who went on to successfully score *Man of La Mancha*) prepared a very upbeat music track, and got the ubiquitous and generously talented Darlene Zito to swing the words.

Then the animation stand's camera movement on and over the selected stills, was choreographed with split-note precision. The "limited animation" result would have delighted Father Kircher—an optical illusion of an optical illusion. With brief scenes—some less than half a second long—the still pictures seemed to move—and undoubtedly sold a lot of nylons.

Of course, imitators quickly moved in—but none ever really captured the particular style and bounce of this original effort.

Appliances

Ours is the most gadget-ridden nation on earth, and television commercials for every sort of major and minor labor-saving device were early denizens of the picture tube. The field slipped easily into the *demonstration* (our brand vs. "Brand X") area. Typical is the 1956 Westinghouse Washer "Dirty Sand Test"—*live,* no less!—included here.

Its length—six and a half minutes of commercial—sets some kind of television record.

To produce such commercials posed herculean logistical problems, usually solved week after week through the brilliant cooperation of agency and network personnel. Occasionally (this was long before the days of video tape recording, and you couldn't do the commercial over), all the careful preparations broke down; at least once Betty Furness found herself locked in mortal combat, coast-to-coast, live, with a recalcitrant Westinghouse product. One wasn't always so "sure." The commercial appears in this section, eloquent testimony to a vanished on-air human equation.

It is refreshing to realize that from TV's earliest days, all realistic (non-animation) demonstration commercials had to combat a healthy American skepticism—force-fed, perhaps, by decades of Hollywood's optical tricks. On TV, the viewer felt one picture might be worth a thousand lies.

This author (who also produced the Shell "Platformate" demonstration commercials during the early '60's) would often spend two-thirds of his commercial minute merely setting up a visually unimpeachable (and therefore proveable) premise.

The "documentary" nature of such commercials gave them a flavor of reality usually reserved on television to news and special event programs, and many advertisers—Timex Watches is an outstanding example—began to use the creative "torture test" form almost exclusively. But note too, in the following pages, that someone else had done it first. Bulova went sailing over the falls, long before Timex jumped into the Pacific on its Acapulco diver.

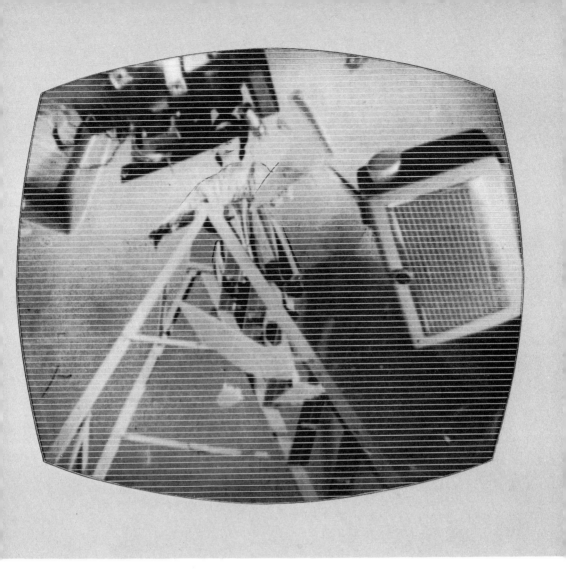

Scene 2   *"Ladder Drop"*

DETAILS

    Live action black-and-white film. 60 seconds. 130 words. Air date 1954.
    Radio Corporation of America, *Advertiser.*
    Kenyon & Eckhardt, Inc., *Agency.*
    MPO Videotronics, Inc., *Producer.*

CREDITS

    Allen Z. Hodshire, Harry Stoddart, Stanley Tannenbaum, Larry Parker,
    Creative.
    Zoli Vidor, *Production.*

"LADDER DROP"

1. OPEN ON MS OF GIRL ATOP 15-FOOT LADDER HOLDING TWO PORTABLE RADIOS. (:03 secs.)

VAUGHN MONROE (V.O.): See these two portable radios?

2. CUT TO LOW FS OF GIRL, SEEN THROUGH GLASS FLOOR. SHE DROPS RADIOS. ONE SHATTERS ON GLASS, THE OTHER REMAINS INTACT. (:04 secs.)

(SOUND: DRUM ROLL)
Well, watch this! Let 'er go, Betsy!
(SOUND: CRASH)

3. CUT TO CU OF MONROE'S HANDS POINTING TO SMASHED RADIO, PICKING UP RCA RADIO. TILT AND PAN TO FRAME MONROE IN MS. (:11 secs.)

Sorry, friend. You old-style portable radios have to go. But look at our new RCA Victor portable radio. (O.C.) Came through without a chip.

4. DISSOLVE TO FS OF PORTABLE ON TABLE. SUPER TITLE: "world's only" OVER RADIO. (:03 secs.)

(V.O.) Here's the world's first and only portable radio—

4A. LOSE TITLE. SUPER TITLES: "non breakable" OVER RADIO, "IMPAC case" BELOW RADIO. (:04 secs.)

—in the non-breakable Impac case. So rugged, it's the only radio case with a—

4B. LOSE TITLE: SUPER TITLE: "5-YEAR GUARANTEE" UNDER RADIO. (:05 secs.)

—five-year guarantee against chipping, cracking or breaking in normal use.

5. DISSOLVE TO MS OF MONROE. HE HOLDS UP RADIO, PUTS IT DOWN ON TABLE. (:04 secs.)

(O.C.) Of course, a tube might jar loose, but that's easily fixed.

6. CUT TO CU OF RADIO ON TABLE. (:04 sec.)

(V.O.) The important thing is, RCA Victor's non-breakable Impac case—

6A. MONROE'S HANDS BANG RADIO ONCE ON TABLE TOP. SUPER TITLE: "NO CHIPPING" OVER RADIO. (:02 secs.)

—means no chipping—

6B. HIS HANDS BANG IT DOWN AGAIN. SUPER NEW TITLE: "NO CRACK-ING" OVER RADIO. (:02 secs.)

—no cracking—

6C. HIS HANDS BANG IT DOWN AGAIN. SUPER NEW TITLE: "NO BREAK-ING" OVER RADIO. (:02 secs.)

—no breaking—

7. DISSOLVE TO ANGLED MCU OF
SEVERAL RCA PORTABLES ON
REVOLVING TURNTABLE. (:13
secs.)

—and, hear that music!
(MUSIC: SYMPHONY ENDING)
It's RCA's great Golden Throat sound.
See the world's only portable with the
non-breakable Impac case, as low as
$27.95.

8. DISSOLVE TO STANDARD RCA
SLIDE LOGO: "HIS MASTER'S
VOICE, etc." (:03 secs.)

At your RCA Victor Dealer's.
(MUSIC: END)

* * *

The bandleader Vaughan Monroe—for RCA Victor—was a holdover from the radio days of the entertainer/spokesman, and served his client well for many years. In this commercial—one of the first of the true demonstration spots—he picks up the pieces of a smashed portable radio ("Let 'er go, Betsy!") to prove the ruggedness of RCA's new Impac case. It's an honest demonstration, by all appearances—no phony shaved sandpaper here. Vaughan is even honest enough to mention that the shock of falling off a ladder might jar an RCA tube loose. Such candor!

Like all early demonstration commercials, there's an over-abundance of titles in this spot—as if the viewer couldn't really believe his eyes, and needed it all spelled out. And the closing scene is really nothing but an RCA Victor logo slide.

Anyway, it told millions of Americans that if they ever dropped their RCA Victor portable radio off a ladder, its Impac case wouldn't shatter.

Scene 3   *"Over the Falls"*

DETAILS

Live action black-and-white film. 53½ seconds. 136 words. Air date 1955.
Bulova Watch Co., Inc., *Advertiser.*
Van Praag Productions, Inc., *Producer.*

CREDITS

Norman Gladney, Arthur Schwartz, *Creative.*
Marc Asch, Fred Perrett, *Production.*

"OVER THE FALLS"

1.	OPEN ON FS OF NIAGARA FALLS WITH SUPERED TITLE: "BULOVA/Clipper/CONQUERS/ NIAGARA FALLS." (:05 secs.)	(SOUND: FALLS) LYLE VAN (V.O.): Can a watch survive the "Niagara Falls Test?"
2.	CUT TO CU OF HAND HOLDING BULOVA WATCH, TIED TO HUGE RUBBER BALL FLOATING ON NIAGARA RIVER. (:02 secs.)	Attached to this heavily-weighted ball—
3.	DISSOLVE TO HIGH PANNING FS OF BALL FLOATING DOWN RIVER OVER EDGE OF FALLS. (:04 secs.)	—can this watch take the full impact of the rocks and landing?
4.	CUT TO LOW TILTING FS OF BALL DROPPING DOWN FACE OF FALLS. (:0½ sec.)	It's going over!
4A.	FREEZE FRAME WITH SUPERED BLACK ARROW POINTING TO BALL. (:0½ sec.)	Watch it!
4B.	UNFREEZE FRAME, CONTINUE TILT DOWN. (:02 secs.)	Down into that raging torrent!
5.	CUT TO HIGH PANNING FS OF BALL BOUNCING AROUND BOTTOM OF FALLS. (:03 secs.)	Buffeted and jolted by the force of that terrific current!
6.	CUT TO CU HAND HOLDING WATCH, STILL ATTACHED TO BALL, IN QUIET WATER. (:02½ secs.)	And here it is, still ticking away!
7.	CUT TO ECU OF SAME TICKING WATCH. (:02 secs.)	The world's greatest watch value.
8.	CUT TO FS NEWSROOM WITH LYLE VAN. (:06 secs.)	(O.C.) I'm Lyle Van. I'm a newscaster, and I covered this Niagara Falls story. This—
9.	TWIN VERTICAL WIPES FROM CENTER FRAME TO REVEAL CU BEAUTY SHOT OF WATCH WITH TITLE BOTTOM FRAME: "BULOVA Clipper/17 JEWELS." (:07½ secs.)	—is the watch. The seventeen-jewel Bulova "Clipper," in the charm and color of natural gold.

10. DISSOLVE TO HIGH CU OF WATCH
    ON MAN'S WRIST. FINGERS
    ENTER FRAME TO FLEX WATCH-
    BAND. (:08½ secs.)

Winds automatically with just the slighest
motion of your wrist. It's anti-magnetic, and
features this handsome expansion band.

11. DISSOLVE BACK TO CU BEAUTY
    SHOT OF WATCH WITH NEW
    TITLES BOTTOM FRAME:
    "BULOVA Clipper/SELF
    WINDING/WATERPROOF/FROM
    $49.50." (:08 secs.)

Now the Bulova "Clipper" is yours to try
for two entire weeks before you pay one
cent. Yours on the easiest of terms.
Complete price from only $49.50.

12. CUT TO ART TITLE: "Easiest/
    Credit/Terms." (:02 secs.)

* * *

Over the years, TV viewers have come to associate Timex Watches with
graphic torture tests that have video taped or filmed the watches still a-tick, after
being subjected to the most terrible kinds of physical abuse. It is interesting to note
that the granddaddy of this form of demonstration was actually a *Bulova*
commercial—with a performance that took place, logically enough, at Niagara Falls.

Handsomely planned and edited—the entire demonstration, entirely
believable, consumes less than fifteen seconds!—this commercial set an economical
style for others to follow. There was even room for six and a half seconds of local
watch dealer identification at the end.

It contained all the ingredients we have come to know so well from the
competitive Timex series that—let us face it—imitates it to a fare-thee-well: the
dramatic locale, the well-known newscaster, and the dripping, still-ticking watch,
sweep-second hand moving, hauled back from torture.

Onward and downward . . . over the falls.

Scene 3D   "Can You Be Sure . . .?"

DETAILS

    Live black-and-white kinescope film. 150 seconds. 290 words. Air date 1954.
    Westinghouse Electric Corp., *Advertiser.*
    McCann-Erickson, Inc., *Agency.*
    CBS-TV Network (N.Y.), *Producer.*

CREDITS

    Betty Furness, *Creative.*
    Worthington Miner, CBS-TV Network, *Production.*

"CAN YOU BE SURE . . . ?"

1. OPEN ON DOLLY IN TO ECU OF "STUDIO ONE" PROGRAM, OPENED TO ART TITLE AND PHOTO: "BALANCING/ACT!" (:05 secs.)

(MUSIC: BACKGROUND THEME)
ANNOUNCER (V.O.): Balancing Act!

2. DISSOLVE TO FS OF WOMAN CARRYING WATER-FILLED DRIP PAN AWAY FROM OPENED, DEFROSTING REFRIGERATOR. SHE SPILLS PAN. (:05 secs.)

BETTY FURNESS (V.O.): Watch it, watch it, look out! Oh, oh, there it goes! Well, emptying messy drip pans—

2A. WOMAN LEAVES FRAME, REAPPEARS WITHOUT PAN. DOLLY IN TO MCU AS SHE EMPTIES FREEZER COMPARTMENT, CHIPS AT ICE WITH KNIFE. (:14 secs.)

—is just part of your job when you're defrosting an old-fashioned refrigerator. First you have to remove all the frozen foods, and then you have to chip or melt away all the frost. It's such a messy job, and so unnecessary, too—

3. CUT TO FS OF FURNESS STANDING ALONGSIDE OF WESTINGHOUSE REFRIGERATOR. (:04 secs.)

—(O.C.) when you own this wonderful new Westinghouse Refrigerator. It always—

3A. SUPER TITLE: "KEEPS ITSELF/ FROST FREE." (:03 secs.)

—keeps itself frost-free.

3B. DROP TITLE. DOLLY IN TO MS AS FURNESS TURNS TO REFRIGE-RATOR AND STARTS TRYING— UNSUCCESSFULLY—TO OPEN DOOR LATCH. (:11 secs.)

Yick! Someone's playing games. Well . . . ordinarily . . . it's completely automatic.

3C. FURNESS AGAIN ASSAULTS DOOR LATCH. (:31 secs.)

There's never anything that you have to do. And, the secret is inside here. Look! I think we left off the current . . . Anyway . . . inside is a magic counter button, and it's the sign of the frost-free freezer. You never have to worry about it, you never have to touch it. You never have to defrost the freezer, or the refrigerator. And here's why. You see, there's a little magic counter button up here, and every time you open and close the door—

3D. THE DIRECTOR HAS NOW
GATHERED HIS WITS—AFTER
HALF A MINUTE—AND ORDERS
HIS CAMERMAN TO DOLLY IN
SUFFICIENTLY TO FRAME OUT
THE REFRIGERATOR DOOR, SO
STAGEHAND CAN FREE IT. THE
CAMERA FRAMES A SOMEWHAT
FRIGHTENED BETTY FURNESS IN
AN UNREHEARSED IMPROPERLY-
LIT "PORE" SHOT. (:08 secs.)

—a small amount of frost enters by the warm, moist air . . . and when the door has been opened and closed enough times . . . that is, about sixty times—

3E. THE CAMERMAN IS NOW PER-
MITTED TO DOLLY BACK TO HIS
NORMAL FS—THE DOOR HAS BEEN
UNLATCHED. (:15 secs.)

—the magic counter button sends a signal that starts the frost-free system to work. You see— the door opens completely automatically! And it wipes every trace of frost away. Even the frost water evaporates automatically. And you see this magic button?

4. CUT TO CU OF FURNESS' FINGER
POINTING TO BUTTON. (:05 secs.)

(V.O.) You never have to touch it. It does the whole job automatically.

5. CUT BACK TO FS OF FURNESS
ALONGSIDE REFRIGERATOR. SHE
CLOSES THE DOOR, POINTS TO
LATCH. (:07 secs.)

(O.C.) And here's something else. Ordinarily, you never have to touch this button here. You see, just a—

6. CUT TO CU OF FURNESS' ELBOW
BANGING DOOR LATCH. DOOR
FINALLY SWINGS OPEN. (:04 secs.)

(V.O.) touch of the elbow—

7. CUT BACK TO FS OF FURNESS
ALONGSIDE REFRIGERATOR. (:08
secs.)

—strike . . . it does it . . . and the magic opener opens it for you. Believe me, that's mighty handy when your hands are full of food.

7A. DOLLY IN TO CU OF FREEZER
CHEST. (:05 secs.)

(V.O.) And just look at all the room you have in this huge refrigerator. Now, this freeze chest holds up to—

7B. SUPER TITLE: "56 POUNDS." (:02
secs.)

—fifty-six pounds of frozen food.

7C. DROP SUPER. DOLLY BACK TO FS
AS FURNESS SHUTS REFRIG-
ERATOR DOOR. (:17 secs.)

(O.C.) That's a two weeks' supply for the average family. And listen . . . your old refrigerator right now is worth a lot more than you think, and your dealer will give you a great big saving allowance on your old refrigerator when you buy any new Westinghouse. So see him tomorrow, won't you? And remember—

7D. SUPER ANIMATED FILM TITLE: —"You can be <u>sure</u> . . . if it's
    "You can be sure . . . if it's/(logo)   Westinghouse!"
    Westinghouse." (:06 secs.)

* * *

This commercial was certainly good for a laugh back in 1954—"Say, did you see how Betty Furness couldn't get the icebox open on TV last night?"—but it also has great historical significance. The jammed refrigerator door latch underlined for Westinghouse—and many other advertisers—the inherent dangers of a live TV commercial performance. As audiences grew and it appeared necessary that the delivery of an expensive TV advertising message had to become letter-perfect, live presentations were slowly dropped in favor of filmed commercials, and the possibility of blown lines or product failure—a nightmare in the earliest days of the medium—gradually became a thing of the past.

Also, film opened up the world outside the studio for advertising exploitation, and motion picture crews and advertising agency producers were soon racing madly all over the world, scattering money as if it was going out of style. There was no more panic—if the cars failed to run the first time, or the watch failed to tick, there was always lots of time—and film—left for another "take."

Something was lost, however: the "now" look of the live commercial. It took almost a decade to recover it, with the advent of video tape recording. Meanwhile, America grew used to the somewhat diffuse, fantasy world of the *filmed* message, where housewives argued girdles over coffee and armored knights pointed lances at refinery workers . . . without a "fluff," ever.

But Betty Furness continued to keep her cool, shortened her skirt, blonded her hair, and eventually became LBJ's Minister of Consumer Affairs.

Act II Scene 8   *"Dirty Sand Test"*

DETAILS

> Live black-and-white kinescope film. 405 seconds. 1015 words. Air date
> 1956.
> Westinghouse Electric Corp., *Advertiser.*
> McCann-Erickson, Inc., *Agency.*
> CBS-TV Network (N.Y.), *Producer.*

CREDITS

> William Scudder, Andrew Christian, J. Wesley Doyle, *Creative.*
> CBS-TV Network, *Production.*

"DIRTY SAND TEST–ACT I"

1. OPEN ON ARTWORK OF SPOTLIGHT WITH TITLE: "WEST-INGHOUSE/STUDIO ONE." (:13 secs.)

(MUSIC: FLOURISH)
ANNOUNCER (V.O.): Right now, something never before attempted on television, an amazing test of automatic washers right here in our studio! Here's Betty Furness, with "The Trial of the Washers."

2. DISSOLVE TO FS OF FOUR AUTOMATIC WASHERS RANGED ALONG WALL, ATTENDED BY FOUR WOMEN AND BETTY FURNESS. THE FIRST WASHER IS UNDER A SIGN: "(logo) Westing-house/REVOLVING/AGITATOR/ LAUNDROMAT/AUTOMATIC WASHER." SECOND WASHER IS UNDER A SIGN: "CENTERPOST/ AGITATOR/AUTOMATIC/X." THIRD WASHER IS UNDER A SIGN: "CENTERPOST/AGITATOR/ AUTOMATIC/Y." FOURTH WASHER IS UNDER A SIGN: "CENTERPOST/AGITATOR/AUTO-MATIC/Z." PILES OF TOWELS AND MEASURING CUPS CAN BE SEEN ATOP EACH WASHER. (:34 secs.)

FURNESS (O.C.): Yes, tonight you're going to see a trial of four of America's leading automatic washers–including the Westing-house Laundromat– to see just how well they wash and rinse your clothes. These four ladies are four leading clubwomen from the New York State and New York City Federation of Women's Clubs, and they're here to represent you, to make sure that each machine gets an absolutely fair trial. They are in no way connected with Westinghouse, its dealers, or its advertising agency. They are—

3. CUT TO CU OF FIRST WOMAN'S PROFILE. SHE TURNS TO CAMERA. (:03 secs.)

—Mrs. Olin Gransom,

4. CUT TO CU SECOND WOMAN'S FACE. (:02 secs.)

Mrs. Kenneth Thayer,

5. CUT TO CU THIRD WOMAN'S FACE. (:04 secs.)

Mrs. Donald Nagg.

6. CUT TO CU FOURTH WOMAN'S FACE. (;03 secs.)

And, Mrs. Arthur Kramer.

7. CUT BACK TO FS OF DEMON-STRATION. (:09 secs.)

Now, ladies, would you each check the inside of your washer to make sure it's completely clean. And then, next, you'll find beside you—

8. CUT TO CU FURNESS' HAND
TOUCHING PILE OF SIX TOWELS
ATOP WESTINGHOUSE LAUNDRO-
MAT. TWO CUPS OF SAND AND A
HALF-CUP OF DETERGENT IN
FRONT OF TOWELS. (:06 secs.)

—six white bath towels, two cups of dirty
sand, and some detergent.

9. CUT BACK TO FS OF DEMON-
STRATION AS LADIES BEGIN
LOADING MACHINES. (:10 secs.)

Now, if you would load those towels into
the machines, and as you do, shake each one
out to make sure that it's clean. Of course,
the ladies can see— and you can't— that—

10. CUT TO MCU OF SECOND WOMAN
LOADING WASHER. PAN RIGHT
PAST THIRD WOMAN TO FOURTH
WOMAN, ALL LOADING. (:11 secs.)

—three of these machines are the automatic
centerpost agitator type of washer. Now,
they're all brand-new models, and they're all
so well-known, that—

11. CUT TO MCU FIRST WOMAN
LOADING WESTINGHOUSE
LAUNDROMAT. (:07 secs.)

—in all fairness, we've masked them off. Of
course, the fourth is the new Westinghouse
Laundromat—

12. CUT BACK TO FS DEMONSTRA-
TION. (:08 secs.)

—with the revolving agitator. Towels all in,
ladies?
LADIES: (O.C.) Yes.
FURNESS: Good. Now, will you toss in
those two cups of dirty sand, and—

13. CUT BACK TO MS OF FIRST
WOMAN NEXT TO LAUNDRO-
MAT, WITH FURNESS IN SHOT.
WOMAN POURS SAND INTO
AGITATOR BASKET. (:03½ secs.)

—that will represent the heavy dirt that you
find in so many of—

14. CUT TO MCU OF SECOND WOMAN
POURING SAND. PAN RIGHT PAST
THIRD WOMAN TO FOURTH
WOMAN, ALL POURING. (:10½
secs.)

—your clothes. And then, toss in the
detergent after that. And then, if you'll be
good enough to close the washers—

15. CUT BACK TO FS DEMONSTRA-
TION AS WOMEN CLOSE
WASHERS, AND SWITCH THEM
ON. (:28 secs.)

—and, when you're all closed, if you'll start
them. All going?
LADIES: All going.
FURNESS: Fine. Now, would you please all
stand right by your washer, until the full
cycle is completed. And that way you—and
you, too— will be able to see exactly how
well each washer gets that dirty sand out of
the towels. Watch for the outcome, at the
end of the next act.

"DIRTY SAND TEST—ACT II"

1. OPEN ON ARTWORK OF SPOT-
LIGHT WITH TITLE: "WESTING-
HOUSE/STUDIO ONE." (:11 secs.)

(MUSIC: FLOURISH)
ANNOUNCER (V.O.): And now, back to
our dramatic "Test of the Washers," in
our live television studio, and . . . the
verdict.

2. DISSOLVE TO FS DEMONSTRA-
TION. (:26 secs.)

FURNESS (O.C.): Earlier in the show, you
saw the beginning of a trial of three
centerpost agitator automatic washers, and
the new Westinghouse revolving agitator
washer. Well, now, each of these machines
has finished its wash and rinse cycles, and
our four clubwomen, from the New York
State and New York City Federation of
Women's Clubs, are ready to unload them.
Why don't we go see?

2A. FURNESS TURNS AND WALKS
TOWARD SECOND WASHER. (:02
secs.)

Let's start with Mrs. Thayer.

3. CUT TO PANNING MS OF
FURNESS AS SHE COMES TO
MACHINE. SECOND WOMAN
OPENS TOP AND REMOVES DIRTY
TOWEL. (:07 secs.)

Mrs. Thayer, would you open your machine,
and take out some of the towels and open
them up, so we can have a good look at
them? Right there.

4. CUT TO CU OF DIRTY TOWEL
BEING LAID FLAT. (:02 secs.)

Oooooh!

5. CUT BACK TO MS OF FURNESS
AND WOMAN BY SECOND
WASHER. WOMAN CONTINUES TO
REMOVE TOWELS. (:06 secs.)

Now as you all saw, each of these machines
was loaded with six towels, two cups of
dirty sand, and—

6. CUT BACK TO CU OF WOMAN'S
HANDS LAYING DIRTY TOWELS
FLAT. (:07 secs.)

—some detergent. Kind of a mess, wouldn't
you say, Mrs. Thayer?

7. CUT BACK TO MS OF FURNESS
AND WOMAN BY SECOND
WASHER. SHE REMOVES LAST
TOWEL, REACHES IN AND PULLS
OUT A HANDFUL OF SAND. (:05
secs.)

MRS. THAYER (O.C.): These towels are
just covered with sand.
FURNESS: They really are.
THAYER: And the bottom of this tub is
just full of sand.

8. CUT TO PANNING CU OF DIRTY
    TOWELS AS TWO HANDFULS OF
    SAND ARE THROWN ON THEM.
    (:05 secs.)

FURNESS: Look at that!
THAYER: Oh, my!
FURNESS: I don't think you'd like your
wash to come out like that, would you,
Mrs. Thayer?

9. CUT TO MS OF FURNESS AND
    THAYER BY WASHER. PAN WITH
    FURNESS AS SHE WALKS TO
    NEXT WOMAN AND WASHER. (:08
    secs.)

THAYER: I should say not.
FURNESS: I wouldn't either. Now let's
check our second agitator washer.
Mrs. Nagg, would you do the same
thing? Would you take your towels—

10. CUT TO CU OF DIRTY TOWELS
    BEING LIFTED FROM WASHER
    AND DUMPED IN PILE. (:12 secs.)

—out, and open them up so we can have a
look at them?
MRS. NAGG (V.O.): They're dirtier than
Mrs. Thayer's.
FURNESS (V.O.): They are not a bit
clean. are they? They look terrible. I
don't think we need to check the
bottom—

11. CUT TO MS OF FURNESS AND
    NAGG BY WASHER. PAN WITH
    FURNESS AS SHE WALKS TO
    NEXT WOMAN AND WASHER. (:12
    secs.)

—of your machine for sand, because I think
it's safely lodged in the towels.!
MRS. NAGG (V.O.): Yes, it's all over
everything. \
FURNESS: Now, why don't we have a look
at our third centerpost agitator machine?
Mrs. Kramer, let's see if you did any better.

12. CUT TO CU OF DIRTY TOWELS
    BEING LIFTED FROM WASHER
    AND DUMPED ON PILE. (:13 secs.)

Would you take your towels out, please?
One at a time? And let's see how they look.
MRS. KRAMER (V.O.): Oh, look at all that
sand in that towel!
FURNESS: That is not attractive—

13. CUT BACK TO MS OF FURNESS
    AND KRAMER BY WASHER. (:02
    secs.)

—(O.C.) is it?
KRAMER (O.C.): I should say not!

14. CUT BACK TO CU OF DIRTY
    TOWELS BEING LIFTED FROM
    WASHER AND DUMPED IN PILE.
    (:10 secs.)

FURNESS (V.O.): And there's still sand in
that, too.
KRAMER (V.O.): Look at that!
FURNESS: Yes, that seems even worse.
Let's see the bottom of your machine. Is
there any loose, down there?

15. CUT BACK TO MS OF FURNESS,
    AND KRAMER REACHING INTO
    WASHER. (:02 secs.)

KRAMER (O.C.): Oh, yes.

16. CUT TO CU OF HANDFUL OF
    SAND BEING THROWN ON
    TOWELS. (:03 secs.)

Look at all that.
FURNESS (V.O.): There certainly is.

17.   CUT BACK TO MS OF FURNESS   (O.C.) Well now, I have a suggestion. Why
      AND KRAMER NEXT TO WASHER.   don't we all go and take a look at the towels
      PAN WITH FURNESS AS SHE   that are coming out of the Westinghouse
      STARTS WALKING BACK TO   Laundromat?
      WESTINGHOUSE LAUNDROMAT.
      (:06 secs.)

18.   CUT TO FS OF FURNESS AND   Now you ladies have just seen with your
      THREE WOMAN WALKING TO   very own eyes just how much sand these
      LAUNDROMAT. DOLLY BACK   centerpost agitator machines left in the
      SLOWLY AND PAN LEFT. (:10   towels.
      secs.)

19.   CUT TO MS OF FURNESS AND   Mrs. Gramson, let's have a look at your
      FIRST WOMAN ALONGSIDE   towels, may we?
      LAUNDROMAT. OTHER WOMEN
      ENTER FRAME. (:04 secs.)

20.   CUT TO CU OF LOADING DOOR   LADIES (V.O.): Oh, look at that! Look at
      OF LAUNDROMAT. IT IS OPENED,   how lovely and beautiful they are! Ohhh!
      AND FOUR CLEAN WHITE   Beautiful and clean! Beautiful!
      TOWELS ARE REMOVED ONE AT   FURNESS (V.O.): And another one, just
      A TIME AND PLACED ON TOP OF   as clean. Each one. There's not a grain of
      THE WASHER. (:15 secs.)   sand. I must say—

21.   CUT TO MS OF FURNESS AND   —(O.C.) I'm very impressed myself.
      LADIES GROUPED AROUND   (LAUGHS) They all look simply wonderful.
      LAUNDROMAT. ANOTHER TOWEL   Well, now—
      IS REMOVED. (:07 secs.)

22.   CUT TO CU HANDS EXAMINING   —(V.O.) Mrs. Gramson, I have a clean cloth
      TOWELS. (:03 secs.)   here.

23.   CUT TO MS OF LADIES AND   (O.C.) I wonder if you would just wipe out
      FURNESS. SHE HANDS GRAMSON   the inside of the Laundromat?
      A CLOTH. (:04 secs.)

24.   CUT TO CU OF LOADING DOOR.   GRAMSON (V.O.): I have one more.
      HANDS REMOVE LAST TOWEL,   LADIES (V.O.): (LAUGH)
      REENTER FRAME WITH CLOTH,   FURNESS (V.O.): Look at that. Not a
      WIPE INSIDE OF BASKET. PAN UP   trace of sand.
      WITH CLOTH AS IT IS PLACED   GRAMSON: Not a trace.
      ATOP TOWELS, PERFECTLY
      CLEAN. (:10 secs.)

25.   CUT BACK TO MS OF LADIES AND   FURNESS (O.C.): Well, now, ladies, you've
      FURNESS AROUND LAUNDRO-   all watched this test. We've all seen it right
      MAT. (:25 secs.)   from beginning to end, together, and you
                                         know it was completely fair and impartial,
                                         and I think I can see that you're pretty
                                         impressed with our Laundromat.
                                         LADIES: (O.C.): Yes. Very much so.
                                         FURNESS: I want to thank each of you
                                         so much for coming with us tonight.
                                         LADIES: Thank you. Goodnight.
                                         FURNESS: Goodnight.

25A. LADIES LEAVE FRAME, PAN WITH FURNESS AS SHE SHUTS LAUNDROMAT LOADING DOOR AND CROSSES TO LEFT FRAME. (:32 secs.)

And as for you ladies at home, if you're in the market for an automatic washer, I'd like to suggest that you go to your Westinghouse dealer, and ask him to let you see this dramatic "sand test" yourself. I'm sure you'll agree that the new Westinghouse Laundromat with the revolving agitator will wash and rinse your clothes much better than old-fashioned centerpost agitator washers. And for the best in laundry equipment, or any appliance, remember—

25B. SUPER TITLE IN SYNC WITH AUDIO: "YOU CAN BE SURE ... IF IT'S/(logo)Westinghouse." (:04 secs.)

—"You can be sure ... if it's Westinghouse!"

* * *

In the earliest '50's, New York City's WOR-Channel 9, one of TV's leading early outlets, found itself with a lot of unscheduled fringe late-night time on its hands. Fifteen minutes of it was purchased for a nightly "educational program on hair care" by Charles Kasher, founder of the Charles Antell cosmetic firm, and now an international film producer. To fill the period, he shot a quarter-hour film of an unreformed Broadway pitchman named Sid Hassman, who stood in front of a camera and tugged at his own bountiful head of hair, performed various sleight-of-hand demonstrations, and waved (and sold by the carload) bottles of Charles Antell's "Lanolin for the Hair."

This "program"—actually a 15-minute commercial—soon made Lanolin a household word in the New York area, and spread it through the other major markets across the country. (A humorous chronicle of this TV "first" was made into a brief film by the author, shown at one of Lincoln Center's Film Festivals but later destroyed at the request of his Lever Brothers client.)

There seems no question that the Antell-Hassman "program" was actually the longest commercial to date in the history of the television medium. The only spots that have arisen since to challenge it were the Ford commercials prepared for the first telecasts of *The Robe* and *Bridge On the River Kwai*. These spots, slightly over ten minutes long, cost a small fortune to create, and introduced a "shoot-the-wad" technique that certainly impressed the advertising industry, but not, apparently the consumer, since Ford has not repeated the style.

So the Antell record, informal as it may be, still stands. (It has undergone some unplanned bobbling. The author experienced one such situation on October 6, 1959, when his live Kayser-Roth commercial on the Jack Paar Show was exploded into ten minutes of premature guerilla theater by Professor Irwin Corey, Elaine May and Mike Nichols.)

But the longest planned (and legitimate) commercial from the earliest days of the medium is undoubtedly this seven-minute, thousand-word spectacular that actually played in two "acts" on the Westinghouse *Studio One* dramatic program over the CBS Network, September 24, 1956. William Scudder of McCann-Erickson conceived the idea of matching the effectiveness of the new Westinghouse Laundromat *tilted drum* agitator against the traditional *well* agitators of three other leading washing machine manufacturers. Vehicle for the test was two cupfuls of dirty sand. Fairness can be judged by the reader when he realizes that sand poured into the Westinghouse drum drained out through the holes in the side as it rotated, whereas the sand in the competing wells really had no place to go.

Against such a predictable result, the "test" was run live in front of three cameras on the *Studio One* stage—in two "acts" to allow for the loading of the machines on camera, then to go through the "wash-cycle" while the program itself progressed, and then a return to the demonstration to show results. Local clubwomen were found who agreed to serve as impartial "judges." Betty Furness held it all together.

No one has attempted anything like it since.

Cars & Trucks

In no other category did the pretentiousness of early television advertising make itself felt as strongly as in this one. A little of the wind has gone out of those sales now, but even in the late '60's, some Detroit manufacturers were still bringing out each year's new models—over eight million individual automobiles—as if they were announcing the Second Coming.

Perhaps because an automobile is the "biggest ticket" consumer product sold on TV, car advertisers felt *their* commercials had to be longer, louder and more elaborately produced—lest their product be confused with some 39¢ breakfast food?

The result was usually a level of pomposity reflected faithfully in much of this particular "Classic" group. It took two decades for at least one Detroit manufacturer to realize that it was probably easier (and cheaper) to sell a car in a TV commercial merely by showing a student driver ramming it into a showering fire hydrant.

A staggering discovery, when one reflects on the strange position of the automobile in American life as both an economic necessity and status symbol. Much of the Hollywood hogwash in auto advertising was precipitated out toward 1960 by the advent of the Volkswagen import, which eventually also showed the way for Ford's Mustang campaign. But most of the auto commercials were bad, bad, bad . . . and haven't gotten too much better. A lot of them still invite you to kill yourself with 280 horsepower that goes from zero to death in six seconds . . . and mightily increases the pollution index en route.

"Commercials for automobiles and gasoline," observed FCC Commissioner Nicholas Johnson in 1970, "sell something more than product. They sell a lifestyle which should not go unchallenged."

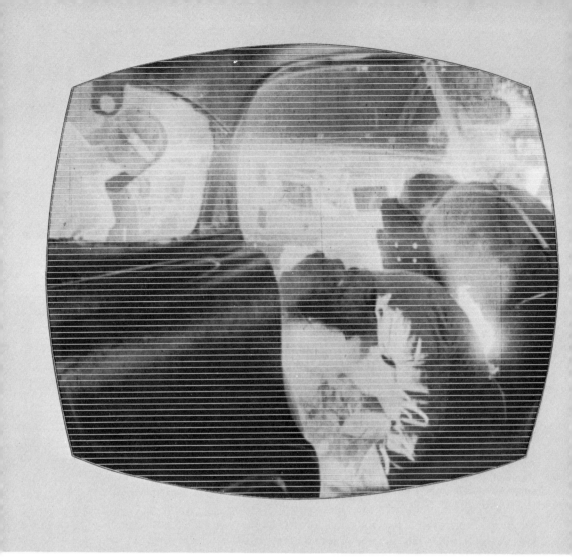

Scene 14   "I Built Me A Dodge!"

DETAILS

Live action black-and-white film. 120 seconds. 190 words. Air date 1955.
Dodge Division, Chrysler Corporation, *Advertiser.*
Grant Advertising, Inc. (Detroit), *Agency.*
VanPraag Productions, Inc., *Producer.*

CREDITS

Robert C. Mack, *Creative.*
William VanPraag, Peter Glushanok, *Production.*

"I BUILT ME A DODGE!"

1. OPEN ON MS OF STEEL FURNACE. (:04 secs.)	(MUSIC: DRAMATIC)
2. CUT TO MCU OF FURNACE. (:01 sec.)	
3. CUT TO MCU OF STAMPING PRESS. (:04 secs.)	MIDDLETON (V.O.): This is a story.
4. CUT TO MCU OF CRANKSHAFT LATHE. (:03 secs.)	A story of industry in action.
5. CUT TO LOW MS OF TURNING GEAR WHEEL. (:03 secs.)	(SINGS) Gonna take me a press,
6. CUT TO HIGH MS OF MAN POURING STEEL. (:03 secs.)	Gonna take me some steel,
7. CUT TO FS OF MAN WITH SHEET OF STEEL. (:03 secs.)	Gonna take my two hands,
8. CUT TO FS OF SHEET IN STAMPING PRESS. (:03 secs.)	And build an automobile!
9. CUT TO FS OF STAMPING COMING OFF PRESS. (:05 secs.)	(SPEAKS) How many dreams can you shape in a minute?
10. CUT TO LOW FS OF AUTOMOBILE ASSEMBLY LINE. (:02 secs.)	An hour?
11. CUT TO LOW CU OF WORKER'S FACE. (:01½ secs.)	Ask the people of Dodge!
12. CUT TO FS OF ASSEMBLY LINE WORKERS. (:03½ secs.)	
13. CUT TO CU OF WELDER IN MASK. (:05 secs.)	(SINGS) Put in a rivet and a weld, And it'll look alive,
14. CUT TO MS OF WELDERS WORKING ON CHASSIS. (:05½ secs.)	Wait till you see this baby drive!
15. CUT TO MCU OF ENGINE ASSEMBLY. (:02½ secs.)	(SPEAKS) What makes an engine go?
16. CUT TO MS OF ENGINE ASSEMBLERS. (:03½ secs.)	Is it stock and steel and copper tubing?

17. CUT TO FS OF ENGINE ASSEMBLY   Or infinite care and experience with
    LINE. (:03 secs.)   men and women working together—

18. CUT TO CU OF ENGINE BLOCK   —to bring metals alive?
    ASSEMBLY. (:02 secs.)

19. CUT TO MS OF PAINT SPRAYING.
    (:01½ secs.)

20. CUT TO LOW CU OF WORKER'S   (SINGS) Turn it up, Henry,
    FACE. (:01 sec.)

21. CUT TO MS LATHE OPERATION.
    (:01 sec.)

22. CUT TO LOW MS OF BLACK   Turn it up, Joe!
    WORKER AT VALVE WHEEL. (:01½
    secs.)

23. CUT TO CU DRILL PRESS OPERA-
    TION. (:01 sec.)

24. CUT TO LOW MS OF GEAR   We'll put'er together,
    ASSEMBLY LINE. (:05 secs.)   Then start to go!

25. CUT TO LOW CU OF WORKER'S   (SPEAKS) Heads up—
    FACE. (:01 sec.)

26. CUT TO TILTING MS OF CAR BODY   —she's coming down! Two months ago,
    BEING LOWERED THROUGH   three tons of unmined ore. Today, a
    OPENING ONTO CHASSIS. (:08 secs.) designer's idea come to life!

27. CUT TO REVERSE ANGLE MCU OF   (SINGS) Put a brand-new body
    BODY DROPPING. (:04½ secs.)   On a brand-new frame,

28. CUT TO HIGH MS OF WORKMAN   Tighten her up and give it a name;
    BOLTING CHASSIS. (:03 secs.)

29. CUT TO ECU OF HOOD DROPPING   Call it a "Dodge"!
    INTO FRAME TO SHOW "Dodge"
    NAMEPLATE. (:03 secs.)

30. CUT TO FS OF CARS COMING OFF   (SPEAKS) It's a proud name. Proud in
    FINAL ASSEMBLY LINE. (:09 secs.) tradition; proud in service. Swift and
                                     mighty—

31. DISSOLVE TO MS RUNNING SHOT   —in action.
    OF SEDAN. (:04 secs.)   (SINGS) I took me a press,

32. CUT TO REVERSE ANGLE MS. (:03   I took me some steel,
    secs.)

33. CUT TO MS RUNNING SHOT OF   I took my two hands,
    CONVERTIBLE. (:03 secs.)

34. CUT TO REVERSE ANGLE MS. (:03   And built an automobile!
    secs.)

35. CUT TO MS RUNNING SHOT OF   I built a Dodge!
    SEDAN. (:03 secs.)

36. IRIS WIPE OUT TO FS SEDAN   I built a Dodge!
    DRIVING AT CAMERA. (:04 secs.)

37. CUT TO ECU "Dodge" NAMEPLATE.
    (:03 secs.)

* * *

In the grand old "John Henry" tradition, Grant Advertising used the Broadway baritone Ray Middleton to tell a musical story of how Dodge Cars Are Put Together. The impressive industrial "scored" photography is by Peter Glushanok (himself a composer of note). It was a change from the usual sticky, romantic new-car-announcement commercial, except that it carried its pretentiousness in the opposite direction.

Shot in the Dodge assembly plant in Detroit, it was one of the few American television commercials—in 1955—to show real people at work, even *one* black man (among fifty on-screen workers!). Glushanok used as little artificial lighting as possible. The result is a ballad commercial in the great tradition of the documentary films of the '30's and '40's, but whisked back to fairyland near the end by a dull series of running shots of the finished Dodge cars.

Credit for almost all the preliminary creative work on this commercial goes to a single Grant man, Robert C. Mack. The music and arrangement is by Gene Farrell.

Scene 45   "Alcan Champs"

DETAILS

    Live action black-and-white film. 230 seconds. 427 words. Air date 1956.
    Chevrolet Truck Division, General Motors Corp., *Advertiser.*
    Campbell-Ewald Inc. (Detroit), *Agency.*
    VanPraag Productions, Inc., *Producer.*

CREDITS

    W. Robert Woodburn, *Creative.*
    William VanPraag, Gilbert M. Williams, Harry Walsh, *Production.*

"ALCAN CHAMPS"

1. OPEN ON BLACK SCREEN. POP ON 6 PAIRS OF ANIMATED HEADLIGHTS IN DIFFERENT AREAS, ONE PAIR AT A TIME. (:05 secs.)	(MUSIC: FLOURISH)
1A. ZOOM WORDS OF TITLE: "TASK/ FORCE/'57" FORWARD FROM INFINITY TO FILL FRAME, IN SYNC WITH AUDIO. (:02 secs.)	CHORUS (V.O.): (SINGS) Task Force '57,
1B. LOSE TITLE. POP ON FULL-FRAME TITLE: "CHEVROLET/TRUCKS/ ARE HERE" IN SYNC WITH AUDIO. (:02 secs.)	Chevrolet Trucks are here!
2. CUT TO LIVE MCU OF HAND HOLDING FLASHLIGHT TRACING ROUTE ON WALL MAP OF ALASKA. (:05 secs.)	Task Force '57, Chevrolet,
2A. ZOOM OUT SUPER TITLE: "CHAMPS/OF THE/ALCAN RUN" FROM INFINITY TO FILL FRAME. (:05 secs.)	Champs of the Alcan Run!
3. DISSOLVE TO PANNING AERIAL FS OF ALASKAN RIVER VALLEY. (:04 secs.)	ANNOUNCER (V.O.): (RECITING) There's a road that lies Under northern skies, Toward the Land of the Midnight Sun.
3A. ANIMATED LINE MAKES A SUPER-IMPOSED TRACING OF HIGHWAY ROUTE. (:02 secs.)	(MUSIC: TRUMPET FLOURISH)
4. CUT TO DIFFERENT AERIAL FS OF HIGHWAY ROUTE. (:07 secs.)	It crosses the crest Of the great Northwest, And it's known as the Alcan Run.
4A. ANOTHER ANIMATED LINE TRACES THE HIGHWAY ROUTE. (:02 secs.)	(MUSIC: TRUMPET FLOURISH)
5. IRIS OUT TO NIGHT MS OF "MILE-POST O" AT DAWSON CREEK. (:04 secs.)	And from Dawson's Creek, With a task force sleek Of the '57 line,

223

6. CUT TO FLOODLIT MS OF TWO   We blazed a way
   MECHANICS CHECKING TRUCK   For—
   ENGINE COMPARTMENT. ONE
   WEARS CHEVROLET-LOGOED
   COVERALLS, THE OTHER AN
   "AAA" BRASSARD. (:02 secs.)

7. CUT TO "CHEVROLET" ESCUTCH-   —Chevrolet
   EON ON HOOD. (:04 secs.)   To conquer the Alcan grind.

8. CUT BACK TO MS OF MEN   Our engines were steeled,
   CHECKING ENGINE. (:01½ secs.)

9. CUT TO CU AAA MAN LOCKING   Our tanks were sealed,
   GAS TANK CAP. (:01 sec.)

10. CUT TO CU DRIVER'S FEET   For once we were under way,
    CLIMBING ON RUNNING BOARD
    INTO CAB. (:02 secs.)

11. CUT TO MCU MAN'S HANDS   Every mile of that ride
    LOCKING GAS TANK CAP. (:02
    secs.)

12. CUT TO HIGH MCU OF TWO MEN   Would be certified
    PUTTING SEAL ON ENGINE HOOD
    LOCK. (:01 sec.)

13. CUT TO CU OF ARM WITH "AAA"   By the seal of the A.A.A.
    BRASSARD ADJUSTING ENGINE.
    (:02 secs.)

14. CUT TO CU OF DRIVER SLAM-   (MUSIC: TIMPANI ROLL)
    MING CAB DOOR. (:01 sec.)

15. CUT TO ECU LOCKED GAS TANK
    CAP. (:01 sec.)

16. CUT TO SLOW DOLLY FS PAST   Cameo Carrier '57!
    LINE OF 6 FLOODLIT TRUCKS.   (MUSIC: TIMPANI)
    EACH TRUCK PULLS AWAY IN   One-Ton Panel '57!
    SYNC WITH NAME. (:22 secs.)   (MUSIC: TIMPANI)
                                     Belt Body Tandem Axle!
                                     (MUSIC: TIMPANI)
                                     And Panel Body, Low Cab Forward!
                                     (MUSIC: TIMPANI)
                                     5-Speed Transmission Tractor-Trailer!
                                     (MUSIC: TIMPANI)
                                     Hyster Trailer, Powermatic!
                                     (MUSIC: TIMPANI)

17. CUT TO FLOODLIT FS OF ROAD
WITH TRUCKS PASSING CAMERA
POSITION. (:17 secs.)

The trucks of the Task Force fleet!
(MUSIC: FLOURISH)
CHORUS: A great new test in every weight
The mighty "six," the great new "eight,"
With all these trucks, all up-to-date,
Chevrolet, the Champion of them all!

18. CUT TO FLOODLIT REVERSE
ANGLE FS OF ROAD WITH
TRUCKS GOING AWAY. (:16 secs.)

(MUSIC: TRUMPET FLOURISH)
ANNOUNCER: Fighting dust, fighting time,
On that long northern climb,
Alone, against all nature's might,
These trucks made by Chevy . . .
Light, medium, heavy . . . .
Roared into the wilderness night.

19. CUT TO NIGHT CU OF RAIN-
COVERED WINDSHIELD. TWO
MEN INSIDE CAB. (:05 secs.)

(MUSIC: FLOURISH)
The lightning flash,
The hailstorm crash,
The rain turned the road to paste.

20. CUT TO RAIN-COVERED WIND-
SHIELD ON SECOND TRUCK. (:04
secs.)

We drove our band through that washed-out
    land
Up into the Yukon waste.

21. DISSOLVE TO FS ALCAN HIGH-
WAY IN EARLY MORNING,
MOUNTAINS IN BACKGROUND.
TRUCK PASSES. (:03½ secs.)

(MUSIC: FLOURISH)
CHORUS: The night is gone and here's the
    dawn

22. CUT TO MS HIGHWAY WITH
TRUCK PASSING. (:02½ secs.)

The bold are coming, clear and strong.

23. CUT TO MS HIGHWAY WITH
MOUNTAINS IN BACKGROUND, 2
TRUCKS PASSING. (:09 secs.)

The greatest champs are pushing on
For Chevrolet, the Champion of them all!
(MUSIC: TRUMPET FLOURISH)

24. CUT TO FS ROAD SEEN THROUGH
CAB WINDSHIELD. (:04½ secs.)

ANNOUNCER: So we made our push
Through the Arctic bush
On that ribbon of mountainous road,

25. CUT TO FS OF HAIRPIN HIGHWAY
TURN WITH 3 TRUCKS PASSING
DOWNHILL. (:04½ secs.)

And we held our stride
On that rugged ride,
In spite of the heavy load.

26. CUT TO CU OF TRUCK WHEELS
PASSING OVER BUMPY ROAD.
(:02 secs.)

(MUSIC: TRUMPET FLOURISH)

27. CUT TO TRACKING FS OF TRUCK
ON HIGHWAY. (:04½ secs.)

Powermatic transmission
Locked in position,
No shifting from "drive" to "low,"

28. CUT TO LOW FS OF 3 TRUCKS   Proving by test
     PASSING ON HIGHWAY. (:04½   That Chevy is best
     secs.)   Wherever a truck can go.

29. CUT TO HIGH CU OF 2 TRUCKS   (MUSIC: FLOURISH)
     BUMPING THROUGH WATER-
     FILLED RUTS. (:04 secs.)

30. CUT TO FS OF TRUCK PASSING   CHORUS: We've got the power beneath the
     DOCK FACILITIES, STEAMER AT   hood
     PIER. (:02½ secs.)

31. CUT TO MS OF TWO MEN WATCH-   To set the pace we knew we could,
     ING TRUCK PASS OFF-SCREEN.
     (:02 secs.)

32. CUT TO HIGH FS OF TRUCKS ON   We're out to tame the great Northwest
     HIGHWAY SNAKING AROUND   For Chevrolet, the Champion of them
     LAKE. (:06 secs.)   all!

33. CUT TO MS OF MOOSE RUNNING.   (MUSIC: TRUMPET FLOURISH)
     (:03 secs.)

34. CUT TO FS OF 3 TRUCKS CROSS-   ANNOUNCER: There were rivers to span
     ING BRIDGE OVER NARROW   With our caravan,
     RIVER. (:02½ secs.)

35. CUT TO RUNNING FS OF ROAD-   And the valleys were wide and deep.
     SIDE SEEN FROM TRUCK CAB.   (MUSIC: TRUMPET FLOURISH)
     (:03½ secs.)

36. CUT TO LOW FS OF HIGHWAY   Though the way was hard,
     WITH TRUCK ON HILLY CURVE.
     (:01 sec.)

37. CUT TO FS HIGHWAY SEEN   With Hydraulic Retard
     THROUGH CAB WINDSHIELD. (:02
     secs.)

38. CUT TO ANGLED LOW FS OF   We held, where the grades were steep.
     TRUCK NEGOTIATING DOWNHILL
     STRETCH OF HIGHWAY. (:03 secs.)

39. CUT TO FS OF DUST BEHIND   (MUSIC: FLOURISH)
     TRUCK, FROM TRUCK. (:02 secs.)

40. CUT TO LOW MCU OF AAA   Statistics say at the Triple A
     ENGINEER HOLDING CLIPBOARD.   It's a 72-hour drive,
     (:04½ secs.)

41. CUT TO FS OF FAIRBANKS   But we roared down into Fairbanks town
     BRIDGE WITH 3 LEAD TRUCKS   In less than 45!
     COMING OFF. (:06 secs.)

42.   CUT TO AAA MAN'S HANDS WITH   (MUSIC: FLOURISH)
      TIMING CLOCK. (:04 secs.)

43.   CUT BACK TO SCENE 41 AS LAST   CHORUS: Champs of the Alcan Run!
      3 TRUCKS LEAVE BRIDGE. (:03
      secs.)

44.   CUT TO CU OF AAA MAN'S HANDS
      SNAPPING TIMING CLOCK. (:01
      sec.)

45.   CUT TO FS OF HIGHWAY   ANNOUNCER: If you haul loads over
      ENTERING FAIRBANKS. TRUCKS   all kinds of roads,
      PASS CAMERA INTO TOWN. (:11   Chevy Trucks are Number One.
      secs.)   They're engineered best,
                                           And proven by test

45A. ZOOM OUT SUPER TITLE: The Champs of the Alcan Run.
      "CHAMPS/OF THE/ALCAN RUN"
      FROM INFINITY TO FILL FRAME.
      (:03 secs.)

45B. LOSE TITLE. ZOOM WORDS OF   CHORUS: Task Force '57,
      TITLE: "TASK/FORCE/'57"
      FORWARD FROM INFINITY TO
      FILL FRAME IN SYNC WITH
      AUDIO. (:02½ secs.)

46.   DISSOLVE TO BLACK POP ON   Chevrolet Trucks are here!
      FULL-FRAME TITLE: "CHEV-
      ROLET/TRUCKS/ARE HERE" IN
      SYNC WITH AUDIO. (:02 secs.)

47.   CUT TO MCU OF RELIEF MAP OF   Task Force '57,
      GLOBE SHOWING ALASKA. (:02
      secs.)

47A. SUPER TITLE: "CHEVROLET" IN   Chevrolet,
      TOP FRAME. (:02½ secs.)

47B. ADDITIVE TITLE: "CHAMPS/OF   Champs of the Alcan Run!
      THE/ALCAN RUN." (:02½ secs.)

                              *   *   *

    This is one of the best of the old-time commercial blockbusters. Three-and-a-half minutes long, with a soundtrack setting *a la* Robert Service, backed by Artie Fields' chorus and half a hundred musicians, as Joel Aldred spins out the 1957 Announcement story for Chevrolet Trucks against the background of the Alcan Highway—making it seem like one of the automotive torture tests of the world.

    Actually, it's not that bad. During World War II, U.S. Army Engineers connected a series of fairly decent wagon roads running through the Canadian

Yukon with a long (and flat) Alaskan outlet. But Army P.R. soon trumpeted it into one of the worst roads on earth, and by 1956, the impression was still not dispelled in the public mind—despite the slowly rising tourist trade.

So Chevrolet ran six loaded trucks over the road (supposedly in only 45 hours!) from Dawson Creek, British Columbia, to Fairbanks, Alaska—1,523 miles. That averages out to almost 35 miles per hour, which is not bad for an unpaved "wilderness road."

VanPraag Productions, who gained a reputation as the top automotive commercial house with work like this, sent a sizeable crew along with the trucks—and presumably was always in the right place at the right time as the AAA-certified trucks thundered by. Or was there ever time for a re-take?

The photography was properly documentary, but a stock shot had to be used for the moose sequence—the Alcan Highway is notoriously shy of wildlife (even mosquitoes!) The camera angles were well chosen; very few scenes had to be adjusted (or faked) later. The passing trucks in Scene 17 were spaced for safety, so soft vertical left-to-right wipes follow each individual truck; since the camera is "tied-off," the effect is hardly noticeable; all the trucks appear to be right behind each other. One doubts whether it rained to-order (Scenes 20 and 21)—this material has all the hallmarks of being staged.

And of course Scene 30 is not on the Alcan at all—nowhere in its 1,500 miles does it pass any water that can accomodate an ocean freighter.

But cavil aside, the overall effect is powerful—and you believe that Chevrolet has proved something, although just what is hard for the viewer to say. Why, for example, were the truck transmissions all locked?

This spot certainly set back innocent tourist auto travel on the friendly Alcan Highway by several light years. Perhaps not by coincidence, its name was changed in the late '50's to the "Alaska Highway," and traffic picked up again.

Scene 22   "Somewhat Subliminal"

DETAILS

> Live action color film. 120 seconds. 162 words. Air date 1958.
> General Motors Corporation, Chevrolet Division, *Advertiser*.
> Campbell-Ewald Co., Inc. (Detroit), *Agency*.
> Universal Studios, Inc. (L.A.), *Producer*.

CREDITS

> Willard Hanes, Kensinger Jones, Fred Lounsberry, *Creative*.
> Will Cowan, *Production*.

"SOMEWHAT SUBLIMINAL"

1. OPEN ON FS OF PLATFORMS SHAPED LIKE CHEVROLET LOGOS, RESTING IN CLOUD LIMBO. PAT BOONE AND DINAH SHORE SKIP IN ACROSS LOGOS FROM OPPOSITE SIDES OF FRAME. (:04 secs.)

    (MUSIC: INTRO)

2. CUT TO MS OF BOONE AND SHORE AS THEY REACH CENTER LOGO AND TURN TO VIEWER. (:08 secs.)

    BOONE & SHORE (O.C.):
    (SING) Hey, have you heard
    About the crazy new way
    To send, a message today?

3. CUT TO CU OF BOONE AS HE STEPS TO LEFT. (:04 secs.)

    BOONE: It's flashed on a screen
    Too quick to see

4. CUT TO CU OF SHORE. (:04 secs.)

    SHORE: But still you get it,
    Subliminally.

5. CUT BACK TO MS (SCENE 2) OF BOONE AND SHORE. THEY DANCE APART OVER NEARBY LOGOS. (:05 secs.)

    BOONE & SHORE:
    Put on your specs,
    Pull up your chair,
    And see if you can see—

6. CUT BACK TO FS (SCENE 1) AS BOONE AND SHORE DANCE TOGETHER AGAIN. (:04 secs.)

    —what's coming through the air?

6A. THEY SIT DOWN AS WHITE CUT-OUT " '59" RISES BEHIND SET. (:02 secs.)

    SHORE: Ladies and gentlemen, the '59 Chevy!

7. CUT TO FS OF CHEVROLET SEDAN (FOR 8 FRAMES-1/3 sec.)

    (MUSIC: STING)

8. CUT BACK TO FS (SCENE 6A). (:02 secs.)

    BOONE: See it?

9. CUT BACK TO CU (SCENE 4) OF SHORE SEATED. (:03 secs.)

    SHORE: Isn't it beautiful?

10. CUT BACK TO CU (SCENE 3) OF BOONE, SEATED. (:03 secs.)

    BOONE: Some car, huh folks?

11. CUT BACK TO CU (SCENE 9) OF SHORE, SMILING. (:02 secs.)

    (MUSIC: STING)

12. CUT BACK TO CU (SCENE 10) OF BOONE, AS HE STANDS. (:04 secs.)

BOONE: (SINGS) That was the '59 Chevy just then,

13. CUT BACK TO CU (SCENE 11) OF SHORE, STANDING. (:04 secs.)

SHORE: All new, all over again.

14. CUT BACK TO MCU OF BOONE AND SHORE MOVING TOGETHER AGAIN. (:08 secs.)

BOONE: In case you missed it, Going by,
SHORE: We're gonna' give you all, Another try

15. CUT TO MS (SCENE 5) AS THEY STEP APART AND SIT DOWN. (:01 secs.)

16. CUT TO FS OF ROTATING SEDAN (FOR 12 FRAMES—½ sec.)

17. CUT BACK TO MS (SCENE 15). THEY CLIMB UP ON CENTER LOGO AND SIT DOWN AGAIN. (:06 secs.)

SHORE: See it?

18. CUT TO MCU (SCENE 14) OF BOONE AND SHORE. (:13 secs.)

SHORE: (SINGS) Now that you've seen,
The new Chevrolet,
BOONE: In a somewhat
Subliminal way,
SHORE: We hope that you'll place
your order right now,
BOONE & SHORE: For the '59 Chevy . . .

19. THEY STAND UP. (:06 secs.)

Here's how:
SHORE: Just go see your Chevrolet
dealer right now.
BOONE: The '59 Chevy's due out—

20. POP ON SUPER TITLE IN TOP FRAME: "THURS. OCT. 16." (:06 secs.)

—Thursday, October 16th, but . . . you can get the details and place your order in advance.

20A. LOSE TITLE AND DOLLY BACK SLOWLY TO FS, REVEALING "CHEVROLET" LOGO IN BOTTOM FRAME. CUT-OUT " '59" DROPS DOWN INTO TOP FRAME. (:09½ secs.)

SHORE: (SINGS) So come right in,
BOONE: And right away,
BOONE & SHORE: To your Chevrolet
dealer . . . For Chevrolet!

21. CUT TO FS OF SEDAN (FOR 8 FRAMES—1/3 sec.)

(MUSIC: STING)

22. CUT BACK TO FS (SCENE 20A). THEY SIT DOWN BACK TO BACK ON CENTER LOGO. (:05 secs.)

SHORE: See it?

23. THEY DISAPPEAR AND ARE   (MUSIC: PLAYOFF)
     REPLACED BY TITLE: "THURS.
     OCT. 16." (:15 secs.)

                              *   *   *

     This frivolous little one-shot musical comedy used two of TV's best-known
talents of the late '50's, engaging in a spoof of the major American communications
bugaboo of that time—"subliminal advertising." Yet that's exactly what this
commercial *does* include. Because the two minutes of Chevrolet song-and-dance
(under Harry Zimmerman's musical direction) are spiced with three—count 'em,
three—genuine fractional-second peeks at the 1959 Chevy—at air time, still eighteen
days in the offing.
     The wonderful mystique of automobile model marketing secrecy was happily
preserved, and viewers "saw"—or thought they saw?—the new Chevy. Campbell-
Ewald used a fresh idea to sell something that wasn't (hardly) even there!
     Three fixed and one dollying camera covered the performers' action
top-to-bottom; their four negatives were edited together later—cuts only. The single
optical effect, other than the titles, is a dissolve, which occurs as a piece of magic
when the camera "ties off" at the end of Scene 22. Dinah and Pat skip out of
frame, their skip is cut out of the negative, and the scene with them dissolves to the
scene without them.
     Again, thank George Méliès. Even today's ghetto kids, playing with 8mm and
16mm documentaries, still have fun with such camera "magic."

Scene 14   "Boy Meets Impala"

DETAILS

    Live action black-and-white film. 120 seconds. 21 words. Air date 1958.
    General Motors Corporation, Chevrolet Division, *Advertiser.*
    Campbell-Ewald Co., Inc. (Detroit), *Agency.*
    Robert Lawrence Productions, Inc., *Producer.*

CREDITS

    Kensinger Jones, Stanley Wilson, *Creative.*
    Willard Hanes, Gerald Schnitzer, Fred Gately, Ernest Fegte, *Production.*

"BOY MEETS IMPALA"

1. OPEN ON NIGHTTIME CU OF SON, DRESSED FOR PROM, HUGGING MOTHER ON DOORSTEP OF PRIVATE HOME. (:02 secs.)

(MUSIC: LIGHT AND CHEERFUL. UNDERNEATH THROUGHOUT)

1A. WIDEN TO MS INCLUDING FATHER WITH SISTER HOLDING CORSAGE BOX. SON TURNS FROM MOTHER, SHAKES FATHER'S HAND, PATS SISTER'S HEAD. (:01 sec.)

1B. DOLLY BACK TO FS AS SON DANCES DOWN FRONT WALK. (:02 secs.)

1C. SON REMEMBERS CORSAGE, GOES BACK TO GET IT FROM SISTER. (:03 secs.)

1D. CONTINUE DOLLY TO INCLUDE FRONT OF SON'S HOT-ROD IN DRIVEWAY. SON STOPS AND REGARDS IT SADLY. (:05 secs.)

2. CUT TO CU OF SON'S SAD FACE. (:01 sec.)

ANNOUNCER (V.O.): (CHUCKLES)

3. CUT TO MS OF FAMILY LOOKING AT EACH OTHER. (:02 secs.)

If it's happened once, it's happened—

4. CUT BACK TO (SCENE 2) CU OF SON'S FACE TURNING TO STARE ELSEWHERE. (:01 sec.)

—a thousand times.

5. CUT TO FS OF FATHER'S OPEN IMPALA CONVERTIBLE FURTHER DOWN DRIVEWAY. (:02 secs.)

(MUSIC: "SEE THE U.S.A." THEME)

6. CUT TO ECU OF SON'S HEAD SHAKING IN ADMIRATION. (:02 secs.)

7. CUT BACK TO (SCENE 3) OF FAMILY LOOKING IN DIRECTION OF IMPALA. (:01 sec.)

8. CUT TO FS OF (THEIR ANGLE ON)
    IMPALA. (:01 sec.)

9. CUT TO MS OF FATHER AND
    SISTER (LOOKING TOWARD
    IMPALA). (:01 sec.)

10. CUT TO CU OF MOTHER (LOOK-
    ING AT FATHER). (:01 sec.)

11. CUT TO CU OF SISTER (LOOKING
    UP AT FATHER). (:01 sec.)

12. CUT TO CU OF FATHER SHAKING
    HEAD NEGATIVELY. (:02 secs.)

13. CUT TO MS OF SON TOSSING
    CORSAGE INTO FRONT SEAT OF
    HOT-ROD AND STARING ACROSS
    ROOF. (:02 secs.)

14. CUT TO HIGH FS OF SON HALF
    INTO HOT-ROD, LOOKING AT
    IMPALA. (:01 sec.)

15. CUT TO CU OF FATHER AND
    MOTHER LOOKING AT EACH
    OTHER. (:02 secs.)

16. CUT BACK TO (SCENE 11) SISTER
    (LOOKING UP AT FATHER). (:01
    sec.)

17. CUT BACK TO (SCENE 14) FS OF
    SON, HOT-ROD AND IMPALA. HE
    TURNS IN FATHER'S DIRECTION.
    (:01 sec.)

18. CUT BACK TO (SCENE 3) OF
    FAMILY. MOTHER AND SISTER
    LOOK AT FATHER. HE SMILES
    AND REACHES INTO HIS POCKET.
    (:04 secs.)

19. CUT TO ECU FATHER'S POCKET
    AS HIS HAND BRINGS OUT
    IMPALA KEYS. (:02 secs.)

20. CUT BACK TO (SCENE 1D) FS OF
    FAMILY ON DOORSTEP. SON
    DASHES BACK UP WALK TO GRAB
    KEYS. (:02 secs.)

21. CUT BACK TO (SCENE 1A) MS OF
FAMILY AS SON PUMPS FATHER'S
HAND, KISSES SISTER AND
LEAVES FRAME. SISTER HUGS
FATHER. (:06 secs.)

22. CUT TO FOREGROUND MS OF
IMPALA AS SON JUMPS INTO
FRONT SEAT. FAMILY WATCHES
FROM BACKGROUND. (:02 secs.)

23. CUT TO REVERSE FS AND DOLLY
RIGHT AS SON LEAPS FROM
IMPALA AND SPRINTS TO
HOT-ROD. (:05 secs.)

24. CUT TO CU OF FRONT SEAT OF
HOT-ROD AS SON REACHES IN,
GRABS CORSAGE. (:01 sec.)

25. CUT TO HIGH CU OF HIS DATE'S
LAP WITH CORSAGE. DOLLY
BACK FROM IMPALA TO SHOW
HER AND SON IN FRONT SEAT.
(:06 secs.)

26. CUT TO CU OF SON'S PROUD
FACE. (:01 sec.)

27. CUT TO CU OF REAR-VIEW
MIRROR SHOWING REFLECTION
OF DATE'S HAPPY FACE. (:01 sec.)

28. CUT BACK TO (SCENE 26) CU OF
SON'S FACE. (:01 sec.)

29. CUT TO MS OF DATE WITH HAIR
BLOWING. (:02 sec.)

30. CUT TO ECU OF "IMPALA" LOGO
ON REAR FENDER AND WIDEN
TO MS AS CONVERTIBLE MOVES
DOWN SUBURBAN STREET. (:04
sec.)

31. CUT TO FS OF IMPALA MOVING
PAST CAMERA. (:05 secs.)

32. CUT TO CU OF CORSAGE IN
DATE'S LAP AGAINST "IMPALA"
LOGO ON GLOVE COMPARTMENT.
(:02 secs.)

33. CUT TO FS OF HIGH SCHOOL   What a gal. What a night. What a car.
     EXTERIOR AS SON PARKS
     IMPALA. ANOTHER COUPLE
     WALKS BY. DOLLY IN TO MS OF
     IMPALA AS BOY CLIMBS OUT AND
     WALKS AROUND (OUT OF
     FRAME) TO OPPOSITE SIDE TO
     HELP DATE OUT. PAN LEFT AS HE
     SHUTS DOOR AND THEY WALK
     AWAY. THEN HE REMEMBERS
     THE CORSAGE AND COMES BACK.
     AS THEY WALK AWAY FINALLY,
     DATE TURNS AND GAZES
     FONDLY AT IMPALA. (:34 secs.)

34. FADE TO BLACK. (:01 sec.)

35. FADE IN GRAY-AND-WHITE   The new Chevrolet!
     "CHEVROLET" LOGO. (:06 secs.)

* * *

At the time it was produced, 1958, this folksy little black-and-white musical family pantomine must have seemed terribly *avant garde*; only 21 words of announcer copy in two whole minutes, with the sell limited to "What a car"! Today, less than a decade after judges cast their "Classic" votes for "Boy Meets Impala," it appears surprisingly dated—an echo from TV's days of lost innocence.

The reason for this probably lies in the fact that like all of TV's automotive advertising efforts, it is over-styled and over-mannered. As mentioned, television commercial makers seem to grow startlingly self-conscious in the presence of consumer items that cost a *lot* of money.

They underplay their own ingenuity. The result is usually a handsomely-financed dull and unimaginative swing from the floor like this one, that connects with very little. This sweet little morality play in 35 scenes was predictably shot on a predictably-lit, enormous sound stage with a huge crew. Its over-rehearsed talent grimaces from 17 different "computerized" camera positions! It is Hollywood on TV—but pre-1940 Hollywood, when "boy met Impala" and "boy got girl." All style, no idea—other than the predictably-forgotten girl's corsage.

Yet each year since the '50's, one or sometimes two automotive commercials have stood up like mountain peaks above all the others. The creative roulette of placing more television advertising dollars against automobiles than any other product can pay off. Thanks to sheer audacity of concept, starkness of creative approach—and huge budget—a few excellent spots left the automotive commercial production maze through an opening wider than that through which they entered. The rest of the industry's efforts got lost in a welter of pomposity and unrelieved two—and often three-minute boredom.

An annually disturbing waste.

Scene 3B   "Balloons, Please!"

DETAILS

Live action black-and-white film. 60 seconds. 148 words. Air date 1958.
Renault, Inc., *Advertiser.*
Needham, Louis & Brorby, Inc., *Agency.*
VanPraag Productions, Inc., *Producer.*

CREDITS

Ken Snyder, Joseph Creaturo, *Creative.*
Mo Kinnan, William VanPraag, Sidney Zucker, *Production.*

"BALLOONS, PLEASE!"

1. OPEN ON FS OF EXECUTIVE WITH ATTACHÉ CASE, ROLLER-SKATING DOWN CITY SIDEWALK. PAN LEFT WITH HIM. (:03 secs.)

(MUSIC: JOLLY THEME)
ANNOUNCER (V.O.): But then—

2. CUT TO SIDE FS OF SKATER ROLLING PAST. PAN LEFT AND REVEAL BACK OF RENAULT DAUPHINE PARKED AT CURB. (:03 secs.)

—there's another handy way to get around, and have fun doing it.

2A. HOLD ON DAUPHINE. SUPER TITLE IN TOP FRAME: "RENAULT/Dauphine." (:01 sec.)

The Renault Dauphine.

3. CUT TO REVERSE MS OF FRONT OF DAUPHINE. (:03 secs.)

The car made in France to make driving fun again.

3A. DISSOLVE IN EXECUTIVE AT WHEEL OF DAUPHINE. (:01 sec.)

Balloons, please!

3B. DISSOLVE IN THREE TOY BALLOONS FLOATING OVER DAUPHINE. PAN LEFT WITH CAR AS IT PULLS AWAY FROM CURB. (:06 secs.)

Now, there's lots to talk about, so let's make the camera go fast. Watch for the fun car, with the balloons.

4. CUT TO HIGH LS OF DAUPHINE SPEEDING THROUGH HEAVY DOWNTOWN TRAFFIC. PAN LEFT WITH CAR. (:05 secs.)

First, see the Dauphine's maneuverability in traffic. Look how it gets around.

5. CUT TO FS OF DAUPHINE DRIVING OFF AROUND BUSY CORNER. PAN LEFT WITH CAR. (:03 secs.)

How it corners. Special axle design does that.

6. CUT TO FS (THROUGH WIND-SHIELD) OF DAUPHINE PASSING TRUCK ON OPEN HIGHWAY. (:06 secs.)

And see how it accelerates, and climbs. Driving economy? Gets up to forty miles a gallon.

7. CUT TO OVERHEAD MS OF LARGE CAR UNABLE TO FIT INTO CURBSIDE PARKING SPACE. IT PULLS AWAY. DAUPHINE (WITH BALLOONS) PULLS UP AND PARKS EASILY. (:12 secs.)

Parking? The big car couldn't get in this space. (MUSIC: WOODEN BLOCK STING) But watch this. With the Renault Dauphine, everybody's an expert. Lots of room for you to park—

8. CUT TO MS OF DAUPHINE AT CURB. (:02 secs.)

—inside. Handy as roller skates—

9. CUT TO MS OF FRONT SEAT INTERIOR WITH SMILING EXECUTIVE. (:02 secs.)

—and twice the fun. Even has a—

10. CUT TO ECU OF EXECUTIVE'S HAND BLOWING HORN AND ADJUSTING SWITCH. (:03 secs.)

—city horn (SOUND: CITY HORN BEEPS) and, a country horn (SOUND: COUNTRY HORN BEEPS).

11. DISSOLVE TO CU OF ANIMATED OUTLINE OF DAUPHINE AND BALLOONS ON GRAY BACK-GROUND. (:01 sec.)

That's the Renault—

11A. CAR SWELLS SLIGHTLY. (:01 sec.)

(SOUND: CITY HORN BEEP)

11B. ZOOM BACK TO FS OF ANIMA-TION REVEALING BACKGROUND AS U.S. MAP. DAUPHINE STARTS TO DRIVE EAST, LEAVING A DASHED BLACK LINE TRAIL. (:01 sec.)

—Dauphine. (SOUND: COUNTRY HORN BEEPS) At any of—

11C. TRAIL BECOMES A RECTANGLE. DAUPHINE FADES OUT. (:02 secs.)

—six hundred sales, service and parts headquarters.

11D. FADE OUT RECTANGLE; REPLACE WITH LOGO: "RENAULT/ Dauphine." (:05 secs.)

Won't you try it?

* * *

At the opposite end of the automobile sales spectrum from Chevrolet's Impala commercial of the '50's was this folksy little black-and-white minute for the French invader, Renault. The mood is all *fun,* marking a real departure (for 1958) by both agency and production house from TV's usual auto-selling approach. The tongue-in-cheek style was eventually also used with telling and prize-winning effect by the competitive Volkswagen agency, Doyle Dane Bernbach.

But Renault was first, with its famous creative image of a swirl of gaily-colored balloons floating over the Dauphine. (In the inscrutable ways of American advertising, it should be added that Needham, Lewis and Brorby, the Renault advertising agency, lost this account just as sales hit a peak. Perhaps

Renault saw the flood of American compacts coming from the major manufacturers to drown the European challenge, and became desperate.)

The commercial begins with a fairly good visual "hook"—an executive roller-skating his way to work. Then come 147 rapid-fire words (compared to 21 for the Impala!) mixed in with Curt Biever's jingling musical background, suggesting that driving can be fun again. They contain a neat bit of creative ingenuousness: "There's lots to talk about," says the announcer, "so let's make the camera go fast," and thereby he legally pardons the "undercranking" that makes the French car import appear faster and more maneuverable than it actually is. (With poetic justice, this is another film technique first developed by George Méliès in Paris, in the 1890's.)

A more original piece of TV creativity (Scene 7) is the overhead shot of the small Dauphine squeezing into a curbside space a larger car has found unsuccess-fully tiny. This single idea has since been exhaustively copied by commercials for compacts, motorcyles and motor scooters—some of which have also won awards.

Scene 30   "Brand New Door"

DETAILS

    Live action color film. 120 seconds. 13 words. Air date 1958.
    General Motors Corporation, Chevrolet Division, *Advertiser.*
    Campbell-Ewald Co., Inc. (Detroit), *Agency.*
    Gerald Schnitzer, Inc. (L.A.), *Producer.*

CREDITS

    Jere Chamberlin, Kensinger Jones, *Creative.*
    Gerald Schnitzer, Karl Struss, *Production.*

"BRAND NEW DOOR"

1. OPEN ON CU STATION WAGON WITH PLATE: "C-1959/CHEVROLET." DOLLY BACK TO MS REVEALING LITTLE GIRL HANGING OUT OPEN REAR WINDOW. (:03½ secs.)

1A. DOLLY FURTHER BACK TO FS REVEALING WAGON IN SHOWROOM. SALESMAN CROSSES IN FRONT OF CAMERA. (:02½ secs.)

2. CUT TO TRUCKING MCU OF FAMILY WITH GROCERIES PASSING OUTSIDE SHOWROOM (FATHER, MOTHER, LITTLE BOY). (:02½ secs.)

2A. TRUCKING SLOWS TO LET PARENTS PASS OUT OF FRAME. BOY PAUSES IN SHOWROOM DOOR TO STARE AT GIRL IN WAGON. (:02½ secs.)

3. CUT TO CU OF BOY SMILING AT GIRL. (:01 sec.)

4. CUT TO CU OF GIRL IGNORING BOY. (:01 sec.)

5. CUT TO CU OF BOY IGNORING GIRL. (:01½ secs.)

6. CUT TO CU OF GIRL STICKING OUT TONGUE. (:01½ secs.)

7. CUT TO CU OF BOY PULLING DOWN HIS EYELIDS. (:01½ secs.)

8. CUT TO MS OF SALESMAN WITH SURPRISED LOOK. (:02 secs.)

9. CUT BACK TO CU OF BOY BREAKING INTO LAUGH. (:01 sec.)

10. CUT BACK TO SALESMAN BREAKING INTO SMILE. (:01 sec.)

(MUSIC: ACCOMPANYING ACTION THROUGHOUT)

11. CUT TO MS OF BOY IN SHOW-
     ROOM DOORWAY LOOKING AT
     WAGON. HE IS JOINED BY HIS
     FATHER. (:02 secs.)

12. CUT TO FS OF SALESMAN AS HE
     CONTINUES TO DEMONSTRATE
     WAGON TO GIRL'S PARENTS.
     (:02½ secs.)

13. CUT TO CU OF BOY'S FATHER'S
     FACE STARING AT WAGON. HE IS
     OBVIOUSLY THINKING OF
     BUYING A NEW CAR. HE TURNS
     AND BECKONS OUT OF FRAME TO
     MOTHER. (:06 secs.)

14. CUT TO MCU OF MOTHER BY OLD
     CAR UP THE STREET. SHE NODS
     BACK. (:01 sec.)

15. CUT TO HIGH MS OF MOTHER
     PUTTING GROCERY BAG IN OLD
     CAR AND TRYING TO SLAM
     DOOR. IT SHUTS ON THE THIRD
     TRY. SHE LEAVES FRAME. (:10½
     secs.)

16. CUT TO MS OF FATHER. MOTHER
     ENTERS FRAME REGISTERING
     DISAPPROVAL. FATHER NODS AT
     WAGON INSIDE SHOWROOM.
     (:04½ secs.)

17. CUT TO REVERSE MS OF WHOLE
     FAMILY STARING INTO SHOW-
     ROOM. (:02 secs.)

18. CUT TO CU MOTHER'S FACE AS
     SHE BEGINS TO DEMONSTRATE
     INTEREST. (:02½ secs.)

19. CUT TO CU OF FATHER'S
     INTERESTED FACE. (:01½ secs.)

20. CUT TO MS OF SALESMAN
     CONTINUING TO DEMONSTRATE
     CAR. (:04½ secs.)

21. CUT TO MCU OF NODDING
     FATHER AND MOTHER. (:02½
     secs.)

22. CUT TO CU OF BOY'S FACE AS HE
    HAPPILY RUBS HIS NOSE. (:02
    secs.)

23. CUT TO CU OF 1959 WAGON
    GRILLE. (:02½ secs.)

24. CUT TO CU OF MOTHER LOOKING
    TOWARD GRILLE. (:02½ secs.)

25. CUT TO CU OF SALESMAN'S
    HAND OPENING DOOR. (:03½ secs.)

26. CUT TO CU OF INTRIGUED LOOK
    ON MOTHER'S FACE. (:01½ secs.)

27. CUT TO SALESMAN'S HAND
    CLOSING DOOR. (:01 sec.)

28. CUT TO CU OF ASTONISHED
    LOOK ON MOTHER'S FACE. SHE
    TURNS TO LOOK UP STREET AT
    HER OWN OLD DOOR. (:02 secs.)

29. CUT TO MCU OF OLD CAR DOOR.
    IT UNLATCHES BY ITSELF AND
    SLOWLY SWINGS OPEN. (:02½
    secs.)

30. CUT TO MCU OF HORRIFIED
    FATHER AND MOTHER STARING
    UP STREET. (:02 secs.)

31. CUT TO MCU OF GROCERY BAG
    TOPPLING OUT OF CAR. (:00½
    sec.)

32. CUT CUT TO ECU OF ROLLING
    ORANGE. (:00½ sec.)

33. CUT TO MS THROUGH WIND-
    SHIELD OF ENTIRE FAMILY NOW
    IN WAGON WITH SALESMAN,
    MOTHER AT WHEEL. (:04½ secs.)

34. CUT TO INTERIOR CU OF FATHER
    WINKING TOWARD SON. (:01 sec.)

35. CUT TO INTERIOR CU OF SON
    RETURNING WINK. (:01½ secs.)

36. CUT TO INTERIOR CU OF
    MOTHER LOOKING OVER HER
    SHOULDER TOWARD THEM. (:02
    secs.)

37. CUT TO EXTERIOR CU OF
     MOTHER OPENING DOOR FROM
     INSIDE. (:02½ secs.)

38. CUT BACK TO INTERIOR CU OF
     MOTHER'S FACE. (:01 sec.)

39. CUT BACK TO INTERIOR CU OF
     SMILING FATHER. (:00½ sec.)

40. CUT BACK TO INTERIOR CU OF
     SMILING BOY. (:00½ sec.)

41. CUT BACK TO EXTERIOR CU OF   ANNOUNCER (V.O.): Yes, fun to see—
     MOTHER CLOSING DOOR FROM
     INSIDE. (:03 secs.)

42. CUT BACK TO INTERIOR CU OF   —fun to drive—
     SMILING BOY. (:01 secs.)

43. CUT BACK TO EXTERIOR MS   —fun to buy. The new—
     THROUGH WINDSHIELD OF
     ENTIRE FAMILY AND SALESMAN.
     (:03 secs.)

44. CUT TO EXTERIOR FS OF WAGON   —Chevrolet!
     ON SUNNY, TREE-LINED STREET.   (MUSIC: "SEE THE U.S.A." MOTIF)
     PAN LEFT WITH CAR AS IT PULLS
     AWAY, MOTHER AT WHEEL. (:10
     secs.)

45. DISSOLVE TO "CHEVROLET"
     LOGO ON GRAY BACKGROUND.
     (:08 secs.)

* * *

In our land of conspicuous consumption, you may wonder why it took so long for an automobile manufacturer (or his advertising agency?) to suggest that an old car should be abandoned for a brand-new one just as soon as its door stuck.

In 1958 it finally happened. Chevrolet announced its next year's line with just such a folksy little two-minute marshmallow. It should really have utilized the talents of Mickey Rooney and Ann Rutherford (with Fay Bainter and Lewis Stone), and starred Jack Oakie as the Car Dealer—instead of some anonymous TV commercial performers.

The video directions hardly begin to describe all the bits of human-interest business with which their director studded this effort. The entire family's mugging—beg your pardon, *miming*—is reminiscent of silent film comedy. The silence, however, provides happy justification for only *thirteen words* of soft sell, probably a record for American TV commercials in which there has not been some form of audio broadcast failure.

Automotive Products

This field, understandably less pretentious than its mother category, offered mainly inferential demonstrations during the early years of the TV medium. Since the viewer could not *see* the product working—inside the motor or elsewhere—the creative work could not be as forthright (or probably as successful) as that of appliance commercials. Copywriters resorted to animation—usually humorous—or highly romanticized "problem + solution" spots.

The result was a great number of TV "also-rans." Only a few Automotive Product commercials were produced with sufficient imagination to poke their heads up into anyone's winners' circle.

Scene 10   *"Dragnet?"*

DETAILS

    Black-and-white animated film. 60 seconds. 121 words. Air date 1953.
    Bardahl International, Inc., *Advertiser.*
    Miller, Mackay, Hoeck & Hartung, Inc. (L.A.), *Agency.*
    Ray Patin, Inc. (L.A.), *Producer.*

"DRAGNET?"

1. OPEN ON ANIMATED ECU OF GAS STATION ATTENDANT'S CAP LABELED "BARDAHL." (:02 secs.)

(MUSIC: DRAMATIC)

1A. IRIS IN SPOTLIGHT (IN TV MASK SHAPE) ON CAP LABEL. ZOOM BACK TO MCU. (:06 secs.)

ATTENDANT (O.C.): This story is true.

2. DISSOLVE TO HIGH FS OF GAS STATION AT NIGHT. CAR PULLS IN TRAILING SMOKE CLOUD. (:04 secs.)

(V.O.) It was 10:37 when he drove in. Light blue sedan.

3. CUT TO LOW CU OF GRILLE AND LICENSE PLATE. ZOOM BACK TO FS OF CAR, DRIVER AND ATTENDANT. (:04 secs.)

License number B6394. Bad shape. He barely made it.

4. CUT TO SIDE MS OF CAR HOOD. ATTENDANT ENTERS FRAME, RAISES HOOD, SMOKE ESCAPES. FOUR PAIR OF EYES POP ON UNDER HOOD IN SYNC. (:09 secs.)

I took one look. It was our old friends Dirty Sludge, Sticky Valve, Gummy Ring, Blackie Carbon. Only one thing to do.

5. CUT TO FS ATTENDANT ON PHONE. (:02 secs.)

I called for Bardahl.

5A. POP ON "BARDAHL," WEARING BLACK HAT AND RAINCOAT. (:02 secs.)

10:43: Bardahl arrived.

6. CUT TO MS OF BARDAHL. HE OPENS RAINCOAT, REVEALING TWO BARDAHL CANS STRAPPED TO HIS CHEST. HE TAKES ONE OUT. (:02 secs.)

Went right to work.

7. CUT TO CU OF MOTOR AS BARDAHL'S HAND ENTERS FRAME WITH CAN AND POURS IT. (:02 secs.)

(MUSIC: DRAMATIC)
Poured one quart of Bardahl in the crankcase.

8. DISSOLVE TO ECU OF CARBURETOR AS HAND POURS IN PINT CAN OF BARDAHL. (:03 secs.)

Fed one pint of Bardahl through the carburetor intake.

9. DISSOLVE TO ECU OF GAS TANK   Added four ounces of Bardahl Top Oil to
    FILLER PIPE. HAND POURS IN   the gas tank.
    CAN. (:03 secs.)

10. CUT TO FS OF CAR WITH HAPPY   At 10:45 we had 'em on the run.
    DRIVER, ATTENDANT AND
    BARDAHL. (:03 secs.)

11. CUT TO HIGH FS OF GAS STATION   Bardahl. Done it again.
    AS CAR PULLS AWAY FROM
    ATTENDANT AND BARDAHL. (:03
    secs.)

12. CUT TO CU OF ATTENDANT AND   AT 10:47, Bardahl turned to me and said:
    BARDAHL. TILT DOWN TO CU OF   BARDAHL (O.C.): New customer?
    SPOTLIT BARDAHL CAN IN   ATTENDANT (O.C.): Yeah.
    ATTENDANT'S HAND. ANOTHER   BARDAHL: He'll be back.
    HAND WITH HUGE RUBBER   (MUSIC: UP TO CLIMAX)
    STAMP ENTERS FRAME TO STAMP
    BOXED TITLE: "SOLD AT
    BETTER/GAS STATIONS,
    GARAGES,/NEW CAR DEALERS."
    (:15 secs.)

* * *

Trading directly off the unparalleled popularity of Jack Webb's early television detective series *Dragnet,* the Bardahl commercials (of which this was the first) made an immediate and deep impression on American viewers. The similarity between this (nicely impressionist) cartoon treatment and the live-action *Dragnet* program was close enough to be good, spoofing fun; not too close to be actionable.

The actors exchanged lines in the laconic style of Jack Webb and Ben Alexander; the time of each event was stated precisely in the manner of a L.A. police report; the private eye Bardahl was the very image of a private eye; and William Bates even took *Dragnet's* G-A-A#-G signature chord and modified it ever so slightly to his own musical devices.

At the end of the commercial, just in case anyone missed the point, a huge cartoon hand comes in with a rubber stamp (!), a direct imitation of *Dragnet's* "MARK IV" hammer-and-anvil signoff. And black-clad Mr. Bardahl, inscrutable as ever, is ready for some other heroic tune-up job.

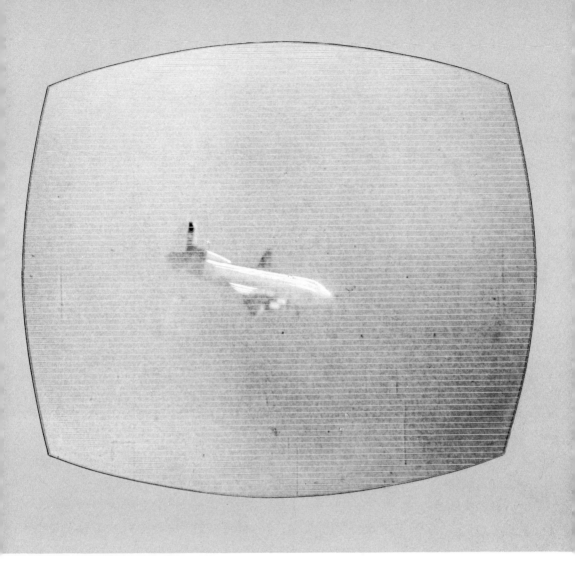

Scene 21   "Plane in Fog"

DETAILS

Live action color film. 187 seconds. 439 words. Air date 1957.
General Motors Corporation (United Motors System), Delco-Remy Division,
Advertiser.
Campbell-Ewald Co., Inc. (Detroit), *Agency.*
VanPraag Productions, Inc., *Producer.*

CREDITS

Art Ross, Edmund Birnbeyer, *Creative.*
Art Ross, Bruce Anderson, William VanPraag, Fred Porrett, Oscar Canstein,
Production.

"PLANE IN FOG"

1. FADE AERIAL LS OF C-124 OVER ALASKAN GLACIER IN CLEAR WEATHER. (:07 secs.)

    (SOUND: PLANE MOTORS)
    ANNOUNCER (V.O.): This is a C-124, the largest transport plane in the Air Force.

2. CUT TO AERIAL LS OF GLACIER. (:04 secs.)

    It's no picnic, flying a payload over country like this.

3. CU TO AERIAL LS OF SNOW-CAPPED MOUNTAIN. (:05 secs.)

    When ice-fog moves in over these mountains, then you're heading for trouble.

4. CUT TO GROUND FS OF AIR FORCE RADAR INSTALLATION. (:04 secs.)

    Enter "G.C.A." . . . Ground Control Approach—

5. CUT TO CU OF SIGN ON BUILD-ING: "1931st AACS SQ./GCA SITE/AUTHORIZED PERSONNEL ONLY." (:01 sec.)

    —the eyes of the Air Force—

6. CUT TO INTERIOR FS OF RADAR EQUIPMENT ROOM WITH FIVE OPERATORS. (:04 secs.)

    (SOUND: RADAR BLEEPS) —
    —guiding planes to safety in bad-weather situations.

7. CUT TO MS OF EMERGENCY POWER GENERATOR WITH "DELCO" BATTERY VISIBLE. (:02 secs.)

    Every precaution is taken—

8. CUT TO CU OF DELCO BATTERY. (:03 secs.)

    —including an emergency standby generator.

9. CUT TO MS OF THREE GROUND CREWMEN SILHOUTTED IN AIRFIELD DOORWAY, WATCHING FOG DRIFTING OVER PLANES. (:04 secs.)

    Uh-uh. Ice-fog's really socking in now.

10. CUT BACK TO AERIAL MS OF C-124 OVER FOGGY MOUNTAINS. (:04 secs.)

    (SOUND: PLANE MOTORS)
    RADAR OPERATOR (V.O.): Five one zero five four. I have you in radar contact.

11. CUT TO CU OF C-124 PILOT'S FACE, LISTENING ON HEADSET. (:01 sec.)

    (SOUND: PLANE MOTORS)
    Ceiling is zero.

12. CUT TO CU OF CO-PILOT'S FACE, LISTENING ON HEADSET. (:01 sec.)

Visibility—

13. CUT TO MS OF PLANE'S RADIO OPERATOR AT EQUIPMENT. (:01 sec.)

—one-sixteenth of a mile, with—

14. CUT TO AERIAL FS OF FOG-SHROUDED MOUNTAINS. (:04 secs.)

—ice-fog. Over.
PILOT (V.O.): Roger. Understand the weather. The ice-fog up here—

15. CUT TO GROUND MS OF FOG-SHROUDED REVOLVING RADAR ANTENNA. (:02 secs.)

—is pretty bad. Let's make it good the first time. Over.

16. CUT BACK TO (SCENE 6) RADAR ROOM. (:03 secs.)

(SOUND: RADAR BLEEPS)
OPERATOR (O.C.): Perform your final cockpit check. Your gear down and locked.

17. CUT BACK TO AERIAL FS OF C-124 AS WHEELS DROP. (:06 secs.)

(SOUND: PLANE MOTORS)
PILOT (V.O.): Roger. Cockpit check. Gear down and locked. Over.

18. CUT BACK TO MS OF RADAR ROOM WITH TWO OPERATORS AND THEIR SCOPES. (:03 secs.)

(SOUND: RADAR BLEEPS)
OPERATOR (O.C.): Roger, five one zero five four. Your pilot controller.

19. CUT BACK TO (SCENE 17) AERIAL FS OF PLANE AS IT STARTS DROPPING INTO FOG. (:06 secs.)

(SOUND: PLANE MOTORS)
ANNOUNCER (V.O.): This what the boys in the Arctic call a "hairy" situation. Our C-124 is—

20. CUT BACK TO (SCENE 11) PILOT'S FACE. (:03 secs.)

—flying totally blind through a treacherous—

21. CUT TO AERIAL LS OF DRIFTING FOG, PLANE HARDLY VISIBLE. (:04 secs.)

—ice-fogged mountain range, completely dependent on G.C.A.—

22. CUT BACK TO (SCENE 18) TWO RADAR OPERATORS. (:01 sec.)

(SOUND: RADAR BLEEPS)
—for its safe landing.

23. CUT TO REVERSE ANGLE ON SINGLE OPERATOR TALKING ON HEADSET. (:01 sec.)

OPERATOR (O.C.): Roger. Your heading is—

24. CUT TO CU OF RADAR SCOPE. (:01 sec.)

OPERATOR (V.O.): —two three five, You're correcting over the—

25. CUT BACK TO (SCENE 21) PLANE IN FOG. (:04 secs.)

(SOUND: PLANE MOTORS)
—on-course last leg. Your heading is—

26. CUT BACK TO (SCENE 15) RADAR   —two three five.
    ANTENNA. (:02 secs.)

27. CUT BACK TO (SCENE 23) SECOND   OPERATOR (O.C.): Now right three
    OPERATOR JOINING THE FIRST.   degrees. Over.
    (:02 secs.)

27A. ROOM LIGHTS BEHIND THEM   (SOUND: EMERGENCY GONG)
    SUDDENLY DIM AND GO OUT.
    (:01 sec.)

28. CUT BACK TO (SCENE 26) RADAR   ANNOUNCER (V.O.): Stand by!
    ANTENNA, WHICH HAS STOPPED   Power failure!
    REVOLVING. (:02 secs.)

29. CUT BACK TO (SCENE 7) AS   All contact with plane lost!
    TECHNICIAN HASTILY OPENS   A switch is turned on. The standby
    EMERGENCY GENERATOR PANEL   emergency—
    AND THROWS SWITCHES. (:06
    secs.)

30. CUT TO CU OF HANDS ON SWITCH   —generator, dependent on—
    PANEL. (:01 sec.)

31. CUT BACK TO (SCENE 8) DELCO   (SOUND: GONG STOPS)
    BATTERY. (:03 secs.)   —battery power, springs into instant action.

32. CUT BACK TO (SCENE 28) RADAR   The life-saving signal (SOUND: RADAR
    ANTENNA. IT BEGINS TO   BLEEPS) is resumed.
    REVOLVE AGAIN. (:03 secs.)

33. CUT BACK TO (SCENE 18) AS
    SECOND RADAR OPERATOR
    ROLLS HIS CHAIR AWAY. (:03
    secs.)

34. CUT BACK TO (SCENE 20) PILOT'S   (SOUND: PLANE MOTORS)
    FACE. (:01 sec.)   OPERATOR (V.O.): Five miles east of the
                                          field.

35. CUT BACK TO (SCENE 12)   Continue heading two four zero at two
    CO-PILOT SMILING. (:02 secs.)   thousand. Over.

36. CUT TO AERIAL FS OF FOG-   PILOT (V.O.) Roger. Nice approach. Going
    SHROUDED RIDGE. (:05 secs.)   to tower frequency.

37. CUT TO ECU OF OPERATOR'S   (SOUND: RADAR BLEEPS)
    HANDS ON SCOPE KNOBS. (:02   OPERATOR (V.O.): The heading is two
    secs.)   three—

38. CUT BACK TO (SCENE 16) FS OF   —eight. You're now over touchdown point.
    RADAR ROOM. (:02 secs.)

39. CUT TO LS VIEW OF FOG-
SHROUDED RUNWAY THROUGH
C-124's WINDSHIELD. (:04 secs.)

(SOUND: PLANE MOTORS)
Take over and complete your landing.
PILOT (V.O.): Roger.

40. CUT TO REVERSE GROUND FS
AND PAN LEFT AS PLANE
TOUCHES DOWN. (:08 secs.)

ANNOUNCER (V.O.) We're home.
(SOUND: TIRE SKID) Another Air Force
mission accomplished. No sweat, thanks to
G.C.A.

41. SOFT-EDGE BOX WIPE OUT TO
PAN ECU OF DELCO BATTERY ON
PASSING AIRFIELD TRACTOR.
(:06 secs.)

(SOUND: TRACTOR MOTOR) Once the
C-124 is safely down, the ground crew rolls
out to greet her.

42. CUT TO FS OF PLANE AS PAIR OF
TRACTORS APPROACHES. (:02
secs.)

Tractors, tow-trucks, forklifts—

43. CUT TO REVERSE HIGH ANGLE
MS OF TRACTORS APPROACHING
PLANE. (:02 secs.)

—and tankers, all dependent on battery
power—

44. CUT TO A DIFFERENT FS OF
PLANE AS ADDITIONAL
TRACTOR AND TWO TRUCKS
APPROACH. (:04 secs.)

—gather around the giant bird, to unload
and service her.

45. CUT TO MS OF FORKLIFT DRIVER
CHARGING A DELCO BATTERY
FROM A CAN OF FLUID ON HOOD.
(:03 secs.)

Fresh power, dependable power—

46. CUT TO CU OF CHARGING OPERA-
TION. (:05 secs.)

—is needed here. Absolutely fresh power,
like the Delco Dry Charge Battery.

47. CUT TO ECU AS DRIVER RECAPS
BATTERY. (:02 secs.)

None of its vital power can waste away—

48. CUT BACK TO (SCENE 46) DRIVER
REMOVING FLUID CAN FROM
HOOD. (:02 secs.)

—because this battery comes bone-dry.

49. CUT BACK TO WIDER SHOT
(SCENE 45) AS DRIVER PUTS CAN
DOWN OUT OF FRAME. (:03 secs.)

Only when fluid is added does a—

50. CUT BACK TO (SCENE 47)
DRIVER'S HAND SWINGING
BATTERY BACK INTO FORKLIFT
MOTOR AND SHUTTING PANEL.
(:05 secs.)

—Delco Dry Charge Battery come to life,
ready for fast starts, (SOUND: PANEL
LATCHING) dependable performance—

51. CUT BACK TO (SCENE 45) DRIVER
     CLIMBING INTO FORKLIFT,
     STARTING MOTOR AND DRIVING
     TOWARDS C-124. (:10 secs.)

—anywhere, under all conditions. When it's
time to replace, make sure you get
(SOUND: FORKLIFT MOTOR STARTS)
all the power you pay for. Power that can't
get old before it's sold.

52. CUT TO CU OF ANOTHER DELCO
     BATTERY ON WORK DOLLY, AS
     FORKLIFT MOVES AWAY IN
     BACKGROUND. (:07 secs.)

Delco Dry Charge Battery, made by the
Delco-Remy Division of General Motors.
Delco—

52A. POP ON SUPERIMPOSED "GM-
     UMS" LICENSE PLATE IN TOP
     FRAME. (:05 secs.)

—available through the United Motors
System and its independent dealers and
distributors.

52B. SOFT-EDGE BOX WIPE TO BLACK.
     (:05 secs.)

* * *

This handsomely photographed "slice-of-life" film commercial with its 52 dramatic intercuts (none more than ten seconds long) offers a perfect latter-day expression of the famous "chase" technique—pioneered in Great Britain by James Williamson in his 1901 *Attack on a China Mission* (two years before Edwin S. Porter's *The Great Train Robbery*).

Rhythmic cutting carries the viewer back and forth between an Air Force plane in an Alaskan ice-fog, and its equally fogbound radar ground control. At a crucial moment during the plane's approach, ground power fails—but emergency power equipment, powered by Delco Batteries, comes alive, and everyone lands safely. Additional Delco equipment is rushed out to service the aircraft. Ta-da!

By any standard—either those of a decade ago when this commercial was produced for insertion in the middle of some forgotten TV spectacular, or of today—this spot is a blockbuster. It was filmed in color not for TV transmission, but probably with an eye on a GM stockholders' meeting. Produced by Van Praag Productions, specialists in the involved logistics of automotive commercial production, "Plane in Fog" required total USAF cooperation—including the otherwise exorbitant transportation cost to Alaska for crew and equipment, which you and I paid for.

This commercial was *post-tracked*—the Alaskan filming was made, blessedly, with silent camera equipment (far easier to handle under difficult location conditions) and filtered voices and effects were added later. Contrapuntal use of radar and plane sounds heightens the realism, and the announcer—wonderful old warhorse Nelson Case—manages his usual blend of high drama and serious sell to convince America's motorists that the only battery product they should ever consider is Delco. (Of the fourteen cast members in "Plane in Fog," Mr. Case was the only one eligible for union residual payments. The rest—GI's—just got their picture on 1957 television.)

Gasoline

There is not too much to say on TV about any branded gasoline,* except that it costs less than the competition (which it never does for very long), or that it promises some special ingredient to make cars run (1) smoother, (2) better, (3) longer, (4) further, (5) cleaner, or (6) all five. The only other sales alternative is to offer some completely externalized inducement to buy. It is not surprising, therefore, that gasoline companies have vacillated historically between "magic ingredients," giveaway prize campaigns, or glassware—as they pump half a billion dollars out of the American Motorist's pocket each *week*.

On rare occasions, the consumer rebels—in unpredictable ways:

The author was for several years Senior Producer in charge of the Shell "Platformate" TV campaign at Ogilvy & Mather—until unexpected public outcries (such as Dick Gregory's in *Playboy:* "Why the white cars always win and the black ones lose?") wrote sudden "finis" to a creative idea on which the client had spent many millions of dollars.**

O tempora! O mores!

---

* According to industry legend, every branded gas pump along the bridge-like, hundred-mile Key West Overseas Highway is serviced once a week from the same huge (and unmarked) gasoline tanker truck.

** Although *Playboy* replied, "It is clear that at least one of the black cars is Jewish, and running on chicken soup."

257

Scene 2   "Dry Bones"

DETAILS

   Black-and-white animated film. 60 seconds. 129 words. Air date 1954.
   Speedway Petroleum Corp., *Advertiser.*
   W. B. Doner & Co., Inc. (Detroit), *Agency.*
   Storyboard Films, Inc., *Producer.*

CREDITS

   John Hubley, *Creative.*
   John Hubley, Arnold Gillespie, *Production.*

"DRY BONES"

1. OPEN ON ANIMATED FS OF ABSTRACT HEAD SHAPE AGAINST WHITE DOT-STUDDED BLACK BACKGROUND (:08 secs.)

(MUSIC: INTRODUCTION)
CHORUS (V.O.): (SINGS)
It's the great new gas called "Powerfuel",
Speedway-79 Powerfuel,

1A. FEATURES AND CAR PARTS FLY INTO FRAME AND SHAPE BECOME DRIVER ON CAR CHASSIS. CAR DRIVES OFF RIGHT FRAME. (:05 secs.)

The "extra" gas you can't surpass,
Speedway Powerfuel.

2. CUT TO PANNING MS OF RUNNING CHASSIS WITH DRIVER. CAR PARTS POP ON OR DROP INTO PLACE AS THEY ARE DESCRIBED IN LYRIC. (:09 secs.)

BASS SOLO (V.O.):
The gas tank connecta to the gas line,
The gas line connecta to the fuel pump,
The fuel pump connecta to the
    carburetor,
And you get more power from—

2A. PAN LEFT AS CAR EXHAUST FORMS TITLE: "POWERFUL" AND THEN EXPLODES. (:01 sec.)

—Powerfuel.

3. CUT TO PANNING CU OF CARBU-RETOR. OTHER PARTS POP ON OR DROP IN AS THEY ARE DESCRIBED IN LYRIC. (:07 secs.)

CHORUS: The carburetor connecta to the
    intake valves,
The valves are connecta to the cylinder
    head,
The cylinder head is connecta to the
    cylinders,

3A. ODOMETER NUMBERS FLASH OVER CYLINDERS. (:01½ secs.)

And you get more mileage from—

3B. TITLE: "POWER/FUEL" REPLACES ODOMETER NUMBERS. (:01 sec.)

—Powerfuel.

4. CUT BACK TO PANNING FS OF RUNNING CHASSIS. POP ON PARTS AS THEY ARE DESCRIBED IN LYRIC. (:07 secs.)

The cylinders connecta to the pistons,
The pistons connecta to the spark plugs,
The spark plugs connecta with the—

4A. PANNING STOPS AS CHASSIS DISAPPEARS BEHIND GAS PUMP LABELED "SPEEDWAY/79/MP." SYMBOLIC GAS DRAINS OUT OF PUMP. (:01½ secs.)

—gasoline,
And you run much smoother—

4B. CHASSIS REAPPEARS FROM BEHIND PUMP, CIRCLES, AND RUNS OFF OUT OF RIGHT FRAME. (:02 secs.)	—on Powerfuel—
5. CUT TO PANNING FS OF RUNNING CHASSIS, DRIVER AT WHEEL. (:01 sec.)	—Speedway 79.
5A. CHILD DROPS ONTO CHASSIS BEHIND DRIVER AND BLOWS UP BALLOON LABELED "HIGHER/ OCTANE." (:02 secs.)	Powerful, higher octane—
5B. PARENTS DROP ONTO CHASSIS BEHIND CHILD. (:03½ secs.)	—Powerfuel, Everybody's raving about Powerfuel,
5C. CHASSIS AND PASSENGERS DETACH FROM OVAL WHEELS AND MOVE OUT OF RIGHT FRAME. WHEELS STOP TURNING; ONE LABELED "SPEEDWAY," THE OTHER "79." (:02 secs.)	Speedway 79.
5D. OVALS MERGE IN CENTER FRAME TO FORM "SPEEDWAY 79" LOGO. DOLLY IN SLOWLY TO MS OF LOGO. (:02½ secs.)	BASS SOLO: So get yourself connected with Speedway . . .
5E. HEADS OF PASSENGERS AND ETHYL CORPORATION LOGO DROP INTO SPEEDWAY LOGO LIKE LOLLYPOP HEADS ON STICKS. (:04 secs.)	CHORUS: Speedway 79!
5F. PASSENGER HEADS DISSOLVE AWAY. ETHYL LOGO REMAINS. (:02 secs.)	(MUSIC: ASCENDING NOTE)

* * *

John Hubley, working under the Storyboard shingle, was commissioned by W. B. Doner to prepare an animated 60-second spot heralding Speedway's new high-test gasoline product.

Against a wonderfully rhythmic musical track by Jack Elliott—itself based on the traditional black spiritual "Dry Bones"—Hubley played with those loose, amorphous little forms that have since become his animation trademark. It is an exercise in track-related graphics, as valid a gasoline-selling message today as the day it was made.

It is indeed art.

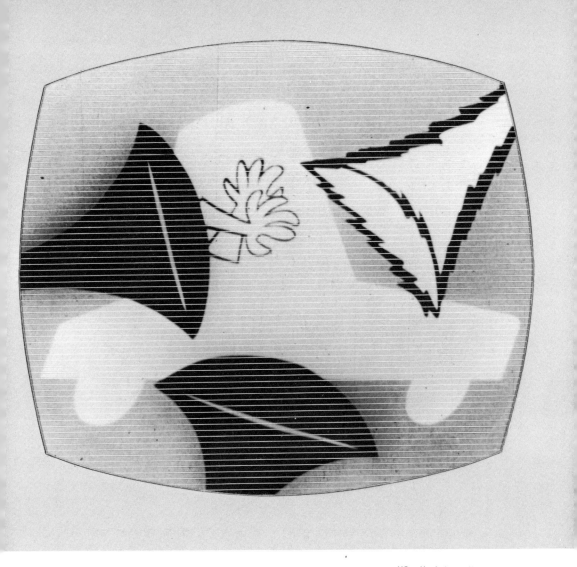

Scene 1E   *"Stalled Auto"*

DETAILS

      Black-and-white animated film. 60 seconds. 21 words. Air date 1957.
      Imperial Esso, Ltd., *Advertiser.*
      MacLaren Advertising, Ltd. (Toronto), *Agency.*
      Shamus Culhane, Inc., *Producer.*

CREDITS
      George Elliot, Shamus Culhane, *Creative.*
      Shamus Culhane, William Hurtz, *Production.*

"STALLED AUTO"

1. OPEN ON AUTOMOBILE STEER-
ING WHEEL IN CENTER FRAME.
(:01 sec.)

(<u>SOUND</u>: AUTOMOBILE MOTOR)

1A. PAIR OF HANDS ENTER FRAME
LEFT-RIGHT AND GRASPS WHEEL.
(:01 sec.)

1B. FADE IN 25 HORIZONTAL
JIGGLING LINES MOVING RIGHT-
LEFT BEHIND HANDS AND WHEEL,
ESTABLISHING SILHOUETTE OF
AUTOMOBILE. (:04 secs.)

1C. LINES STOP JIGGLING. (:01 sec.)

(<u>SOUND</u>: MOTOR STOPS)

1D. LINES VIBRATE AND BREAK UP
INTO DASHES. (:01 sec.)

(<u>SOUND</u>: MOTOR GRINDS AND
STALLS)

1E. FADE IN VIBRATING HORN
ABSTRACTION IN LEFT FRAME.
HANDS LEAP OFF STEERING
WHEEL. (:01 sec.)

(<u>SOUND</u>: MANY DISCORDANT HORNS)

1F. OTHER HORNS ENTER FRAME.
GRAY BACKGROUND REPLACES
DASHED LINES. STEERING WHEEL
DISAPPEARS AND HANDS START
TO PRAY. (:03 secs.)

(<u>SOUND</u>: OTHER DISCORDANT HORNS)

1G. "ESSO EXTRA" LOGO RECTANGLE
COMES BOUNCING INTO LEFT
FRAME. EVERYTHING ELSE
DISAPPEARS. (:02 secs.)

(<u>MUSIC</u>: TEMPLE BLOCK ROLL)

1H. RECTANGLE STOPS AND
VIBRATES. (:02 secs.)

(<u>MUSIC</u>: BASS DRUM, AND CYMBAL
ROLL)

1I. GRAY SQUARE APPEARS BELOW
RECTANGLE, WITH "STOPS"
HAND-LETTERED IN BLACK. (:01
sec.)

(<u>MUSIC</u>: TWO BLOCK NOTES)

1J. "COOL" POPS ON IN WHITE. (:01
sec.)

(<u>MUSIC</u>: TWO BLOCK NOTES)

1K. "WEATHER" POPS ON IN BLACK. (:01 sec.)

(MUSIC: TWO BLOCK NOTES)

1L. "STALLING" POPS ON IN BLACK. (:01 sec.)

(MUSIC: TWO BLOCK NOTES)

1M. GRAY SQUARE TURNS BLACK AND ZOOMS UP TO FILL SCREEN. LETTERING TURNS WHITE. (:01 sec.)

(MUSIC: SNARE DRUM ROLL)

1N. "STOPS" IS UNDERLINED IN WHITE. (:02 secs.)

1O. BACKGROUND TURNS WHITE. LETTERING TURNS BLACK. "COOL" IS UNDERLINED IN BLACK. (:02 secs.)

(MUSIC: 7 BLOCK NOTES)

1P. TONAL VALUES ARE REVERSED AGAIN. "WEATHER" IS UNDER-LINED IN WHITE. (:01 sec.)

(MUSIC: 7 COWBELL NOTES)

1Q. VALUES ARE REVERSED AGAIN AS "COOL" REMAINS WHITE. ITS UNDERLINE TURNS BLACK. (:02 secs.)

(MUSIC: DRUM, BLOCK AND COWBELL ROLL)

2. CUT TO SPINNING ABSTRACTION OF BLACK, GRAY AND WHITE LINES. (:01 sec.)

(MUSIC: CYMBAL CRASH)

3. ABSTRACTION METAMORPHOSES INTO A HEAVY BLACK ARROW POINTING RIGHT. (:01 sec.)

(MUSIC: SNARE DRUM ROLL)

3A. GRAY OVALS SLIDE RIGHT-LEFT THROUGH FRAME BEHIND ARROW. (:03 secs.)

3B. "IMPERIAL ESSO DEALER" LOGO OVAL SLIDES RIGHT-LEFT INTO FRAME, BOUNCING OFF HEAD OF ARROW. (:02 secs.)

(MUSIC: BASS DRUM)

3C. ZOOM LOGO UP TO FILL SCREEN. (:02 secs.)

3D. ZOOM LOGO BACK AGAIN, TO BECOME CAP OF SCRATCHED-IN DEALER ABSTRACTION. (:01 sec.)

(MUSIC: SNARE DRUM, BLOCK AND COWBELL ROLL)

3E. SCRATCH IN GASOLINE PUMP ABSTRACTION. (:02 secs.)

3F. ESSO LOGO RECTANGLE POPS
    ONTO PUMP. DEALER'S HAND
    POINTS TO LOGO. HE TALKS. (:02
    secs.)

DEALER: Fill 'er up with Esso Extra
Gasoline—

3G. LOGO SPINS UP OFF PUMP TO FILL
    FRAME. (:01 sec.)

(MUSIC: DRUM, BLOCK AND COWBELL
ROLL)

3H. REVERSE LOGO TONAL VALUES.
    (:01 sec.)

3I. ZOOM LOGO BACK AND ADD
    HANDLETTERED "STOPS COOL/
    WEATHER/STALLING" UNDER-
    NEATH. (:03 secs.)

—the gasoline which stops cool weather
stalling.

4. CUT TO ABSTRACTION OF BLACK.
    GRAY AND WHITE LINES. (:01 sec.)

(MUSIC: DRUM, BLOCK AND COWBELL
ROLL)

5. ABSTRACTION METAMORPHOSES
    INTO ABSTRACT GASOLINE PUMP.
    (:01 sec.)

5A. ABSTRACT AUTOMOBILE
    GASOLINE TANK SLIDES RIGHT-
    LEFT INTO FRAME. (:05 secs.)

5B. HOSE ON PUMP ANIMATES TO FILL
    TANK. (:02 secs.)

Fill up with Esso Extra and . . . GO!

5C. PUMP SLIDES RIGHT-LEFT OUT OF
    FRAME. (:01 sec.)

(SOUND: AUTOMOBILE MOTOR)

5D. FADE IN DASHED HORIZONTAL
    LINES AGAIN, MOVING RIGHT-
    LEFT, FORMING AUTO
    SILHOUETTE (WITH TIRES, HANDS
    AND STEERING WHEEL) AROUND
    GASOLINE TANK. (:02 secs.)

5E. FADE OFF EVERYTHING BUT THE
    GASOLINE TANK AGAIN. FADE
    JUGGLING LETTERS OF "ESSO
    EXTRA" INTO TANK. (:01 sec.)

(MUSIC: DRUM, BLOCK AND COWBELL
ROLL)

* * *

This busily-choreographed black-and-white animation commercial is an
advertising agency art director's dream—only 21 spoken words. (Three years later,
the advertiser—Imperial Esso of Canada—took the deep plunge with an animation
spot, "Oil Heat Cat," that contains no words at all, only *meows* and *purrs,* and was

awarded first prize in its category at the 1961 TV Commercials Festival, plus other international honors.)

"Stalled Auto" carried forward handsomely the role of pure graphics in television advertising. Its functional combinations of sliding cels and full animation use a syncopated reversal of black, white and shades of gray values. The ear is arrested with strange musical sound combinations of bass and snare drums, cymbals, tuned wooden temple blocks and cowbells.

Although the Canadian advertising agency creating "Stalled Auto" bears a similar name to that country's foremost film abstractionist—McLaren—the spot was actually produced in New York, by Shamus Culhane. Mr. Culhane's other TV commercial work in the late '40's and early '50's included the two earlier "Classics" in animation, the Ajax pixies and the sexy Muriel cigar. He may be even better remembered for those designs than for his 1956 screen-credit tailpiece to Mike Todd's *Around the World in 80 Days*. In that film, his creative inspiration set a style in motion picture main-titling that is still in vogue.

Scene 1A   "They Oughta' Advertise"

DETAILS

   Black-and-white animated film. 60 seconds. 111 words. Air date 1958.
   Standard Oil of California, Inc., *Advertiser.*
   Batten, Barton, Durstine & Osborn, Inc., *Agency.*
   Elektra Film Productions, Inc., *Producer.*

CREDITS

   Richard Mercer, Jack Goldsmith, *Creative.*
   Rocco Dellarso, Abe Liss, *Production.*

"THEY OUGHTA' ADVERTISE"

1. OPEN ON ANIMATED FS OF HY
    FINN'S LIVING ROOM AS HE
    TUNES TV SET. (:01 sec.)

1A. FINN IGNORES "CHEVRON/
    SUPREME" LOGO APPEARING ON
    TUBE. PAN RIGHT AS HE WALKS
    AWAY. (:01 sec.)

ANNOUNCER (V.O.): When new—

1B. CHEVRON LOGO COMES UP OFF
    PICTURE TUBE IN CLOUD OF
    ANIMATED SPARKLES, FOLLOW-
    ING FINN. (:02 secs.)

(SOUND: FIREWORKS) —Chevron
Supreme Gasoline burst on the scene—

1C. FINN IGNORES CLOUD AND
    DISAPPEARS THROUGH DOOR. (:02
    secs.)

2. SWISH PAN RIGHT TO FS OF FINN
    AT REFRIGERATOR, POURING
    GLASS OF MILK. (:04 secs.)

—the American Motorist greeted it with rare
enthusiasm—

3. CUT TO MS OF FINN AS HE YAWNS
    AND DRINKS MILK. (:05 secs.)

—and exuberance.
FINN (O.C.): YAWNS.
ANNOUNCER (V.O.): He digested each
amazing fact—

4. CUT TO FS OF FRONT STEPS. PAN
    RIGHT AS FINN MOVES DOWN TO
    CAR, IGNORING AIRSHIP IN
    BACKGROUND WITH BLINKING
    "NEW CHEVRON/SUPREME" SIGN.
    (:04 secs.)

—gave his undivided attention to each
communique.

5. CUT TO CU OF FINN IN CAR. (:02
    secs.)

(SOUND: MOTOR STARTS) He learned
that—

5A. PAN RIGHT AND DOLLY OUT AS
    CAR STARTS ROLLING DOWN
    HIGHWAY PAST SERIES OF
    "CHEVRON SUPREME SUPER
    PREMIUM" SIGNS AND BILL-
    BOARDS, WHICH FINN IGNORES,
    CAR PASSES "CALSO/STATION"
    LOGO WITH (LITERAL) GASOLINE
    PUMP. (:07 secs.)

—new Chevron Supreme is a super-premium
fuel that will deliver all the mileage, all the
better performance built into his car.

5B. CAR BUCKS AND STOPS, OUT OF
    GAS. (:01 sec.)

6. SWISH PAN LEFT, BACK TO CALSO   He was drawn irresistibly —
    STATION AND PUMP. (:01 sec.)

6A. FINN ENTERS FROM RIGHT   — to the Calso Station.
    CARRYING GASOLINE CAN. (:02
    secs.)

7. CUT TO CU OF FINN AND PUMP. HE   Without hesitation, he said . . .
    REGISTERS SOME SURPRISE, THEN   FINN (O.C.): Fill 'er up.
    SMILES AND SPEAKS. (:04 secs.)

7A. DOLLY OUT TO FS AS DELIGHTED   (SOUND: PUMP CLANKS AND
    PUMP METAMORPHOSES INTO   GURGLES)
    SPARKLING CLOUD, FILLING   ANNOUNCER (V.O.): And from —
    FINN'S GAS CAN. (:04 secs.)

7B. CLOUD METAMORPHOSES BACK   — that moment on, an invisible bond was
    INTO PUMP AGAIN. DOLLY IN AS   formed between the American Motorist —
    FINN EMBRACES AND KISSES IT.   (SOUND: KISS)
    (:06 secs.)

7C. DOLLY OUT TO FS AS ANIMATED   — and this great super-premium gasoline.
    HEARTS RISE FROM PUMP.   (SOUND: RIPPING)
    "CALSO/STATION" LOGO SLIDES
    BACK INTO UPPER LEFT FRAME
    AS FINN RIPS PUMP OFF BASE AND
    CARRIES IT OUT TO RIGHT. (:03
    secs.)

8. CUT TO FS OF FINN PLACING PUMP   Try Chevron Supreme, a super-octane fuel
    IN REAR SEAT OF HIS CAR. PAN   (SOUND: MOTOR STARTS) for today's
    RIGHT AS HE DRIVES AWAY. (:06   horsepower.
    secs.)

9. CUT TO PANNING CU OF FINN IN   FINN (O.C.): You know, this stuff is great.
    CAR MOVING DOWN HIGHWAY   They oughta' advertise it.
    PAST BACKGROUND OF CHEVRON
    SIGNS, WHICH HE STILL IGNORES.
    (:03 secs.)

9A. STOP PAN AS CAR SLIDES OUT
    PAST MS BILLBOARD: "CHEVRON/
    SUPREME/GASOLINE/CALSO/
    STATIONS." DOLLY OUT TO FS OF
    BILLBOARD. (:02 secs.)

                            *   *   *

In the late '50's, when Standard Oil of California first began marketing their
gasoline nationwide, it was decided to drop the regional connotation of "Calso
(*Cal*ifornia *S*tandard *O*il)" and introduce a new name (and design), "Chevron."

It was also a period of extreme car fender design, so California Standard's advertising agency, Batten, Barton, Durstine & Osborn, promptly invented the symbolic TV cartoon character "Hy Finn." This jolly and somewhat befuddled motorist, drawn with big nose, flat head, wide smile, straw hat and bow tie, captured all the sweet confusion of the Chevron name change.

Hy's original tongue-in-cheek indifference, believably conveyed by the famous voice of Paul Ford, caught the pleased attention of television viewers throughout the expanding Chevron market area. Hy soon became the symbol for all California Standard gasoline advertising, in print as well as TV.

The stark simplicity of Elektra Productions' black-and-white animation (styled by the late Abe Liss) is typical of the "UPA brand" of motion picture cartooning pioneered in the '50's by Stephen Bosustow. This semi-abstract technique rapidly grabbed the imagination—and pens—of animators on both Coasts, mainly because it lent itself so admirably to the gray-scale problems of television, and TV's somewhat dull light source.

This original Hy Finn "announcement" commercial is enlivened by the contrastingly portentious tones of the late Westbrook Van Voorhis, at one time the exclusive "voice" of the *March of Time*.

Consumer Services

It is small surprise that this category, offering the commercial creator—be he art director, copywriter or agency producer—freest rein to imagination, should have slipped so early into *animation* ... where all things are possible and the reality of the television picture helps make even the wildest idea somewhat believable.

Banks and utilities soon discovered the P.R. benefits of making their representative television "customer" as non-ethnic and non-identifiable as possible. So there he and she are, going their animated way through all kinds of exaggerated adventures in the search for higher savings interest rates, more easily obtainable mortgages, and ever more efficient phone and power service.

The fact that—almost two decades later—mortgages are practically unobtainable and phones hardly work has nothing to do with television.

Scene 1A   "Instant Money"

DETAILS

    Black-and-white animated film. 20 seconds. 33 words. Air date 1955.
    Bank of America, *Advertiser.*
    Johnson and Lewis, Inc. (San Francisco), *Agency.*
    Storyboard Films, Inc. (L.A.), *Producer.*

CREDIT

    John Hubley, *Creative-Production.*

"INSTANT MONEY"

1. OPEN ON PANNING FS OF ANIMATED TREMBLING MAN WALKING THROUGH BANK LOBBY. (:08 secs.)

(MUSIC: XYLOPHONE)
ANNOUNCER (V.O.): Do you have money jitters?

1A. HE STOPS AT COUNTER AND SILENTLY GESTURES TO BANKER BEHIND IT. BANKER TURNS TO SHELF WITH MONEY JARS LABELED WITH "$'s" AND SIGN: "INSTANT MONEY". ZOOM TO SHELF AS HE REMOVES JAR, ZOOM BACK AS HE POURS IT INTO COFFEE CUP AND HANDS IT TO MAN. (:04 secs.)

Ask the obliging Bank of America for a jar of soothing "instant money" . . . m-o-n-e-y–

1B. PAN LEFT TO MAN. "$" RISES IN STEAM FROM CUP. MAN DRINKS, STOPS TREMBLING, JUMPS WITH DELIGHT. (:04 secs.)

–in the form of a convenient personal loan.
(SOUND: MAN GULPING)
(MUSIC: GUITAR CHORUS)

2. CUT TO MS JAR SHELF. "$" CIRCLE ZOOMS OFF A JAR TO CENTER FRAME, METAMORPHOSES INTO BANK OF AMERICA "Timeplan" SEAL. (:04 secs.)

Available now at Bank of America.
(MUSIC: GUITAR STING)

* * *

In the era before the "creative types" in advertising agencies had learned enough to start telling their suppliers how to do it all, Storyboard Productions, always innovative with animation, was powerfully innovative with content. Here John Hubley is again among the earliest to spoof—commercials. TV's instant-pick-me-up of a cup of steaming coffee is transformed, through the undisputed magic of animation, into the happiness of a bank loan. This commercial is another example of the post-Disney style that was Hubley's trademark before he came East.

This brief "reminder" advertising was used at station breaks by the Bank of America, who did nicely with it for a long time. This was before young people burned banks in California.

Scene 3D   *"Chalk Talk"*

DETAILS

    Black-and-white animated film. 60 seconds. 179 words. Air date 1955.
    New York Telephone Company, *Advertiser.*
    Batten, Barton, Durstine & Osborn, Inc., *Agency.*
    Elektra Film Productions, Inc., *Producer.*

CREDITS

    Les Collins, Hal Algyer, Larry Berger, *Creative.*
    Abe Liss, *Production.*

"CHALK TALK"

1. OPEN ON BLACK SCREEN WITH WHITE HAND-LETTERED TITLE: "This is the/story of." POP ON DOTS OVER THE "i's." (:03 secs.)	(MUSIC: RHYTHMIC) ANNOUNCER (V.O.): This is the story of—
1A. TILT DOWN AND SCRATCH ON ANIMATED MAN'S FACE IN LEFT FRAME. POP ON TITLE: "Jock" UNDER FACE. (:01½ secs.)	—a man named Jock,
1B. SCRATCH ON WOMAN'S FACE IN RIGHT FRAME. POP ON TITLE: "Mary" UNDER FACE. (:02 secs.)	His loving wife Mary—
1C. TILT DOWN TO MS ALARM CLOCK. IT SPINS AROUND AND FALLS FLAT. (:02½ secs.)	—and their alarm clock. It failed to go off,
1D. POP ON TITLE: "My Word!" IN LEFT FRAME. (:01 sec.)	My word, what a fuss!
1E. TILT DOWN TO JOCK'S FACE. (:01½ secs.)	Poor Jock overslept
1F. POP ON TITLE: "and missed his" IN BOTTOM FRAME. BUS ENTERS AND LEAVES FRAME LEFT TO RIGHT, WIPING TITLE, AS JOCK'S FACE SLIDES OUT TOP FRAME. (:01½ secs.)	And missed his bus.
2. POP ON WHITE TITLE ON BLACK: "But." (:01 sec.)	But—
2A. TILT DOWN TO MARY'S FACE. (:01 sec.)	—Mary was ready, With the—
2B. YELLOW PAGE LOGO SLIDES UP INTO FRAME IN FRONT OF MARY'S FACE. (:01 sec.)	—Yellow Page guide;
2C. SLIDE PHONE UP INTO FRAME NEXT TO MARY'S FACE. (:01 sec.)	Called a cab,

2D. POP ON TITLE: "sent him off" IN TOP FRAME. CAB ENTERS AND LEAVES FRAME LEFT TO RIGHT, WIPING TITLE. MARY'S FACE AND PHONE SLIDE UP OUT OF FRAME, LEAVING YELLOW PAGE LOGO. (:02 secs.)	Sent him off on his ride.
3. TILT UP TO MARY'S FACE AGAIN. YELLOW PAGE LOGO SLIDES DOWN INTO FRAME. (:02 secs.)	Then she decided To find where to buy
3A. POP ON VARIOUS PRODUCT SYMBOLS IN LOWER FRAME. (:03 secs.)	Some brand-name products She wanted to try,
3B. MARY'S HAT SLIDES ACROSS RIGHT TO LEFT IN TOP FRAME. (:02 secs.)	She found neighborhood dealers In the Yellow Page Book,
3C. HAT PICKS UP MARY'S FACE EN ROUTE AND SLIDES OUT LEFT FRAME WITH IT. (:01 sec.)	And went on her way,
3D. POP ON TITLE BOTTOM FRAME: "that's all it took." (:02 secs.)	That's all it took.
4. POP OFF YELLOW PAGE LOGO. DISSOLVE TITLE INTO NEW TITLE: "down at the office" (:02 secs.)	Down at the office,
4A. TILT DOWN TO JOCK'S FACE. "TYPE OUT" TITLE: "G-o-o-d-b-y-e." POP ON 12 SYMBOLIC TYPEWRITER KEYS. SLIDE TITLE OUT LEFT FRAME. (:04 secs.)	To Jock's dismay, He saw that his typist Was leaving that day
4B. POP ON TITLE IN RIGHT FRAME IN DASHED BALLOON: "employment/ agency." POP OFF TITLE. BALLOON SWINGS INTO DASHED QUESTION MARK. (:05 secs.)	An employment agency He'd used before (But forgotten the name of)
4C. MOVE UP 12 TINY GIRLS' FACES TO REPLACE TYPEWRITER KEYS. (:01 sec.)	Had girls galore.
4D. SLIDE GIRLS' FACES UP OUT OF FRAME. (:02 secs.)	So to find out the name, Jock took a fast look
4E. SLIDE UP YELLOW PAGE LOGO NEXT TO JOCK'S FACE. (:03 secs.)	In the time-saving Classified Telephone Book.

4F. SLIDE JOCK'S FACE OUT OF TOP
    FRAME. A DASHED LINE FORMS A
    HOUSE OUTLINE AROUND
    YELLOW PAGE LOGO. MAID'S
    FACE SLIDES PARTIALLY OUT
    FROM BEHIND LOGO. TILT DOWN
    TO LOSE ENTIRE SCENE. (:04 secs.)

Meanwhile, back at the ranchhouse,
The maid had looked in the Classified,
And made a date to have the clock made to
ring.

5. POP ON CLOCK. SLIDE TITLE UP
    INTO FRAME AND OUT THE TOP:
    "you/be/smart/too." (:01 sec.)

You be smart, too.

5A. "oo" OF "too" REMAINS IN FRAME,
    AS EYES. SLIDE UP YELLOW PAGE
    LOGO. (:04 secs.)

If you're looking for something,
Here's what to do,
Use the Yellow Pages!

5B. SLIDE UP TITLE: "The First Place To
    Look/ . . . For Anything" INTO
    BOTTOM FRAME. (:03 secs.)

The first place to look for anything!

5C. POP ON TELEPHONE CENTER
    FRAME. (:02 secs.)

(MUSIC: PLAYOFF)

* * *

One of the favorite telephone company creative advertising techniques during
the 1920's and '30's—for some unknown reason—was the *rebus*. There may have
been some valid connection between that ancient communication form and the
supplied visual imagery of a telephone conversation. Perhaps a memory of those
phone company *rebuses* crossed the minds of the agency and production company
when they first sat down to plan this simple, fast-moving commercial.

The polarity has been reversed on the art; it was all drawn with brush and
India ink on rough-textured paper, and then produced as a white-on-black negative,
giving the effect of chalk sketches on a huge blackboard. The close-up camera gives
the appearance of moving all around the blackboard, picking out the separate
illustrative images to the beat of Jack Easton's finger-snapping musical score.

As a somewhat matter-of-fact predecessor of the highly mnemonic "Let Your
Fingers Do the Walking . . . ," it was highly effective.

TOTAL U.S. TV ADVERTISING EXPENDITURES, 1958

(Source: *BAR Reports*)

	Total TV	Spot	Network
AGRICULTURE	$ 1,378,154	$ 1,350,000	$ 28,154
Feeds, Meals	774, 154	746,000	28,154
Miscellaneous	604,000	604,000	–
ALE, BEER & WINE	50,502,987	44,214,000	6,288,987
Beer & Ale	46,172,656	40,299,000	5,873,656
Wine	4,330,331	3,915,000	415,331
AMUSEMENTS, ENTERTAINMENT	771,616	559,000	212,616
AUTOMOTIVE	58,840,855	7,376,000	51,464,855
Anti-Freeze	1,170,251	112,000	1,058,251
Batteries	884,984	131,000	753,984
Cars	46,119,575	4,134,000	41,985,575
Tires & Tubes	4,112,266	1,554,000	2,558,266
Trucks & Trailers	2,354,178	132,000	2,222,178
Miscellaneous Accessories & Supplies	2,583,525	1,313,000	1,270,525
Automotive Institutional	1,616,076	–	1,616,076
BUILDING MATERIAL, EQUIPMENT, FIXTURES, PAINTS	17,675,494	2,789,000	14,886,494
Fixtures, Plumbing, Supplies	562,000	562,000	–
Materials	3,623,716	656,000	2,967,716
Paints	2,792,760	1,185,000	1,607,760
Power Tools	275,996	59,000	216,996
Miscellaneous	452,903	327,000	125,903
Industrial Materials Institutional	9,968,119	–	9,968,119
CHEMICALS, INSTITUTIONAL	404,969	–	404,969
CLOTHING, FURNISHINGS, ACCESSORIES	17,215,439	13,241,000	3,974,439
Clothing	13,793,587	11,269,000	2,524,587
Footwear	2,694,327	1,445,000	1,249,327
Hosiery	556,499	497,000	59,499
Miscellaneous	171,026	30,000	141,026
CONFECTIONS & SOFT DRINKS	40,254,724	28,237,000	12,017,724
Confections	21,191,973	12,039,000	9,152,973
Soft Drinks	19,062,751	16,198,000	2,864,751

	Total TV	Spot	Network
CONSUMER SERVICES	26,325,054	14,605,000	11,720,054
Dry Cleaning & Laundries	81,000	81,000	–
Financial	2,298,209	2,181,000	117,209
Insurance	9,717,696	2,773,000	6,944,696
Medical & Dental	151,000	151,000	–
Moving, Hauling, Storage	317,000	317,000	–
Public Utilities	9,838,706	7,099,000	2,739,706
Religious, Political, Unions	2,302,089	1,224,000	1,078,089
Schools & Colleges	135,000	135,000	–
Miscellaneous Services	1,484,354	644,000	840,354
COSMETICS & TOILETRIES	126,107,799	46,749,000	79,358,799
Cosmetics	14,291,147	8,133,000	6,158,147
Deodorants	10,393,933	3,426,000	6,967,933
Depilatories	365,560	295,000	70,560
Hair Tonics & Shampoos	25,099,209	8,674,000	16,425,209
Hand & Face Creams, Lotions	6,634,264	2,813,000	3,821,264
Home Permanents & Coloring	19,399,683	5,890,000	13,509,683
Perfumes, Toilet Waters, etc.	2,191,874	1,704,000	487,874
Razors, Blades	10,523,583	1,904,000	8,619,583
Shaving Creams, Lotions, etc.	7,397,084	1,694,000	5,703,084
Toilet Soaps	26,257,410	10,744,000	15,513,410
Miscellaneous	3,554,052	1,472,000	2,082,052
DENTAL PRODUCTS	34,330,671	14,467,000	19,863,671
Dentifrices	29,026,972	11,132,000	17,894,972
Mouth Washes	3,631,484	2,455,000	1,176,484
Miscellaneous	1,672,215	880,000	792,215
DRUG PRODUCTS	98,224,639	44,626,000	53,598,639
Cold Remedies	20,347,749	12,863,000	7,484,749
Headache Remedies	28,592,976	7,792,000	20,800,976
Indigestion Remedies	14,925,100	8,988,000	5,937,100
Laxatives	8,510,764	3,082,000	5,428,764
Vitamins	8,654,652	2,825,000	5,829,652
Weight Aids	2,199,936	1,917,000	282,936
Miscellaneous Drug Products	14,115,792	6,285,000	7,830,792
Drug Stores	877,670	874,000	3,670
FOOD & GROCERY PRODUCTS	243,515,420	135,687,000	107,828,420
Baked Goods	30,600,235	26,469,000	4,131,235
Cereals	38,943,194	11,552,000	27,391,194
Coffee, Tea & Food Drinks	49,040,909	32,140,000	16,900,909
Condiments, Sauces, Appetizers	9,521,787	5,515,000	4,006,787
Dairy Products	19,639,043	7,853,000	11,786,043
Desserts	6,646,848	2,023,000	4,623,848
Dry Foods, (Flour, Mixes, Rice, etc.)	20,544,486	8,314,000	12,230,486
Fruits & Vegetables, Juices	17,818,420	9,429,000	8,389,420
Macaroni, Noodles, Chili, etc.	2,984,184	1,934,000	1,050,184
Margarine, Shortenings	12,691,659	6,673,000	6,018,659
Meat, Poultry & Fish	9,973,214	6,366,000	3,607,214
Soups	4,107,958	461,000	3,646,958
Miscellaneous Foods	10,040,510	6,420,000	3,620,510
Miscellaneous Frozen Foods	1,878,973	1,454,000	424,973
Food Stores	9,084,000	9,084,000	–
GARDEN SUPPLIES & EQUIPMENT	880,638	661,000	219,638

	Total TV	Spot	Network
GASOLINE & LUBRICANTS	27,979,209	24,479,000	3,500,209
Gasoline & Oil	26,911,209	23,411,000	3,500,209
Oil Additives	858,000	858,000	–
Miscellaneous	210,000	210,000	–
HOTELS, RESORTS, RESTAURANTS	521,705	423,000	98,705
HOUSEHOLD CLEANERS, CLEANSERS POLISHES, WAXES	46,098,594	29,650,000	16,448,594
Cleaners, Cleansers	31,581,500	24,051,000	7,530,550
Floor & Furniture Polishes, Waxes	9,097,030	4,146,000	4,951,030
Glass Cleaners	1,883,042	392,000	1,491,042
Home Dry Cleaners	1,001,519	405,000	596,519
Shoe Polish	1,456,653	148,000	1,308,653
Miscellaneous Cleaners	1,078,800	508,000	570,800
HOUSEHOLD EQUIPMENT–APPLIANCES	18,996,479	4,621,000	14,375,479
HOUSEHOLD FURNISHINGS	5,353,509	2,926,000	2,427,509
Beds, Mattresses, Springs	1,807,881	1,671,000	136,881
Furniture & Other Furnishings	3,545,628	1,255,000	2,290,628
HOUSEHOLD LAUNDRY PRODUCTS	76,237,980	29,940,000	46,297,980
Bleaches, Starches	6,648,628	4,814,000	1,834,628
Packaged Soaps, Detergents	67,510,561	23,217,000	44,293,561
Miscellaneous	2,078,791	1,909,000	169,791
HOUSEHOLD PAPER PRODUCTS	15,153,884	5,163,000	9,990,884
Cleansing Tissues	2,170,063	1,411,000	759,063
Food Wraps	4,970,803	1,417,000	3,553,803
Napkins	1,914,937	347,000	1,567,937
Toilet Tissue	3,558,086	755,000	2,803,086
Miscellaneous	2,539,995	1,233,000	1,306,995
HOUSEHOLD GENERAL	10,257,185	4,101,000	6,156,185
Brooms, Brushes, Mops, etc.	524,372	430,000	94,372
China, Glassware, Crockery, Containers	1,456,429	356,000	1,100,429
Disinfectants, Deodorizers	3,599,480	1,090,000	2,509,480
Fuels, (heating, etc.)	488,000	488,000	–
Insecticides, Rodenticides	2,143,821	821,000	1,322,821
Kitchen Utensils	272,362	89,000	183,362
Miscellaneous	1,772,721	827,000	945,721
NOTIONS	415,720	384,000	31,720
PET PRODUCTS	11,665,699	4,411,000	7,254,699
PUBLICATIONS	1,559,069	757,000	802,069
SPORTING GOODS, BICYCLES, TOYS	5,209,243	3,045,000	2,164,243
Bicycles & Supplies	335,905	35,000	300,905
Toys & Games	3,497,873	2,819,000	678,873
Miscellaneous	1,375,465	191,000	1,184,465

	Total TV	Spot	Network
STATIONERY, OFFICE EQUIPMENT	2,834,817	149,000	2,685,817
TELEVISION, RADIO, PHONOGRAPH, MUSICAL INSTRUMENTS	11,495,606	1,501,000	9,994,606
Antennas	163,844	108,000	55,844
Radio & Television Sets	6,245,688	208,000	6,037,688
Records	1,732,149	750,000	982,149
Miscellaneous	3,353,925	435,000	2,918,925
TOBACCO PRODUCTS & SUPPLIES	93,443,822	31,119,000	62,324,822
Cigarettes	89,248,461	28,164,000	61,084,461
Cigars, Pipe Tobacco	3,413,776	2,562,000	851,776
Miscellaneous	781,585	393,000	388,585
TRANSPORTATION & TRAVEL	5,641,358	2,937,000	2,704,358
Air	2,471,600	1,469,000	1,002,600
Bus	2,125,111	666,000	1,459,111
Rail	702,000	702,000	–
Miscellaneous	342,647	100,000	242,647
WATCHES, JEWELRY, CAMERAS	20,550,151	4,459,000	16,091,151
Cameras, Accessories, Supplies	9,177,184	290,000	8,887,184
Clocks & Watches	5,064,188	1,925,000	3,139,188
Jewelry	413,794	160,000	253,794
Pens & Pencils	4,918,875	1,988,000	2,930,875
Miscellaneous	976,100	96,000	880,110
MISCELLANEOUS	8,517,912	7,144,000	1,373,912
Trading Stamps	892,000	892,000	–
Miscellaneous Products	4,133,912	2,760,000	1,373,912
Miscellaneous Stores	3,492,000	3,492,000	–
TOTAL	$1,078,360,401	$511,770,000	$566,590,401

APPENDIX B

TOTAL U.S. TV ADVERTISING EXPENDITURES, 1969

(Source: *BAR Reports*)

	Total TV	Spot	Network
AGRICULTURE & FARMING	$ 5,052,200	$ 4,020,300	$ 1,031,900
APPAREL, FOOTWEAR & ACCESSORIES	49,466,100	16,959,600	32,506,500
Apparel Fabrics & Finishes	2,183,200	930,600	1,252,600
Footwear	11,866,000	6,860,600	5,005,400
Hosiery	8,117,400	3,755,900	4,361,500
Ready-to-wear	8,662,500	3,198,800	5,463,700
Underwear, Foundations & Bras	16,840,900	2,096,900	14,744,000
Misc. Apparel, Accessories & Notions	1,796,100	116,800	1,679,300
AUTOMOTIVE	191,672,300	56,053,000	135,574,300
Passenger Cars	140,311,500	43,543,300	96,768,200
Tires & Tubes	21,972,000	5,910,600	16,061,400
Trucks & Mobile Homes	5,885,400	478,800	5,406,600
Misc. Auto Accessories & Equipment	23,458,400	6,120,300	17,338,100
BEER & WINE	78,684,700	56,084,200	22,600,500
Beer & Ale	68,584,600	48,553,800	20,030,800
Wine	10,100,100	7,530,400	2,569,700
BUILDING MATERIALS, EQUIP-MENT & FIXTURES	20,264,900	6,808,700	13,456,200
Building Materials	2,655,700	243,500	2,412,200
Equipment, Fixtures & Systems	6,810,900	3,507,700	3,303,200
Protective Coating & Finishes	10,798,300	3,057,500	7,740,800
CONFECTIONERY & SOFT DRINKS	131,079,000	92,929,300	38,149,700
Confectionery	53,720,600	34,274,600	19,446,000
Soft Drinks	77,358,400	58,654,700	18,703,700
CONSUMER SERVICES	35,564,900	14,492,000	21,072,900
Engineering & Professional Serv. & Misc.	14,894,400	203,000	14,691,400
Financial	17,381,300	11,172,600	6,208,700
Schools & Colleges	3,289,200	3,116,400	172,800
DRUGS & REMEDIES	289,006,300	73,130,800	215,875,500
Medical Equipment & Supplies	8,141,600	4,944,300	3,197,300
Medicine & Proprietary Remedies	273,394,000	67,526,700	205,867,300
Misc. Drugs & Remedies	7,470,700	659,800	6,810,900

	Total TV	Spot	Network
ENTERTAINMENT & AMUSEMENT	36,412,800	22,128,200	14,284,600
Amusements & Events	1,359,300	1,225,700	133,600
Motion Pictures	4,055,500	–	4,055,500
Restaurants & Drive-Ins	30,998,000	20,902,500	10,095,500
FOOD & FOOD PRODUCTS	519,798,300	245,810,000	273,988,300
Bakery Goods & Snack Foods	68,000,000	30,740,700	37,259,300
Canned Goods	55,217,100	26,938,400	28,278,700
Cereals	87,489,400	30,376,100	57,113,300
Coffee, Tea & Cocoa	60,248,400	44,459,700	15,788,700
Dairy Products	18,372,000	11,478,700	6,893,300
Flour & Prepared Baking Mixes	22,543,400	6,184,400	16,359,000
Frozen Foods	35,019,900	19,344,400	15,675,500
Fruit & Vegetable Juices	23,247,300	5,676,100	17,571,200
Fruit & Vegetables–Fresh	6,350,800	2,289,400	4,061,400
Health, Dietary & Infants' Foods	26,081,600	14,375,100	11,706,500
Meats, Poultry & Fish–Fresh	15,543,400	6,356,000	9,187,400
Packaged Foods	27,787,700	13,538,600	14,249,100
Seasoning & Condiments	31,427,100	12,630,800	18,796,300
Shortening & Oils	31,080,300	15,868,600	15,211,700
Sugars, Syrups & Jellies	7,379,600	4,000,600	3,379,000
Misc. Ingredients	3,561,000	1,363,800	2,197,200
General Promotion & Combination Copy	449,300	188,600	260,700
GASOLINE, LUBRICANTS & OTHER FUELS	78,128,400	45,387,300	32,741,100
HORTICULTURE	5,958,400	3,117,600	2,840,800
HOUSEHOLD EQUIPMENT & SUPPLIES	110,081,000	51,232,300	58,848,700
Household Paper Products	43,645,800	28,184,800	15,461,000
Insecticides, Disinfectants & Deodorizers	20,410,400	7,740,700	12,669,700
Major Appliances	24,708,700	7,722,700	16,986,000
Small Appliances & Equipment	15,148,400	6,353,500	8,794,900
Misc. Accessories & Supplies	6,167,700	1,230,600	4,937,100
HOUSEHOLD FURNISHINGS	26,921,500	7,463,600	19,457,900
Floor Covering	10,575,100	2,133,100	8,442,000
Furniture	3,808,200	2,130,600	1,677,600
Household Fabrics & Finishes	9,139,600	3,136,000	6,003,600
Misc. Household Furnishings	3,398,600	63,900	3,334,700
INDUSTRIAL DEVELOPMENT & FREIGHT	4,997,400	552,200	4,445,200
INDUSTRIAL MATERIALS	6,198,200	189,800	6,008,400
INSURANCE	34,423,900	6,585,700	27,838,200
JEWELRY, OPTICAL GOODS & CAMERAS	41,273,200	4,542,600	36,730,600
Cameras & Photographic Supplies	25,790,900	3,841,100	21,949,800
Jewelry, Watches & Optical Goods	15,482,300	701,500	14,780,800

	Total TV	Spot	Network
OFFICE EQUIPMENT, STATIONERY & WRITING SUPPLIES	20,431,300	4,149,700	16,281,600
PET & PET SUPPLIES	48,782,400	23,556,600	25,225,800
PUBLISHING & MEDIA	16,329,000	13,218,200	3,110,800
RADIOS, TELEVISION SETS & MUSICAL INSTRUMENTS	43,963,300	23,880,700	20,082,600
Musical Instruments	730,100	594,800	135,300
Records & Tape Recordings	3,982,100	3,901,400	80,700
Radios, TV Sets, Phonographs & Recorders	38,063,100	18,919,800	19,143,300
Misc. Components & Supplies	1,188,000	464,700	723,300
SMOKING MATERIALS	213,386,300	39,842,400	173,543,900
Cigarettes	201,846,500	37,376,300	164,470,200
Cigars & Tobacco	10,949,700	2,246,800	8,702,900
Misc. Smoking Materials & Accessories	590,100	219,300	370,800
SOAPS, CLEANSERS & POLISHES	250,396,200	96,699,600	153,696,600
Soaps & Detergents	105,966,000	39,056,400	66,909,600
Cleansers, Polishes & Laundry Preps.	144,430,200	57,643,200	86,787,000
SPORTING GOODS & TOYS	63,826,600	35,084,000	28,742,600
Games, Toys & Hobbycraft	59,248,400	32,819,500	26,428,900
Sporting Goods	4,578,200	2,264,500	2,313,700
TOILETRIES & TOILET GOODS	411,680,200	136,087,800	275,592,400
Cosmetic & Beauty Aids	57,371,900	24,087,900	32,564,000
Dental Supplies & Mouthwashes	93,451,700	25,431,000	68,020,700
Depilatories & Deodorants	48,661,800	15,951,700	32,710,100
Hair Dressings & Accessories	108,676,300	41,878,300	66,798,000
Shaving Goods & Men's Toiletries	64,601,400	18,962,700	45,638,700
Toilet Soaps	29,810,000	6,606,700	23,203,300
Misc. Toilet Goods	9,107,100	2,449,500	6,657,600
TRAVEL, HOTELS & RESORTS	55,844,200	31,146,800	24,697,400
Airlines	46,147,100	25,839,000	20,308,100
Buses	3,918,100	1,876,000	2,042,100
Car Rental	4,389,600	2,768,000	1,621,600
Resorts & Hotels	1,159,200	444,500	714,700
Steamships	9,700	9,700	–
Travel Services	220,500	209,600	10,900
MISCELLANEOUS	23,287,500	4,292,000	18,995,500
TOTAL	$2,812,865,500	$1,115,445,000	$1,697,420,500

TOP 50 U.S. TELEVISION ADVERTISERS
1969 Expenditures

Over $100 million

1. Procter & Gamble   2. General Foods Corp.   3. Colgate-Palmolive Co.

Over $50 million

4. Bristol-Myers Co.   5. American Home Products Corp.

Over $25 million

6. Warner-Lambert Pharm. Co.
7. Lever Brothers Co.
8. Gillette Co.
9. William Wrigley, Jr. Co.
10. Coca-Cola Co.
11. Kellogg Co.
12. General Mills, Inc.
13. Kraftco Corp.

14. General Motors Corp.
15. International Tel. & Tel. Corp.
16. Alberto-Culver, Inc.
17. Nestle Co., Inc.
18. Johnson & Johnson
19. Loew's Theatres
20. C.P.C. International, Inc.
21. Pepsico, Inc.

Over $10 million

22. R. J. Reynolds Foods, Inc.
23. Standard Brands, Inc.
24. Sterling Drug, Inc.
25. Standard Oil Co. of Ind.
26. Scott Paper Co.
27. Philip Morris, Inc.
28. Norton Simon, Inc.
29. Carnation Co.
30. Shell Oil Co.
31. Miles Laboratories, Inc.
32. American Can Co.
33. Carter Wallace, Inc.
34. Triangle Publications, Inc.
35. Royal Crown Cola Co.
36. Jos. Schlitz Brewing Co.

37. De Luxe Topper Corp.
38. Standard Oil Co. of N.J.
39. United Air Lines
40. British-American Tobacco Co., Ltd.
41. Quaker Oats Co.
42. Ralston-Purina Co.
43. Heublein, Inc.
44. American Express Co.
45. American Airlines, Inc.
46. Anheuser-Busch, Inc.
47. Chesebrough-Ponds, Inc.
48. Mobil Oil Corp.
49. Atlantic Richfield Co.
50. Seven-Up Co.

APPENDIX D

WORLD'S FIRST COMMERCIAL

(August 28, 1922, Station WEAF, New York City)

ANNOUNCER: This afternoon, the radio audience is to be addressed by Mr. M. H. Blackwell of the Queensboro Corporation, who, through arrangements made by the Griffin Radio Service, Inc., will say a few words concerning Nathaniel Hawthorne and the desirability of fostering the helpful community spirit and the healthful, unconfined home life that were Hawthorne ideals. Ladies and gentlemen, Mr. Blackwell:

MR. BLACKWELL: It is fifty-eight years since Nathaniel Hawthorne, greatest of American fictionists, passed away. To honor his memory, the Queensboro Corporation, creator and operator of the tenant-owned system of apartment homes at Jackson Heights, New York City, has named its latest group of high-grade dwellings "Hawthorne Court."

I wish to thank those within the sound of my voice for the broadcasting opportunity afforded me to urge this vast radio audience to seek the recreation and daily comfort of the home, removed from the congested part of the city, right at the boundaries of God's Great Outdoors, and within a few minutes by subway from the business section of Manhattan.

This sort of residential environment strongly influenced Hawthorne, America's greatest writer of fiction. He analyzed with charming keenness the social spirit of those who had thus happily selected their homes, and he painted the people inhabiting those homes with good-natured relish.

There should be more Hawthorne sermons preached about the utter inadequacy and general hopelessness of the congested city home. The cry of the heart is for more living room, more chance to unfold, more opportunity to get near Mother Earth, to play, to romp, to plant and to dig.

Let me enjoin upon you as you value your health and your hopes and your home happiness, get away from the solid masses of brick, where the meager opening admitting a slant of sunlight is mockingly called a light shaft, and where children grow up starved for a run over a patch of grass and the sight of a tree.

Apartments in congested parts of the city have proven failures. The word "neighbor" is an expression of peculiar irony—a daily joke.

Thousands of dwellers in the congested district apartments want to remove to healthier and happier sections, but they don't know and can't seem to get into the belief that their living situation and home environment can be improved. Many of them balk at buying a house in the country or the suburbs, and becoming a commuter.

They have visions of toiling down in a cellar with a sullen furnace, or shoveling snow, or of blistering their palms pushing a clanking lawnmower. They can't seem to overcome the pessimistic inertia that keeps pounding into their brains that their crowded, unhealthy, unhappy living conditions cannot be improved.

The fact is, however, that apartment houses on the tenant-ownership plan can be secured by these city martyrs merely for deciding to pick them—merely for devoting an hour or so to preliminary verification of the living advantages that are within their grasp. And this, too, within twenty minutes of New York's business center by subway transit.

Those who balk at building a house or buying one already built, need not remain deprived of the blessings of the home within the ideal residential environment, or the home surrounded by social advantages and community benefits, where "neighbor" means more than a word of eight letters.

In these better days of more opportunities, it is possible under the tenant-ownership plan to possess an apartment-home that is equal in every way to the house-home, superior to it in numberless respects.

In these same better days, the purchaser of an apartment-home can enjoy all the latest conveniences and contrivances demanded by the housewife, and yet have all the outdoor life that the city dweller yearns for but has deludedly supposed could only be obtained through purchase of a house in the country.

Imagine a congested city apartment lifted bodily to the middle of a large garden within twenty minutes travel of the city's business center. Imagine the interior of a group of such apartments traversed by a garden court stretching a block, with beautiful flower beds and rich sward, so that the present jaded congested section dweller, on looking out of his windows, is not chilled with the brick and mortar vista, but gladdened and enthused by colors and scents that make life worth living once more.

Imagine an apartment to live in at a place where you and your neighbor join the same community clubs, organizations and activities; where you golf with your neighbor, tennis with your neighbor, bowl with your neighbor and join him in a long list of outdoor and indoor pleasure-giving, health-giving activities.

And finally imagine such a tenant-owned apartment, where you own a floor in a house the same as you can own an entire house, with a proportionate ownership of the ground, the same as the ground attached to an entire house; but where you have great spaces for planting and growing the flowers you love, and raising the vegetables of which you are fond.

Right at your door is such an opportunity. It only requires the will to take advantage of it all. You owe it to yourself and you owe it to your family to leave the hemmed-in, sombre-hued, artificial apartment life of the congested city section and enjoy what nature intended you should enjoy.

Dr. Royal S. Copeland, Health Commissioner of New York, recently declared that any person who preached leaving the crowded city for the open country was a public-spirited citizen and a benefactor to the race. Shall we not follow this advice and become the benefactors he praises? Let us resolve to do so. Let me close by urging that you hurry to the apartment home near the green fields and the neighborly atmosphere, right on the subway without the expense and trouble of a commuter, where health and community happiness beckon—the community life and friendly environment that Hawthorne advocated.

Glossary of Broadcast

Advertising Terms

The 500-odd terms herein are in common use in the various broadcast advertising disciplines. They have been compiled with an eye towards simplicity; fuller explanation of many would require treatment the length of this entire book.

AAAA "4 A's"–American Association of Advertising Agencies. A trade association, setting professional standards and determining general policy.

A & B rolls "Checkerboarded" film or video tape footage, overlapped to permit *dissolves* between rolls.

A & B winds Emulsion coating on different sides of the film base.

above-the-line Creative production costs, as distinct from technical ("below the line") production costs. Derived from some early estimating format.

Academy aperture Frame standard established by the Academy of Motion Picture Arts and Sciences; distinct from the "TV safety" area projecting scannable picture information in terms of the average home receiver mask.

acoustic recording Early non-electronic recording.

across the board Throughout the week.

action Movement before a camera. Also: the director's call for such movement.

A.D. Assistant Director; indispensable "detail man" on set or location before, during and after production.

adjacencies Commericals aired before and after a particular commercial.

ad lib From *ad libitum* (Lat.); to improvise material without rehearsal.

Advertising Council Semi-official group organizing and funding creation of non-profit "public service" national advertising.

affidavit Sworn station statement affirming broadcast of a commercial.

affiliate Radio or TV station contractually tied to a network for specific hours of network programming.

A.F.M. American Federation of Musicians; the musicians' union.

A.F.T.R.A. American Federation of Television and Radio Artists; union covering all radio and video tape performers, including acting talent, singers and sound effects artists.

aided recall Research technique utilizing "clues" to help an interviewee remember a viewed commercial.

air check Film, video tape, or audio tape of a commercial actually recorded "off-the-air." For use as a file copy, or by competitive advertisers.

alternate sponsorship Weekly rotation of commercial messages within a sponsored program to afford shared costs, with "major" and "minor" commercial appearances.

ambient light General light not directed at the subject.

American Television Commercials Festival An annual award presentation.

amplify To increase level.

analyze Break down soundtrack flow for limited animation photography

angle of view Diameter of picture information passing through a specific lens. (Lenses range from *telephoto* to *fisheye*.)

angle shot Any camera position not directly head-on to subject.

animatic See: *limited animation*.

animation Frame-at-a-time photography of slightly differing artwork (usually cartoon drawings). Projection at speed (24 fps) gives illusion of actual motion. See: *limited animation*.

animation camera Vertically-mounted camera over a horizontal table; the movements of both are carefully coordinated. (Called *rostrum camera* in Britain.)

announcer Commercial "pitchman" or program introducer.

answer print First composite (picture and sound) print from a completed negative. Used for evaluation and correction.

aperture Variable opening in camera shutter through which each frame of film is sequentially exposed.

apple, full (half) On set, a strong box (or half box) used to raise the height of props or performers.

ARB American Research Bureau.

arc Brilliant electrical discharge used behind an optical lens system in theatrical projection equipment.

Arri From *A*rens' and *R*ichter's ingenious, lightweight "Arriflex" reflex motion picture camera, initially used in the Wehrmacht. Now an international cinematographic work-horse in both 35mm and 16mm versions.

art card 11″ x 14″ cardboards, usually hot-pressed with type and/or designs for photography by the TV camera.

ASA (Emulsion speed rating of) American Standards Association.

ASCAP American Society of Composers, Authors and Publishers; trade guild to protect music performing rights.

aspect ratio Numerical ratio of film picture width to height, normally 1.33 to 1.

attenuate To decrease levels.

audience flow Statistical breakdown showing number of TV viewers (1) held from the previous program, (2) tuning from another channel, (3) initially turning on their set.

audience share Percentage of all receivers in use tuned to your program.

Audimeter A. C. Nielsen's electronic rating device, installed in their sample homes.

audio (Lat.="I hear.") Relating to the sound portion of a broadcast. See *mix*.

audio tape Non-sprocketed ferrous oxide-coated tape in ¼", ½" and 1" widths used in electronic sound recording.

Auricon Self-blimped 16mm sound-on-film (single system) camera.

availabilities Commercial advertising time segments open for purchase. Also refers to talent availability for specific booking, or for non-competitive product work.

baby legs Short tripod for low camera angles.

background BG; in *audio,* a continuing sound source played at a subdued level; in *video,* the setting behind the actors.

backlight Illumination directly behind the camera subject. See: *rimlight*.

backtiming Audio recording technique for perfect cueing of two elements.

back-to-back Two units of broadcast material transmitted without interruption.

baffle Acoustical correction panel.

balance Adjustable relationship between two or more broadcast elements.

Balopticon TV chain projector, manufactured by *Ba*usch and *Lo*mb, handling 4" x 5" opaque art-cards (*balops* or *telops*) rather than transparent slides.

barn doors Hinged panels on a spotlight to direct or limit the beam.

barney Protective camera cover.

base Film material on which emulsion is coated. Formerly cellulose nitrate, now non-flammable acetate, with thicknesses ranging from 0.0003" to 0.0009."

base light See: *fill light*

basic network Minimum number of a network's affiliate stations contracted for national advertising.

bear trap Spring clamp used to anchor set pieces.

beep(s) Interrupted *tone* signal used in *cueing*.

below-the-line Technical production costs, as distinct from creative ("above-the-line") production costs. Derived from some early estimating format.

billboard Brief announcement at the beginning and/or end of a broadcast, identifying sponsor(s).

binaural Two tracks on a single audio tape.

bipack Expose one piece of film from two other *combined* pieces.

bird's nest Mass of jammed film in the camera.

bit Brief creative "business." Also: a minor role.

blimp Soundproof camera housing.

blocking Roughing out camera and cast positions and movement in advance of final performance.

bloop See: *beep*.

blooper Announcer error.

blow up To enlarge optically.

BMI Broadcast Music, Inc.; trade guild to protect music performing rights.

boom Cantilevered camera pedestal. Also: elevated support for a microphone.

brightness range Relative brightness values within a scene.

bridge Sound or music link between two audio sections of a broadcast.

brightness Comparative intensity of surface-reflected illumination (measured in foot-Lamberts).

broad 2,000-watt light. Also: *double-broad, half-broad.*

brute Large arc spotlight.

buckle Camera film path jam.

bumper Extra tail footage.

busy Over-elaborate, distractive.

butt splice Non-overlapping film join.

buy Successful *take.*

buy-out One-time flat talent payment restricted to certain minor categories of union performance, not to be compensated thereafter by re-use fees.

b/w Black-and-white.

call letters International system of broadcast signal identification. Usually beginning with *W* east of the Mississippi, *K* to the west.

camera rehearsal Dress rehearsal, blocking camera movement and switching.

can Container for film elements. (*in the can:* completed). Also: a 1000-watt lamp and housing.

cans Headphones.

capstan Motorized recorder spindle transporting tape.

cartridge Tape container. Also: a *cassette.*

CATV Community Antenna Television.

cel(l) (From *celluloid.*) Transparent sheet used for a single animation drawing or portion thereof.

chain Separate TV console mixing source.

changing bag Portable "darkroom" for location film magazine loading.

channel Officially assigned TV broadcast frequency, usually 6 Megahertz wide.

cheat Non-realistic camera position.

check print Quick "slop" print from completed optical picture (only) negative to check mechanical printing errors.

cherry picker Motorized adjustable high-angle camera position with a bucket for the operator.

China Girl Identical piece of negative of an American girl, used in all U.S. film laboratories as a color printing standard.

china marker Wax-based film pencil.

chroma-key Video tape matteing process.

ciné-board 16mm limited animation version of a storyboard, photographed from the storyboard artwork itself.

cinema verité Documentary film style imposed on non-documentary filming.

Cinex Fifteen-frame strip of film of a selected scene with each frame printed in slightly different colors, for balancing purposes.

class (A,B,C,D) Broadcast advertising time periods, graded by size of audience.

clapstick See: *slate.*

clear Arrange necessary permission(s).

clip Short length of film.

closed-circuit Non-broadcast transmission of a television signal to a receiver.

close-up CU; the actor's *face.*

coaxial cable TV signal transmission cable, affording low power loss at high frequencies.

coincidental interview Telephone research technique: "Are you viewing?"

color balance Proper selection of magenta, cyan and yellow elements to give the most effective picture.

color bars See: *test bars.*

color temperature Measurement of color balance of a light source.

commercial Broadcast advertising message.

compatability Reception of either color or black-and-white TV signal on a color or black-and-white receiver

composite Single film print containing both picture and sound track.

cone Huge reflector for lighting large set areas, from 750 to 5,000 watts.

console Desk-like control and switching unit.

contact print Motion picture print made from a negative of the same width in direct contact with raw stock.

continuity Non-commercial broadcast material. Also: numerically-ordered scenes in a shooting script.

contrast Degree of difference between light and dark areas.

control room Special smaller room for direction and switching, separated from the performing studio by soundproofed windows and audio lock.

cookie Light-and-shadow mask. From *kukaloris* (Gr.).

copy platform Basic creative plan to exploit particular reputed value(s) of a product.

core Unflanged plastic hub for storing 35mm and 16mm film.

cord off Indicate or mark a particular section of film footage.

corporate campaign Advertising campaign charged with developing a complete corporate "image," as apart from selling a particular product.

cost-per-thousand CPM; broken-down cost of reaching 1,000 viewers with any particular piece of broadcast advertising. Used primarily for comparison with other media.

costume house Rental agency for talent wardrobe.

coverage Sets-*in-use* reached by (different levels of) a broadcast signal. (*Circulation:* indicates *all* families—one set to a family.)

crab dolly Four-wheeled camera mount on which all wheels can swivel synchronously for sidewise movement.

crawl Program credits moving up the screen.

credits Creative personnel identification. Also: performance "points" to establish music royalties.

crop To frame-out part of camera subject.

cross-fade One audio source arising out of another.

crosstalk Undesired electronic signal interfering with a desired one.

cue Signal to begin presentation of a new element.

cue card Script material written on an off-camera card in the performer's view.

cue sheet Written collection of sequential cues.

cume Cumulative audience; total number of viewers exposed to a commercial.

cut Editing or switching to a new broadcast element directly from a previous one (no fades or dissolves).

cutaway Editor's "insurance" shot.

cut-in Local station material inserted in a network feed.

cutoff Portion of transmitted TV picture not visible behind home receiver masks.

cyan Greenish-blue element of a color film print.

cycle To repeat sections of animation.

dailies One-light positive prints processed overnight from negative material exposed the previous day.

DB's Delayed broadcast; programs—usually on 16mm film—broadcast over stations with no direct network cable or microwave link. Also: *decibels.* One *db* is the smallest change in sound volume that the human ear can detect. (Named after the inventor of the telephone.)

db meter Control device to measure audio level.

degauss Erase tape in a magnetic field.

demographics Breakdown of broadcast audiences by varying statistical characteristics.

depth of field Inside and outside distances from a particular setting of the camera lens, within which a subject remains in focus.

deuce 2,000-watt floodlight.

diary Research technique utilizing a personal viewer log.

DIN (Emulsion speed rating of) Deutsche Industrie Norm.

diopter lens See: *proxar.*

director In-charge person on a set or in a studio.

disc Grooved audio recording. Also: video tape slow-motion equipment.

dissolve (lap) Fading into a new scene while fading out of an old one.

distortion Electronic departure from a desired signal.

documentary Unrehearsed film of actual events.

dolly Wheeled camera mount of varying complexity. See: *crab dolly.* Also: the screen move of such a mounted camera (altering parallax).

double print Printing each frame twice to halve the speed of an action.

double system Sound and picture recorded separately.

draw cards Art cards in a special holder.

dropout TV picture streak, caused by video tape irregularities.

dropout compensator Complex electronic device to eliminate the above.

dry run Rehearsal without costumes or camera facilities, etc.

dual track See: *binaural.*

dub Copy of a magnetic recording.

dubber Equipment for playing back magnetically-recorded sprocketed film.

dubbing Duplicating audio or video tape masters. Also: adding lip-synchronized dialogue to existing video (called *looping* on the West Coast).

dupe Copy.

echo chamber Device for adding artificial reverberation to an electronic recording signal.

edge number Multi-digit identification number applied by the film manufacturer to each foot of raw stock.

editor Production house specialist charged with piecing together a commercial from varied visual and sound elements.

electron beam recording Improved video tape-to-film transfer technique.

electronic recording Conversion of sound waves into recorded electrical impulses.

emulsion Light-sensitive coating placed on a film base.

end slate Slate photographed (upside-down) at the end rather than the beginning of a take, for expediency.

equalize To electronically alter frequency characteristics of any audio source.

erase To wipe away recorded electromagnetic patterns.

establishing shot Master opening scene identifying location and/or relationship of on-camera talent.

E.T. Electrical transcription; obsolete term identifying a broadcast recording disc.

exterior Outside of a set or location.

extra close-up ECU; the actor's *features.*

extras Talent used to "people" a scene.

fact sheet Copy points used by an *ad-lib announcer.*

fade-in In *video,* to come slowly out of black to an image. In *audio,* to come slowly out of silence to a sound.

fade-out Reverse of the above.

fader See: *pot.*

FCC Federal Communications Commission.

feedback Audio howl caused by a microphone picking up its own speaker.

fill light Light source supplying general illumination.

filmstrip Sequence of individual 35mm frames, shown singly in a special projector.

filter In *video,* deliberate alteration of a film image by a shaded or tinted glass over the camera lens. In *audio,* deliberate constriction of recorded frequencies to achieve a tinny or bassy effect.

fine cut Final, approved work print.

finegrain Special raw stock with a finer-grained emulsion and more transparent base, used for quality duplication of original material.

fisheye Extremely wide angle lens, usually used for comic close-up effects.

flag On set, a mask to keep stray light out of the camera lens.

flat Lacking video contrast. Also: a flat piece of scenery. Also: with no equalization (see *equalize*).

flip cards Art cards on a special "loose-leaf" stand.

floor manager Director's representative on the floor of a TV studio, usually connected by headphones to the control room.

fluff Announcer error.

fogged Light-struck, spoiled film.

follow shot Camera dolly following a moving subject.

follow spot Spotlight doing the same thing.

footage Film measurement reference: 16 frames to each 35mm foot; 40 frames to each 16mm foot.

foot candle Luminance standard for projection.

force Push exposures beyond normal ratings in developing.

frame n., An individual motion picture film unit. Also: the TV tube image. v., To adjust a TV camera for better subject positioning.

frame line Thin horizontal line dividing frames.

frames-per-second FPS; film speed through the camera.

free-lance Self-employed individual, usually creative.

freeze frame An individual motion picture negative frame, reprinted as a positive without change many times. Also: the identical visual effect achieved by a video tape disc recorder.

frequency Transmission wavelength. Also: average number of viewer impressions.

fringe time Broadcast time periods preceding or following prime time.

from the top Rehearsal from the very beginning of a performance.

front projection Studio background effect, achieved by projecting (from the front) a location slide or film on a huge Scotchlite screen behind the actors (and on the actors themselves).

FTC Federal Trade Commission.

full coat 35mm sprocketed film completely coated with ferrous oxide for multiple-track recording.

full shot FS: the actors and the entire background.

gaffer Set electrician.

gamma Developed film characteristics in respect to contrast.

gate, film Projector opening through which all light passes through the film onto the screen.

gate, sound Projector light "valve" reading the optical film soundtrack.

generation Duplicate copy, usually made with some loss of quality.

glass shot Obsolete painted effect that preceded optical matteing.

glitch Random TV picture disturbance.

golden time Sunday, holiday or any other special overtime compensated under union agreements at more than normal (1½ X) overtime rates.

go to black To fade from an image to a black screen.

gray scale Ten-point intensity scale for evaluating shading of a black-and-white television picture. [Note: Nos. 1 (pure white) and 10 (pure black) cannot be adequately reproduced on a TV tube.]

grip Film crew member charged with lifting or carrying.

guide track Temporary sound track, prepared only as a guide for subsequent photography.

hand-held (camera) Not mounted on a tripod or dolly.

head Beginning of a reel of tape or film. Also: tape recording magnet.

headphones Tiny wired speakers worn over each ear.

head shot Framing the actor's head and shoulders.

helical scan Miniaturized "diagonal" video tape recorder usually utilizing ½″ or 1″ tape.

hiatus Planned interruption of a broadcast schedule, usually to extend an advertising budget.

high-band Higher-frequency (10 megacycles) improved color video tape recording; or, the VTR for such recording. (Note: *LOW-band* video tapes can be played back on a *high-band* VTR.)

hi-con High-contrast black-and-white film for optical work.

high hat Tripod extension for high camera angles.

high key Having a narrow range of bright exposure values.

hot press Imprinting technique utilizing highly-reflective foil instead of ink.

hue Color wavelength.

iconoscope Early TV camera pickup tube.

I.D. Channel/station identification period. Also: a brief commercial for use during this period.

idiot card See: *cue card.*

I.D., local Local "tag" sponsorship of a national commercial.

image orthicon I.O.; older type of TV camera pickup tube.

ink-and-paint "Fill-in" stage in full animation.

inky Small spotlight.

insert Close-up shot of an inanimate object.

integrated A TV commercial advertising format, claiming (somewhat arbitrarily) a relationship between the two (or more) products being advertised, thus obtaining a lowered pro-rata time cost.

integration Editing of a commercial into a television program.

interlock Synchronous 35mm or 16mm projection-and-playback of separated work picture/work track; the projector or projection system for this purpose.

internegative Finegrain optical color negative made from interpositive materials.

interpositive Finegrain color positive made from a selected section of original camera negative. Used to make an internegative.

ips Inches per second, measuring tape travel.

iris Adjustable mask controlling amount of light passing through a lens. Also: *diaphragm.*

jenny Generator.

jump cut Formerly a bad edit. Now, *nouvelle vague.*

key light Apparent principal light source supplying shadows and form to a subject. Usually a single spot.

kicker Light used to obtain reflections from a performer's eyes or teeth.

kinescope Poor-quality filmed record of a television (tube) program image.

lavalier Microphone worn around the neck, leaving the hands free.

leader Identifying non-projected head and tail section that sets up and "leads" all film from feed to take-up reel, through the projection mechanism. *Academy leader* contains countdown cueing indications in "seconds" (formerly in "feet"), etc., according to standards of the Academy of Motion Picture Arts and Sciences

level In *audio,* volume of sound. In *video,* amount of light.

library music See: *stock music.*

light grid Metal framework suspending lights over a set.

lily Photographic gray-scale guide, similar to *test bars.*

limbo Scene with no recognizable background. See: *sweep; no-seam.*

limited animation Frame-at-a-time cinematography with slightly-moved artwork and/or camera. Projection at speed (24 fps) gives illusion of actual motion. See: *stop-motion.*

lip sync(hronization) Simultaneous recording and photography of an on-camera speaker (or other sound source). See: *dubbing.*

live Non-recorded broadcast material.

location Non-studio photographic area, supplying backgrounds not otherwise available.

log Written record of broadcast schedule performance.

logo Logotype; concise graphic design usually incorporating a manufacturer's name.

long shot L.S.; same as *full shot.*

loop Length of film spliced head-to-tail for continuous projection. Also: the section of film between picture and sound gates.

loose Subject framing with much top and side space. See: *tight.*

low band Lower frequency (5 megacycles) video tape recording; or, the VTR for such recording. (NOTE: *HIGH-band* video tapes cannot be played back on a *low-band* VTR.)

low key Having a wide range of dark exposure values.

magazine Film roll container.

magenta Purplish-red element of a color film print.

magnetic recording Audio recording effected by changing the polarity of microscopic particles of ferrous oxide on a film or tape.

mag stripe Clear 35mm sprocketed film with a strip of ferrous oxide for recording a single track.

major sponsor Advertiser with the most commercials in a multiple-sponsored program.

makegood Free station re-run of a badly-transmitted or omitted commercial.

marketing All aspects of product distribution and sales.

master Original final version.

master control "Nerve center" control room.

matte, matting Optical or electronic combination of two images, making them appear to be photographed by a single camera.

matte ride Visually undesirable outlines around a matted element.

M & E Film music and (sound) effects audio tracks.

medium Means of communicating an advertising message.

medium close-up MCU; the actors are waist-up.

medium shot MS; the actor's whole bodies are in frame.

Mitchell Workhorse American studio camera. Most common model is the *BNC,* a non-reflex version.

mix, audio Session in a sound studio electronically combining two or more audio elements into a single sound track.

mobile unit Vehicle used for transmitting a broadcast signal from a location.

monaural Full-track ¼" audio tape.

monitor Any television receiver connected to a transmission source by wire.

montage Visual blending of several scenes. Also (in Europe): the film editing process.

MOS "mit-out sound"; silent film.

Moviola Film-and-sound editing machine.

multiple image Frame composed of several different picture sources.

NAB, NARTB National Association of (Radio & Television) Broadcasters; a trade standards group.

narrator Often used synonomously (and incorrectly) with *announcer,* cf.

needle Indicator on a db meter dial.

needle drop Stock music description for usage of licensed materials.

negative Film with reversed tonal (and color) values.

net See: *scrim.*

network One of three huge combines supplying programming and advertising material to U.S. broadcast stations. Also: the stations so interconnected for the purpose of broadcasting programs.

N.G. No good!

noise Unwanted sound or picture interference.

no-seam Limbo setting unrolled from a huge horizontal roll of paper. (Also: *no-scene.*)

notch Shallow cue-cut in negative edge for timing purposes.

off-camera Where a speaker is heard but not seen. See: *voice-over.*

on-camera OC; where a speaker is both heard and seen.

one-light print Positive film material printed with no scene color corrections.

on ones (twos, threes, etc.) Animation photography of the *same* frame once, twice, three times, etc.

O & O's Broadcast stations *o*wned *and o*perated by a network (limited by FCC ruling to 5 TV, 7 radio).

OOP Out-of-pocket (expense).

OOT Out-of-town.

open end Program or commercial with no specific scheduled completion time. See: *I.D., local.*

open up Enlarge an aperture.

optical house Facility for processing final film negatives to include all editing and titling effects.

optical negative Final printing negative (picture).

opticals Colloquial term for wipes, dissolves, superimpositions and similar transitional effects.

optical track Final printing negative (sound).

optical view finder Camera device permitting the operator to see, frame *and focus* the picture he is taking.

origination point Network feed point, usually New York or Los Angeles.

out-of-frame Not in view. Also: projecting a portion of two frames.

outtakes Rejected versions.

overcrank Operate a motion picture camera at faster-than-normal frame speed, producing a "slow-motion" effect.

overscale Fee in excess of union minimums.

paint pots Control console color dials.

pan (From *panoramic.*) Camera movement from a fixed position along a horizontal axis. See: *tilt.*

pan(chromatic) master Positive b/w finegrain made from a color negative, used for making a b/w dupe negative.

participation Shared sponsorship.

patch Plug-in connection between two electronic lines.

peg bar Device for registering sequential animation cels.

pedestal Electronic calibration of TV picture black levels.

pencil test Rough animation, photographed to check movement.

persistence of vision Human optical phenomenon on which all motion picture and TV illusion is based, taking place when a succession of static images occurs at a greater frequency than the optic nerve can comprehend.

piggyback Broadcast combination of unrelated commercials.

playback Retrieval of previously-recorded material.

plumbicon Improved TV camera pickup tube.

polarity Positive or negative values in a TV picture.

pop (on, off) To instantaneously add or subtract new optical picture information (usually titles) to the frame.

position Location of a commercial within a program format.

positive Projectable film with true tonal and color representation.

pot(entiometer) Console control dial.

pre-emption Displacement of a scheduled broadcast by one of greater importance.

pre-mix Preliminary mix to reduce the number of ingredients of a final mix.

presence Feeling of physical or psychological immediacy.

prime time Three hours of a station's broadcast day when its audience is at a peak. On both coasts, usually from 8:00 to 11:00 p.m. (with FCC Waivers).

print Positive copy from a film negative. Or: space advertising in newspapers and magazines.

printer Optical machine for exposing a film negative/print.

print-through Excess residual magnetism transferred from one tape layer to the next, producing a "ghost" sound.

prism lens Special optical device for producing multiple images "in the camera."

process shot Same as *matteing*.

production house Facility specializing in preparation of film or video tape commercials.

producer In-charge person preparing any broadcast project for production, and directly responsible for its economic success or failure.

product protection Guaranteed (but varying) time interval between competitive commercials.

promo(tion) Commercial for a broadcast station or a program thereon.

props Properties; owned or rented set furnishings.

protection High-quality duplicate master material.

proxar Supplemental screw-on lens elements to shorten focal length.

public domain P.D.; status of a creative work whose copyright restrictions have expired.

pull back Camera dolly move away from the subject.

pullup Frame distance between picture and sound gates. 20 frames in 35mm; 26 frames in 16mm.

punchmark Visual film cue(s) created with a hole-punch.

purchase proposition Unique putative superiority of an advertised product. See: *unique selling proposition, copy platform*.

push in Reverse of *pull back*.

quadruplex Standard video tape recording method utilizing four rotating heads.

racking over Shifting a non-reflex camera lens into the viewfinder position.

Radio Advertising Bureau RAB; a trade development organization.

raster Illuminated area of the picture tube.

rate card Broadcast station's advertising charges, broken down by time of day, length, and frequency.

rating Percentage of all sets in a market tuned to a specific program/channel.

rating points Percentage of potential market audience tuned to a specific channel for a specific broadcast.

raw stock Unexposed film.

rear projection Studio background effect, achieved by projecting (from the rear) a location slide or film on a huge screen behind the actors.

reduction print Smaller-width print, projected down from a larger-width negative.

reel Flanged wind-up device for film or tape storage.

reflector Large mirror-like device for re-directing sunlight.

registering Aligning the separate images of a TV color camera.

registration pin Mechanism for holding each camera film frame rock-steady during exposure.

release print Final film print delivered to a station for broadcast use.

remote Location broadcast.

reportage Blend of *documentary* and *cinema verité* filming.

residual Talent re-use payment.

reversal processing Procedure in which the in-camera film produces a *positive* image, eliminating the extra negative step.

rewinds Pair of devices for rapidly transferring film from one reel to another.

rig Loosely—*v.*, to set up; *n.*, set-up equipment.

rimlight Illumination from *high* behind the camera subject. See: *backlight.*

Roget, Peter Mark The man who compiled the *Thesaurus* and also developed the theory of *persistence of vision* (1824).

roll Start cue.

room tone Studio ambient noise level.

rotoscoping See: *traveling matte.*

rough cut Initial assembly of work print, usually overlength.

run-through Loose rehearsal.

rushes See: *dailies.*

saturation Heavy bombardment of broadcast audiences with an advertising message.

scale Minimum union rate of pay.

scan Transforming an image into electronic elements.

scatter plan Carefully random advertising schedule.

scene Setting for a particular piece of action.

score Write a music track against a picture.

scratch off Animation technique, printed and projected backwards to make removed material "appear."

scratch print Deliberately damaged (scratched) sample stock shots; the original negative is maintained intact for subsequent print purchase.

scratch track See: *guide track.*

Screen Actors' Guild SAG; the performers' union covering film talent.

Screen Extras' Guild SEG; the extras' union for film.

scrim Gauze light diffuser.

script girl All-important "set secretary."

segué To fade one audio element into another.

selected take Accepted version. See: *outtakes*

set Studio arrangement to suggest the real background of a particular scene.

share (of audience) Percentage of all sets-in-use tuned to a specific program/ channel.

shoot n., a filming; *v.,* to film.

shooting date Day of filming.

short end Unexposed raw stock at tail of reel.

shutter Rotating segmented disc in both camera and projector.

signature A musical device denoting a particular product or advertiser.

silent speed Exposure speed of obsolete silent film; 16 fps. See: *sound speed.*

silk See: *scrim.*

single perf(oration) 16mm film with sound track on one side.

single system Sound and picture recorded on the same film.

16mm Film stock 16mm wide.

skip frame Printing every other frame to double the speed of an action.

slate Small board containing full production/scene information, photographed before each take. A hinged clapstick provides visual/sound synchronization.

slide Transparency mounted on a drum and projected into a *chain* for broadcast.

slop print See: *check print.*

slow motion See: *overcrank.*

SMPTE Society of Motion Picture Technicians and Engineers.

sneak To unobtrusively add a new audio element.

snoot Spotlight attachment to direct the beam.

snorkel Long, thin camera lens mirror attachment.

snow Electronic interference in a TV picture.

sonic cleaner Film cleaning apparatus utilizing sound waves.

sound effects SFX; real or imitated sounds, produced or played back on cue behind dramatic action.

sound-on-film SOF; not silent.

sound reader Editing machine for translating optical or magnetic sound tracks.

sound speed Exposure speed of sound film; 24 fps. See: *silent speed.*

sound stage Soundproofed filming or video taping area in a studio or production house.

sound track Audio portion of a film or video tape.

special Specially-scheduled one-time program.

special effects Creation of fantastic camera illusions.

spec(ification) sheet Technical equipment information.

speed Emulsion sensitivity to light.

spider Small camera dolly. Also: a multi-socket electrical outlet cable.

splice v., to join two different pieces of film or tape; *n.,* the joint.

splicer, film Mechanical device to accomplish the above with film.

splicing block The same, with tape.

split screen Frame printed from or composed of two different (usually vertical) picture sources.

sponsor Broadcast advertiser.

spot Colloquial term for any broadcast commercial. Also: a spotlight.

spot television Local, non-network commercial advertising time, purchased directly from the broadcast station involved.

sprocket Gear tooth in a film transport system.

spun See: *scrim.*

squeeze To anamorphize a film negative.

"start" mark Physical mark at the head of a piece of film, used for synchronization.

station break Pause in program transmission for FCC-required call-letter identification. Usually at half-hour intervals; usually filled with various-length commercials.

steps See: *test bars.*

"sticks" Camerman's call for slate sound synchronization.

still A single photograph.

stock music Previously-recorded "library" music licensed for commercial background re-use. Also called *canned music.*

stock shots Previously photographed motion-picture footage licensed for commercial re-use.

stop motion Frame-at-a-time motion picture photography of three-dimensional subjects, moved slightly between exposures. Projection at speed (24 fps) gives illusion of actual motion. See: *limited animation.*

storyboard Two-dimensional visualization, usually on paper in separated frames, of the video and audio portions of a planned television commercial.

studio Soundproofed room for creating broadcast material. Also: general term for a large filming facility.

sun gun Small portable light source.

super(imposition) Addition of one source of picture information (usually titling) over another.

swish pan Image-blurring pan shot, usually used as a transition to a similar shot in reverse.

switcher VTR control panel. Also: see *technical director.*

sync(hronization) Exact matching of video and audio elements.

synchronizer Editing machine for accomplishing the above.

sync pulse (Inaudible) servo signal added in audio tape recording to drive playback equipment at a constant speed.

system, on See: *closed-circuit.*

table-top Close-up inanimate camera work.

tag Additional end element, usually local sponsor identification.

tail End of a reel of tape or film.

take (1,2, etc.) Individually filmed or taped versions of the same material.

tally light Pilot light atop a TV camera indicating it is transmitting its image.

tearing Irregular horizontal displacement of TV linearity.

technical director TD; engineer handling all TV control-room console operations. Also called: *switcher.*

Telco line (or patch) Telephone company connection.

telecast Television broadcast.

telephoto Extremely narrow angle lens, usually used for close-ups at sporting events.

Teleprompter Patented roll-up script cueing device, readable (by way of 45° half-silvered mirror) directly "through" the camera lens.

Television Bureau of Advertising TVB; a trade development organization.

telop See: *balop.*

test bars Bar-shaped color patterns used in video tape leader for lining up playback. Formerly b/w *steps*.

35mm Film stock 35mm wide.

tied-off Locked camera position.

tight Subject framing with no top and side space. See: *loose*.

tilt Camera movement from a fixed position along a vertical axis. See: *pan*.

time-lapse Single-frame photography at precise periodic intervals.

timing Control of light through a negative element during film printing.

title Line of type on the tube.

tone 1000-cycle cueing signal marking beginning and end of an audio track.

track See: *sound track*. Also: dolly rails.

traffic Control of commercial requirements for broadcast advertising.

transfer Film made from a video tape.

transparency Transparent positive still film, suitable for broadcast transmission.

traveling matte Non-stationary matte that may also change shape.

treatment Rough script outline.

trim Unused head and tail portions of a selected film take.

truck Sidewise *dolly* movement.

two-shot, three-shot Two persons in frame, etc.

UHF Ultra high frequency; secondary TV broadcast band above 300 megacycles.

undercrank Operate a motion picture camera at slower-than-normal frame speed, producing a "speed-up" effect. See: *overcrank*.

unique selling proposition USP; unique putative superiority of an advertised product. See: *purchase proposition, copy platform*.

unit manager Network employee with coordination responsibilities for advertising material in a particular program.

up-cut Edit tightly.

vault Film storage facility.

VHF Very high frequency. Original TV broadcast band from 30 to 300 megacycles.

video (*Lat.*= "I see.") Relating to the picture portion of a broadcast.

video analyzer Complex electronic device to establish correct color balance for an optical negative.

video tape Ferrous oxide-coated tape in ½″, 1″ and 2″ widths, used in electronic picture-and-sound recording.

video tape recorder VTR; equipment used for recording and playing back video tape. See: *high band, low band*.

vidicon TV camera tube of moderate sensitivity.

voice over A speaker's voice heard over anything except a moving picture of the speaker. See: *off-camera*.

wild spot See: *spot television*.

wild track Recording non-synchronized sound.

wipe Optical effect using a line or shape to generate a new scene.
work print Picture sequence assembled by a film editor for approval.
wow Unintentional audio pitch change during playback.
wrap To finish; to put away equipment.

xenon Motion picture lamp containing xenon gas for truer color projection.

zoom lens Variable focal length lens originally designed to eliminate lens changing, now used almost exclusively to produce the effect of rapid (or slow) camera movement toward or away from a subject, with no change in parallax.